Changing corporate culture is heavy-duty stuff.

This isn't the sort of challenge you take on simply because it sounds good. Or because it's the "in thing" to do these days.

You do it because you *have* to in a desperate attempt to survive. Or if you're lucky—and smart enough—you do it *before* you have to, knowing you must if the organization is going to maintain a competitive edge in today's rapidly changing marketplace.

Most organizations don't have the foresight to change their culture before the world forces it on them. Some start, then don't have enough determination to see the effort through. Others keep tinkering with their culture, but the world of change outruns them. These companies lose control over their destiny.

Some that recognize the need to change deceive themselves, thinking they can achieve a cultural transformation without pain and chaos. But it just doesn't work that way. As this handbook points out, overhauling the culture is an agonizing process. Still, if you carry out culture change correctly, the payoff is worth the price of admission. It's also a lot less painful than having the marketplace slowly drive a stake into the heart of the organization.

Follow the guidelines given here, and you can achieve dramatic culture shifts in record time. It's the best way to protect the organization's future.

# High-Velocity Culture Change

*A Handbook for Managers*

Price Pritchett
&
Ron Pound

PRITCHETT

Printed in the United States of America

ISBN 978-0-944002-13-1

# Table of Contents

# Don't Let the Existing Culture Dictate Your Approach.

"... you'll have trouble creating a *new* culture if you insist on doing it in ways that are consistent with the *old* one."

Your approach to changing the culture should be highly out of character for the organization. Choose methods that stand in stark contrast to standard operating procedures. From the very outset you must free yourself from the existing culture and conceive a plan of action that starts to liberate the organization from its past.

Culture change moves at a slow crawl if the existing culture gets to call the shots on methodology. Or to put it another way, you'll have trouble creating a *new* culture if you insist on doing it in ways that are consistent with the *old* one. Remember, the old culture is designed to protect itself, not to bring about its own demise.

This sounds obvious. You'd think people would see the logic for deliberately violating the culture that's in place. After all, not following the rules is a good way to signal that the rules are being changed.

But organizations keep falling into the trap of letting the existing culture dictate the terms and conditions regarding how the change will be carried out. Instead of drawing up a course of action that is deliberately foreign to the existing culture, they're prone to adopt a strategy that is too compatible. The organization's ingrained way of operating is allowed to determine the "legitimate" methods for changing the culture.

This makes no more sense than trying to win a war while letting the enemy design your battle plans. So why does it happen?

It happens because culture wields great power over what people consider permissible and appropriate. The embedded beliefs, values, and behavior patterns carry tremendous voltage. The culture sends its current into every corner of the organization, influencing virtually everything. If you're not careful, the old culture will permeate your game plan for change like a lot of bad wiring, and will short-circuit your chances for success.

It just doesn't make sense to try to change culture according to the old rules. The rules themselves are part of the problem. You should choose a change strategy that runs contrary to cultural habits. Defy tradition. Disregard the managerial norms that safeguard the established (but outdated) way of doing business. Flout the values and symbols that are relics of an antiquated culture, because that itself is symbolic in a very important way.

Your style, technique, and overall strategy for culture change should be alien to the status quo.

# Focus on the Future.

"Analyzing your
present culture
is like going to
history class, when
you could learn
more valuable stuff
from studying
the future."

Don't get bogged down in the endless task of "culture analysis." Culture change should be guided by where the organization needs to go, not by where it's been.

We don't have time to sit around and sift through the sands of our history, trying to figure out the intricate details of who we are and how we became that way. It's a seductive exercise, but it simply takes too long. Sometimes it's just a stalling tactic. Or a safe way to camouflage resistance to change. But above all, it's just an unnecessary drill.

Instead of wasting precious time contemplating the organization's navel, trying to sort out precisely what the existing culture is, simply get clear on what it *needs* to be. Analyzing your present culture is like going to history class, when you could learn more valuable stuff from studying the future. Take your instruction from tomorrow—that's where you'll find the answers you need.

A quick scan of the future tells us, for example, that the organization's very survival depends on speed. Competitive advantage will come from being faster than the next guy. The race is to the swiftest. Don't burn up precious time and waste resources looking backward.

We already know, simply from staring toward tomorrow, what we need to start shooting for in terms of culture change. The window to the future gives better guidance than the mirror. This is a time for action, not introspection.

Rather than dwell on trying to understand the existing culture, start doing those things that help the culture change.

# Deliberately Destabilize Your Group.

"... you must hit with enough shock effect to immobilize the old culture at least temporarily."

Don't try to sneak up on people with culture change. Be terribly obvious. This is no time for subtlety or a low-keyed approach.

Something has to hit the organization hard enough to shatter the status quo. And it should make enough noise to command people's attention. If your work group is already shaken up, you can take advantage of that situation. Otherwise, you must fracture the old culture yourself. That's how you create the opening for change. If there isn't a crisis already, management has to create one.

Heavy-duty intervention is required because corporate culture has a very strong immune system. Unless you can overwhelm its defenses—weaken the culture somehow—it launches a fierce counteroffensive. Usually it wins.

You might get the needed shake-up if you restructure, downsize, relocate, or merge the group. Maybe it destabilizes things enough if you add a significant number of people, shift personnel on a large scale, or revamp the compensation system. But somehow you must hit with enough shock effect to immobilize the old culture at least temporarily.

Attempts at incremental change—"tweaking" the culture—ordinarily die for lack of energy. If you try to go slow, bureaucracy and resistance to change will cancel out your efforts. So get radical. Take action that turns heads. Let your opening moves leave no doubt that the old culture is incompatible with what's to come.

If you think you can pull off major culture change without a serious shake-up, you're kidding yourself. Don't even consider culture change unless you're willing to hit hard, go fast, and follow through.

# Care Harder.

"It's time for 'tough love.' Caring harder. Caring enough to take the company through the tough, unpopular struggle of culture change so it can survive."

Any serious attempt at culture change puts you under tremendous pressure. Unless you genuinely care for the organization—and for its people—you wouldn't put yourself through this ordeal.

"Caring," however, often gets misconstrued in this highly charged emotional climate. People will question your motives, criticize your approach, and condemn you personally. Some will say you're cutthroat and callous, pointing to your actions as proof that you don't care about employees.

All the blame and negative feelings could cause you guilt and self doubt. Just don't confuse caring with keeping people happy. It's possible to care deeply for every single employee. But you can't please every person even under *routine* circumstances, much less during deliberate culture change.

Your behavior may not look compassionate or humanistic at close range. But a long-term perspective, and respect for the big picture, can reveal that high-velocity culture change is the most caring move you could make. We've entered an era where the organization must adopt a "do what works" mentality instead of trying to live out a "do what feels good" philosophy. Companies are faced with more uncontrollables these days. The management options aren't the same as before. We used to have easier alternatives to choose from, and in times past it was acceptable to settle for gradually evolving culture change.

But those days are dead and gone. Now we're living in a world of accelerating change, and the manager's job is to help the organization keep up. If the culture doesn't adapt—*rapidly*—everybody loses.

It's time for "tough love." Caring harder. Caring enough to take the company through the tough, unpopular struggle of culture change so it can survive.

Trying not to disturb people, seeking to appease everybody by taking it slow and easy, can be the cruelest move of all.

# Disarm the Old Culture.

"You must seize control of the energy—turn it to your advantage—so it can't be used to fortify and perpetuate the old culture."

Organizations hit by change experience a power surge. There's a burst of new energy as the destabilization rouses people like a wake-up call. The old culture goes on red alert.

The new energy that's generated will either work for you or against you. You need to make a preemptive strike and focus the energy on driving culture change. Unless you move quickly, people will spend their new energy in ways that interfere. They'll waste it on self-protective behavior. Or even worse, it will fuel resistance to change. You must seize control of the energy—turn it to your advantage—so it can't be used to fortify and perpetuate the old culture.

Energy gravitates toward clear goals, so start by giving your people a clear aiming point. Tell them precisely what you're shooting for in terms of culture change. Be frank. Specific. Don't talk in generalities or get fuzzy in stating the objectives. You can't afford to allow any room for confusion.

Energy also dislikes uncertainty and is drawn to determination. So don't be tentative. Show commitment to the new culture and you further disarm the old one.

Set higher standards. Challenge your people with more demanding job requirements. When you "raise the bar," you focus that high-octane energy toward desired results and away from resistance to change.

Don't try to calm people or settle things down. You need to keep the energy level high. Just pay attention to where all that energy is going. Don't let it be used as a weapon by the old culture. It's almost impossible to create a significantly different culture unless you strip the old one of its power.

# Change the Reward System.

"If you *don't* make significant changes in the reward system, you'll actually reward resistance."

Culture change is hard to come by unless people can see a big payoff for behaving in different ways. Sticking with the old culture must start to hurt. Buying in to the new culture must bring pleasure. Then you have a decent chance of actually changing things.

If you *don't* make significant changes in the reward system, you'll actually reward resistance. Remember, the existing culture developed, and is now sustained, by the present setup. Don't expect employees to change their behavior significantly unless you make it worth their while.

Restructure the rewards and sanctions to make them consistent with the new priorities, goals, and values. Reinforce the behavior you want. Make it painful and unpleasant for people who hang on to the habits you're trying to break. Send very clear signals regarding how you expect people to behave. Then don't settle for anything else.

Don't contaminate the reward system by giving to everybody whether they're deserving or not. People may feel they're "entitled" to raises, promotions, perks, appreciation, attention, etc., but now is the time to destroy the entitlement mind set. Put all rewards out of reach of those people who don't contribute to the new culture. And if no one qualifies, well, so be it.

Let's face it—today's marketplace has changed *its* reward structure. It doesn't reward companies simply for showing up, or for "trying." The real world rewards *results.* Organizations will take a financial beating if they don't change their cultures so they measure up in terms of quality, speed, and innovation. Likewise, employees who don't contribute enough to culture change should get hit in *their* pocketbooks.

Remember, though, there are many coveted rewards that don't carry dollar signs. You need to change what you celebrate, what you honor, and who you hold up as heroes. Also be conscious of what you're rewarding with your precious time and attention. Don't reinforce the whiners, complainers, and "squeaky wheels" by responding to their noise with more personal support from you. Instead, dote on those who are self-sufficient, who don't gripe, and who readily shoulder responsibility for helping drive the change. Give these people the bigger budgets. Put them in the favored positions. Provide them more of your day-to-day attention.

If you want to figure out how well your reward system is working, it's very simple. Just look at what people keep doing. If their behavior hasn't changed enough—if you're still stuck in the same old culture—you need to make bigger changes in your rewards and sanctions.

# Keep Score.

"Measure change, reward results, and you'll see the whole organization take a different attitude."

What gets measured becomes important. When people see you're serious enough about culture change to track progress and keep score, they have to take it seriously, too. Measure change, reward results, and you'll see the whole organization take a different attitude.

Keeping score means more work for you. But it makes a statement about your personal investment in this process of culture change. If you're not willing to give some extra effort, why should your people? If nobody is going to the trouble to *measure* results, why expect employees to *produce* results? The only way you can hold your people personally accountable for culture change is to keep close tabs on what you want them to treat as important.

Track progress so you can see where the program is bogging down. So you'll know where the resistance lies. Until the new culture becomes second nature, the gravitational pull of the old culture influences people to revert to their old habits. If you don't pay close attention, they relax. Their minds drift. Their behavior goes back on automatic pilot, and back to a work pattern governed by the old culture. Keeping score keeps them honest.

Monitor people's performance so you know where to allocate rewards and sanctions. Measurement is what provides you data for feedback to your people. Good results should be celebrated. Poor results should be used like a spotlight to expose employees, leaving them no place to hide.

Be careful, though, that you don't create more bureaucracy to monitor the process of culture change. Keep score, but keep it simple.

# Promote the Vision.

"The change effort needs to become a cause, a crusade, and your job is to champion the vision."

Understand that culture change is terribly jarring to people. They get disoriented. Demoralized. Dispirited. The tendency is to drift, confused and aimless, unless there is an aiming point that captures their imagination. There must be a vision that holds their attention and hooks their hearts.

The change effort needs to become a cause, a crusade, and your job is to champion the vision. Strong advocacy is called for all up and down the chain of command.

The leaders at the very top need lieutenants who are closer to the troops—managers who can recruit support from the masses. Culture change cannot be achieved by the efforts of a handful of executives alone. The job is too big. The campaign must draw its strength from many—people like you—who carry heavy influence with lower-level employees. The fact is, you interact with the bulk of the workforce far more—usually more directly, and more powerfully—than the distant, top-level executives do. Top executives can conceive the vision, but managers like you are the midwives who must help give it birth.

If you withhold your support, playing the role of critic or doubter, you undermine not only top management but even yourself. Employees watch you intently. They are alert to the smallest clue that you are not committed. All you have to do is sit on the fence, second-guess top management, or give only lukewarm support. Seeing this, your people lose heart. Fear, doubt, and resistance to change rush in to fill the vacuum created by their loss of faith in the vision.

Align your work group with the culture change by keeping the vision alive. Promote it. Sell the dream. Help your employees see the invisible. Give the vision drama, glory, and excitement.

The vision must be like a beacon, a clear beam of light that defines where the culture is headed. Help make it compelling so that—like "magnetic north"—it has the power to pull the entire organization in its direction.

# Free the People.

"Free your people from bureaucracy, and you'll find it much easier to enlist their support for culture change."

A culture revolution calls for liberation of the people. You must free them from "the system," the rules of the "establishment," the old habits of the status quo. If you can break the chains of this bureaucracy, you break the back of the old culture.

Bureaucracy is your #1 enemy. When you announce you're going to change things, you essentially kick the bed where this ugly giant sleeps. It wakes up mad . . . scared . . . and determined to screw up your plans. Bureaucracy is a formidable adversary—sneaky, well positioned, self-righteous, skilled at justifying its existence. Bureaucracy is the gatekeeper of tradition, the legacy of "the way we were," the Bill of Rights for your old corporate culture.

Your people will have difficulty contributing to the new cause so long as they are imprisoned by bureaucracy. You must move quickly to break the shackles of bureaucratic stuff. Be bold. Launch an all-out frontal assault on the status quo.

Get rid of worn-out rules. Eliminate outmoded and unnecessary policies and procedures. *Simplify.*

Do away with old rites and rituals that entrench the existing culture. Kill off the sacred cows that stand in the way of culture change. Break with tradition when it's clearly incompatible with how the organization needs to operate.

Free your people from bureaucracy, and you'll find it much easier to enlist their support for culture change. You get their attention. You gain their respect. And you clear the way for them to show initiative and to implement new and better strategies. Stripping away bureaucracy literally forces people to change the way they do business.

Culture revolution can't succeed without help from the lower echelons. So help employees break out of the bureaucratic prison.

# Crank Up the Communication Effort.

"Standard communication procedures simply won't cut it."

You need a tremendous amount of high-quality communication to sustain a culture change. Managers typically underestimate the effort that is required. They rely on the normal communication practices and patterns, failing to consider that those methods were never designed for times like this. Standard communication procedures simply won't cut it.

Consider the situation at hand. First, people need to hear the logic, the rationale, behind the decision to change the culture. Give them an airtight case, based on hard facts about the marketplace and the firm's competitive position. Next, they want to know what's coming, and how they'll be affected personally. You must give them a clear understanding of what's expected regarding new ways of work. You need to sell people on the purpose, preach hope, and explain the part they're expected to play in the change strategy. The vision must be articulated. Then promoted with the zeal of a crusading evangelist.

And it doesn't stop there. You can't afford to let up. Don't relax.

Talk up the new culture on every possible occasion—in meetings, memos, presentations, company publications, or the casual give-and-take of everyday interaction with others. Culture change needs lots of cheerleading.

Keep the dialogue going. Nonstop two-way communication is needed to offset the ambiguity, counteract the confusion, shift attitudes, and keep people on course. You can't presume that your message stuck just because you said it more than once. Stress and confusion are distracting. People forget. Some don't hear you in the first place. Others warp or deny messages. Information which is very familiar to you needs to be repeated time and again, more than you would ever believe is necessary.

You must get across to your people what management *really* wants. Employees are always struggling to sort out which ideas, plans, and instructions to take seriously. They can handle only so much. The question is, out of all the possible courses of action and things to do, what can they safely ignore? Management must send signals that are clear enough, strong enough, to make the company's intentions clear.

Any communication gaps are going to cause you trouble. So don't leave an information vacuum. Bad news, rumors, and worst-case thinking will fill the void. If you get lazy or careless about communication, employees will lose their bearings and the organization will start to drift. In that atmosphere the culture begins to revert back to its old ways.

Good communication can't guarantee success in your efforts to change the corporate culture, but poor communication guarantees you'll fail.

## Expect Casualties.

"If it does so happen that you hang on to all your people, it's either a near miracle or a sure sign of bad management."

Watching a corporate culture change is like walking through a war zone. You see misery. Wreckage. Trauma. And casualties. The upheaval will be enormous, and some people won't make the cut. If it does so happen that you hang on to all your people, it's either a near miracle or a sure sign of bad management.

Ordinarily you can expect the breakout to look something like this. A good 20% of the people will buy in to the culture change immediately. They'll embrace the idea, enjoy the challenge, and help drive the effort. Another 50% of the group will be undecided . . . on the fence . . . slow to commit themselves one way or the other. The remaining 30% will be anti-change, pure and simple, and that attitude isn't likely to go away.

So you have some tough decisions to make.

First you have to figure out which group to spend your precious time on. Will it be on the group that makes the most racket? Will it be on the main pockets of resistance? That would be a mistake. You'd end up focusing on the negative-minded 30% where you have the worst odds of converting anyone. Some people simply will not wake up and smell the coffee. These people will soak up most of your time and still be an obstacle to the change effort. You're better off (and they probably are, too) if you get rid of them. If you can't release them, at least remove them from the mainstream. Position them where they will do the least damage.

Then turn your attention to the "undecided." You'll probably find that this 50% is already leaning in the right direction. Watching the body count add up in the anti-change group has a way of helping onlookers make up their minds in a hurry. Plus, by not throwing away your time in a fruitless effort to salvage people who won't respond, you end up with a lot more time to woo these fence-sitters.

Actually, you don't have to get rid of *people* to change the corporate culture, but you do have to get rid of wrong *behavior*. Employees need to understand this. They can stay. But their old behaviors that conflict with the new cultural objectives have to go. If they insist on hanging on to the old, non-adaptive behavior, then they have to go with it.

Casualties cause fear. But that's better than complacency. At least fear ratchets up the emotional energy, and you can use that to fuel the change effort.

Be willing to sacrifice those people whose attitude and behavior could sabotage the culture change. Better to lose them than to put the whole company's survival at risk.

# Demonstrate Unwavering Commitment.

"People have to believe you're dead serious about this endeavor and determined to see it through."

Major culture change does not occur unless it's driven by deep convictions. The new culture must be pursued with a raw and burning passion. *Relentlessly.* Culture transformation requires a unique chemistry of determination, courage, audacity, and fierce spirit.

Success doesn't come if the leaders approach this as a purely intellectual exercise. The effort must be fired with emotion. There must be an investment of heart and soul—that's where commitment draws its power.

You don't do a taste test on culture change to see if you like the flavor of it well enough to go beyond the sample. This is not something you dabble at. If you're tentative, people won't take you seriously. Or, if they do, they can mount an even bigger counteroffensive. You have to hit hard or you'll never overcome organizational inertia and the inevitable resistance to change.

It's crucial, at the very outset, to *prove* to people that you're going to change the culture. You can't accomplish this with actions that reflect vanilla commitment. Early moves must be bold, dramatic, totally out of character so far as the old culture is concerned. It only makes it harder if you try to ease into things. Determine your best point of attack, and go cold turkey. Never waver.

People have to believe you're dead serious about this endeavor and determined to see it through. This calls for audacious acts. You need to throw your body across the railroad tracks. You want them to shake their heads and say, "Management would never have done *that* unless they meant business."

The second gut check comes when trouble hits. Somewhere in the course of events there'll be setbacks, and they will be blamed on culture change. You'll begin to doubt the wisdom of it all, second-guess your approach, and lose sleep worrying that the organization could crash and burn. You'll have many critics and few people cheering you on. This is when the effort must be sustained through sheer force of will.

Quitting would come easy when the situation gets messy and painful. But instead of caving in to the pressure, amp up your efforts. Rather than retreat, reach deep down inside yourself for the strength to carry on.

Keep the faith. Persevere. Give it time to work. If you fail to follow through because you grow weary or lose your nerve, you will cause a relapse. You will end up with the same old culture. But the people will be more scared, demoralized, resentful, cynical, and confused. Any subsequent attempts at culture change will be even harder.

# Involve Everyone.

"Your job is to give everyone in your group personal accountability for transforming the culture."

Many people would prefer not to be bothered with the idea of changing the corporate culture. It's not that they're against the idea per se. They simply don't want to worry with it. Sounds like more work. Or maybe they just don't give a hoot about this new pet program higher management has dreamed up. They'd rather delegate responsibility *upward* for making it work. Often employees don't make any personal connection with the culture change initiative, and just want to be left alone to follow their normal work routines.

But people who aren't for change will be against it—inadvertently, perhaps, but their intent is not the issue. What matters is whether they are behaving in ways that help transform the culture, or doing things that cause the old culture to persist.

Your job is to give everyone in your group personal accountability for transforming the culture. Make it perfectly clear that they, too, must play a constructive role in this process. If you don't specifically assign your people the responsibility for culture change, many of them will not treat it as their responsibility.

You must *insist* on involvement. Mobilize everyone. The rallying call should cut across every sector of the company. Top to bottom. And the entire organization should start to vibrate.

The idea is to make this a pervasive, all-inclusive, organization-wide movement. Don't piecemeal it. The core group of culture change advocates needs to reach critical mass as rapidly as possible, and at the onset you can't know for sure where all that support might come from. So recruit involvement and backing from every corner of the organization. To the extent that you exclude employees, or allow them to watch from the sidelines, you invite apathy and increase the odds of resistance to change.

The culture change effort can't benefit from benchwarmers or spectators. All your people need to be active players and have their heads in the game.

# Make Structural and Administrative Changes.

"Breaking worn-out habits and fighting bureaucratic practices are empty acts if you don't offer employees something better."

You can break the rhythm of the bureaucracy and strip away much of its power. You can interrupt old work patterns to further loosen the grip of the existing culture. But then what?

Breaking worn-out habits and fighting bureaucratic practices are empty acts if you don't offer employees something better. You need to come up with dynamic reforms. Make changes that focus people's attention on the vision. Channel their energy into activities that persistently nudge the culture in the right direction.

Without fresh, potent strategies that push toward the new cultural objectives, the ghosts of the old culture will quickly return to haunt the halls. There must be structural changes to reflect the new values. To institutionalize the vision. Administrative processes and procedures must be altered to mirror the changes you seek in people's attitudes and action. The new cultural ideas must be embodied in new practices that clearly improve operating effectiveness.

The right kind of structural changes provide a constant reminder that a culture shift is underway. People simply can't miss it. You might design a flatter, leaner organization in order to control costs and gain speed. Or to push responsibility and accountability down to much lower levels. Realign functions to break down departmental barriers and improve cross-company communications. Develop self-directed teams to spark creativity, initiative, and innovation. Or change to an organizational structure that permits more intimacy with customers. Just make sure your changes are big and beneficial.

Administrative changes? You want something that snaps. Throw away a shelf of policy and procedure manuals in favor of a brief set of key guidelines. Totally alter the approval process to require two signatures instead of ten. Install powerful programs such as "best practices" or "workout" that bring empowerment and innovation. Re-engineer work processes to make quantum leaps in customer service, product development, inventory turns, etc.

Choose structural and administrative changes that are basically incompatible with the old culture and that reinforce the new one. Make them powerful enough to nurture the right behavior until the desired culture is sustained through force of habit.

# Provide a Living Example.

"You will find no better way to coach employees on what the new culture must look like than by how you carry yourself."

Consider yourself on display. Realize that, for better or worse, you *will serve* as a role model for subordinates. Let your attitude and actions serve as a constant point of reference for employees struggling to make the right changes in their job behavior.

Take pains to live out the new cultural imperatives. Hour by hour, day by day. Deliberately go about your management duties with a style and manner that leave no doubt about your acceptance and endorsement of the culture shift. Your behavior should convey, unequivocally, that you are a disciple of change. You can make no stronger statement about your belief in the culture change than to embrace it—*embody* it—yourself. You will find no better way to coach employees on what the new culture must look like than by how you carry yourself.

This is not an easy drill. It requires a conscious effort.

To begin with, employees need to see you make some dramatic, high-profile changes yourself—in your priorities, attitude, or overall management approach. Startle people. Make a hard, right-angle turn or two in how you do things. You must be obvious.

You also must respect the need for immediacy. The organization can't afford to have managers give themselves months or years to catch the spirit and gradually bring their behavior into alignment with the culture being sought. Neither does it work if managers say one thing and do another—i.e., telling subordinates to change, but failing to lead them by example. Such hypocritical behavior will kill your credibility and sabotage the culture change.

Walking your talk puts muscle into your requests and directives. If your behavior portrays the new culture, then by all rights it's fair for you to expect employees to do likewise. And they can't accuse you of having a double standard if you need to reprimand or discipline them.

Show enthusiasm, not grudging compliance. Just as your behavior influences the actions of others, the spirit with which you do it colors their attitudes. Any negativism coming from you legitimizes it for them. Employees should be able to get a refresher course on the new culture any time they need it just by watching you work.

# Achieve Hard Results in a Hurry.

"Ultimately, culture change lives or dies by dollar signs. It's a language everyone understands."

The importance of quick wins cannot be overstated. Culture change needs to produce a tangible payoff in short order. It's crucial that you obtain early proof that the effort is well conceived and is, in fact, working.

Count on it—the first symptoms of culture change aren't going to make you sleep any better at night. Negative effects will precede the positive. People usually misconstrue the situation, failing to remember that problems are the number one by-product of progress.

Everybody will be watching, worrying that the situation might spin out of control. Some will firmly believe the idea was doomed from the start. The anti-change crowd will roll their eyes and point to all kinds of trouble, insisting that this is a dumb plan that's being poorly implemented. The longer you go without good evidence that the benefits will exceed the costs, the easier it is for them to argue that the effort should be aborted.

The commercial argument convinces best. It's hard for the critics to argue with success when you can measure it in hard dollars. This means you must manage the business such that you engineer some quick financial victories. It's absolutely essential that you come up with ways to wring more money out of the operation. For now, financial successes are like giving blood plasma to a trauma victim. Come up with more money, and give culture change the credit. Ultimately, culture change lives or dies by dollar signs. It's a language everyone understands.

There are, of course, many other ways to measure success. But stick with hard results. Tangible performance improvements. Stuff you can quantify—like productivity, quality, increased market share, better yields, quicker delivery, higher customer satisfaction, shorter product development cycles, etc.

Don't get sidetracked trying to prove the value of culture change with soft data. Intangibles—things like morale, trust, loyalty, stress levels, or job satisfaction—will give a false reading on how culture change is going. These indicators will be heading in exactly the wrong direction. Morale craters. Attitudes sour. Trust evaporates quicker than an early morning fog. Stress levels hit all-time highs. Not many people will say they're having fun. But culture change is like going in for surgery—nobody does it for the thrills.

Just remember, hard results talk louder than intangibles. Resistance to change always slows a bit when it looks like top management just might be right after all. Deliver hard results in a hurry, and you buy some time for culture change to build momentum.

## Bring in a New Breed.

"You want pistols, hot-blooded people bent on making their mark. Not mild-mannered, conforming types who will succumb to the awesome power of the existing culture."

Turnover has its virtues. Used correctly, it gives you a chance to reconstitute the workforce. The simplest, most straightforward solution to transforming the corporate culture is to switch out people. Nothing else has the potential to so quickly change the chemistry of the culture.

Take downsizing. Do it in a discerning manner, and you can reduce the size of the resistance forces. Second, you make room for replacements that have the characteristics needed to establish the new culture. That's important, because it's not easy to change culture without new blood.

Don't hesitate to fire nonperformers and offload the anti-change people. It's far harder to convert the resisters than to bring in new people who'll embrace the new culture. The organizational immigrants arrive more open-minded, and assume it's *their* job to adapt. Incumbents, on the other hand, too often can't find it in themselves to change their stripes. Outsiders come in excited, happy, eager to please. And while these newcomers are intent on proving themselves in the new culture, insiders can be guilty of presuming that the new culture should prove itself to them.

Outsiders arrive in a responsive mood. They're more open than incumbents are to establishing new work habits. Outsiders come in focusing their energies and abilities on producing results. Insiders, meanwhile, worry too much about "me issues" and waste energy resisting change.

New hires, since they haven't been nesting in the existing trees, are willing to hack down the cultural forest. They bring a fresh perspective, and can expose your people to new ways of thinking and working. They come in without any investment in the old culture and its power structure. They aren't locked in to its traditions, values, or beliefs. That alone can make a big difference.

But you also should bring in a new *breed.* Break out of your conventional selection/placement practices and find people who clearly do *not* fit the existing corporate mold. Recruit purposefully. Hire very selectively. You want pistols, hot-blooded people bent on making their mark. Not mild-mannered, conforming types who will succumb to the awesome power of the existing culture.

Organizations tend to hire in their own image, and you must avoid that trap if you plan to restaff in ways that reshape the culture. The idea, again, is to overcome insularity, insider arrogance, and the "not invented here" syndrome. Hire mavericks. Renegades. Some Walt Disney types with creativity and natural curiosity. Seed the organization with people whose overall makeup will drive the culture in the right direction. Bringing in a new breed makes a powerful statement about the kind of behavior it will take to survive in the culture that is coming.

# Don't Trust Loyalty.

"Loyalty is a
treacherous thing
in a world
of rapid change."

Be wary of people who take pride in being "loyal" employees. Loyalty is a treacherous thing in a world of rapid change. You need to examine the object of people's loyalty. Analyze their actions as well as their motives. Then determine whether this is the kind of "virtue" the organization can afford.

Loyalty to the *organization* has value, assuming it gets demonstrated in the proper manner. Loyalty to the *culture*, on the other hand, can present a variety of serious problems. Many companies are in trouble because people are defending an outdated culture instead of looking out for the organization itself. They're not changing their values, priorities, beliefs, and behaviors in order to make the outfit stronger and more competitive for these changing times. Instead, they're busy trying to perpetuate a culture that's killing the company.

Some employees are innocent at heart. They become company traitors by default, letting their commitment to the old culture blind them to the desperate need for change. These are the people whose hero worship has them emulating old role models that are wrong for today. The accidental traitors haven't realized that some of the traditions and values they still hold precious now interfere. By not uncoupling from old, established cultural habits in how business gets carried out, they've become enemies of the organization.

Other so-called loyalists are not so guileless. They use loyalty as a coverup for more devious, self-serving acts. It shouldn't come as a surprise. "I'm only being loyal to the culture" makes a great hiding place for resistance to change. People who feel threatened, or those who clearly stand to lose in all the upheaval, don't mind fighting a little dirty to keep things the way they are. These are the deliberate traitors.

Sometimes you have a tough time distinguishing between the two types of loyalists. It helps if you can, though, because they deserve different treatment. The accidental traitors might be turned by education. Or persuasion. But you handle the deliberate traitors best by first exposing their behavior for what it is, and then drawing a line in the sand. Make it clear that if they step over that line with more of their manipulative behavior, they will feel the sting of sanctions. Then make your words stick.

The bottom line on all this, of course, is that loyalty isn't everything it's been cracked up to be. You're better off with *aloyalty* to the culture, because it needs to be a moving target, constantly changing to keep up with the outside world.

## Build a Power Base.

"... you can develop a reputation as public enemy #1 and still prevail if you have a good supporting cast."

You can't take on the old culture and win unless you surround yourself with a core group of strong supporters. You need talented, tough-minded flankers you can count on to help you launch the effort. Fill the key slots with allies. Create a coalition of like-minded people so you have a base of power that enables you to carry out big changes.

The right kinds of moves are guaranteed to cause stiff opposition. Your popularity rating will go into free fall. But you can develop a reputation as public enemy #1 and still prevail if you have a good supporting cast.

Give your best people the big jobs. As for the others who wield power but want you to fail, deal with them such that they are disconnected from their main constituencies. Reassign them. Fire them. Or neutralize them somehow. Remember that money is power. The more you make your adversaries dependent on you for funding their financial needs, the more you gain control.

Be willing to bring in gunslingers from the outside. You may need to do it simply to get the talent and personality strengths needed to produce a different culture. But it also may represent the best way to create your alliance. Outsiders come on board looking forward, not backward. They're not emotionally invested in the old way of doing things. They can back you fully, because they have no conflicting personal ties to others in the organization. And usually outsiders find it much easier than incumbents to get excited about creating a new culture.

Keep in mind that the people who are uncommitted don't strengthen your power base. Even the lukewarm supporters represent a threat, because keeping them in key roles deprives you of the opportunity to surround yourself with true advocates. When you come under fire you'll wish for highly committed allies.

# Encourage Eccentricity.

"You need radicals.
Rebels.
Revolutionaries.
People who howl
at the moon."

Setting out to change the culture is like taking on an army of secret police. You know the enemy is everywhere, ready to crack down on the people who don't conform. Cold-blooded and forever watchful, culture cannot tolerate the unconventional. The more eccentric or out of the ordinary someone behaves relative to existing cultural standards, the more ruthless the response.

Sometimes the rebuke is mild—a mere slap on the wrist to get the offender's attention. But sometimes the reprisal is swift and vicious. Either way, the end result is the same. People whose behavior ranges beyond the traditional cultural boundaries are forced to comply, exiled to the fringes of the organization, or rejected outright. Only a few—usually the strong ones with enough talent to make them precious—are indulged and allowed to remain in the mainstream of the organization. The culture tolerates them out of its own selfish interests, yet still considers them misfits.

Born of the status quo and committed to its defense, culture has many weapons at its disposal. It is engineered to protect itself through various mechanisms that develop over the years—bureaucracy, hiring and promotion practices, the reward system, and plain old peer pressure. The existing culture never hesitates to use its mighty arsenal, even against the innocents who inadvertently step out of line.

Your job is to help break the culture's stranglehold on behavior. You must legitimize unconventional acts. Encourage employees to operate "outside the dots." Run interference for the mavericks and renegades, protecting these cultural outlaws from the retaliation that is sure to come. Give them enough running room to prove what a powerful contribution they can make.

The old culture is sitting on vast resources, stifling priceless creativity and innovative energies. Liberate the employees from cultural constraints. Turn their fresh ideas and initiatives loose and aim them straight at the marketplace. Tease out the hidden talents and traits that lie dormant in your people. Bring more of their mighty potential into play.

You cannot achieve culture change without the influence of "deviant" behavior. You need radicals. Rebels. Revolutionaries. People who howl at the moon. Be eccentric yourself, and encourage eccentricity in others.

"If you're going to break the grip of the old culture, seize control of the schools. That's one of the basic rules followed by revolutionaries."

The old culture has the edge until employees learn how to do things differently. Human nature is such that, for the most part, people stick with what they know how to do, particularly in situations marked by ambiguity and stress. It looks like resistance to change. But to be more precise, they're resisting having to fumble along, look awkward, and go on guesswork.

Employees are better equipped to break old habits if you teach them new routines. Training builds confidence, competencies, and a willingness to change. Give people new techniques—a skill package consistent with what the new culture calls for—and you position them to contribute.

People also are more willing to embrace new values and beliefs if they comprehend the situation. Educate them. Provide a penetrating, well-rounded orientation on the circumstances driving the changes. They need to know the dynamics that are at work, and that culture change is a quest for a competitive edge. Ultimately, a strategy for survival. Show them specifically how they can help carry out the transformation. Many of them would give up before they ever managed to break the code on their own.

The education and orientation effort giving the rationale for change doesn't have to be an indictment of the old culture. Rather than merely bad-mouthing it and putting people on the defensive, give due credit to the old culture and its successes. Honor the past. Then help people see how the transformation is the necessary next step to take, considering the company's heritage and the situation at hand.

Keep in mind that in virtually any social system—businesses included—schools are the voice of the establishment. If you're going to break the grip of the old culture, seize control of the schools. That's one of the basic rules followed by revolutionaries. Redirect training to put it in service of the culture shift. Everything about the training and education, from content to how it's conducted, should reflect a sweeping change in priorities, values, and beliefs.

# Go Flat Out.

"Start out fast
and keep
trying to pick
up speed.
*Leave skid marks*."

There are various good reasons for a high-velocity approach to culture change. There are no valid arguments for going slowly.

It's troubling to hear people talk these days about how it takes five, ten, or even fifteen years to transform the corporate culture. No question you could use that much time. But the disconcerting thing about that line of thought is that it creates a self-fulfilling prophecy. People start accepting the idea that they need a decade or better to pull this off, and their chances of beating that time frame disappear. The job expands to fill the time they mentally have allowed.

Don't tell yourself you've got that long. Sure, you certainly could use the time if you had it. But the blunt truth is the world doesn't look like it's going to be that generous. The pace of change is so intense, and still accelerating. Long before you reach a five- or ten-year finish line, the world will take matters into its own hands. The *world* will reshape your culture, or else leave the organization to die a slow death in the marketplace.

Significant culture change should start to occur in weeks or months. Not years. Start out fast and keep trying to pick up speed. *Leave skid marks.*

Speed may scare you, giving you the feeling that you're too reckless. That you could lose control. But lack of speed is what lets problems get out of hand. Tentativeness and fear cause more mistakes than quickness.

Implementing change at high speed keeps the old culture off balance. Bureaucracy has to eat dust. The emotional energy level remains high. Speed creates a sense of urgency, and is also a sign of commitment. But beyond all that, you must maintain a sizzling pace in order to make the necessary cultural adjustments before the marketplace beats you up.

Speed, of course, is a relative term. What is "fast?" People operate with very different frames of reference. Organizations vary greatly in their cruising speeds. Some types of businesses are notoriously slow. So let's put it this way—speeding up doesn't mean you're fast. You could still be dragging, steadily losing ground to the world's accelerating rate of change.

Start out throwing gravel. Don't even think of trying to carry out culture change at anywhere near the company's usual pace. You can go faster than you think you can. When you get to the other end of this exercise—when you look back and reflect on how it has gone—you'll say you should have done it even faster.

# Additional Corporate Culture Handbooks

### *Culture Shift: The Employee Handbook for Changing Corporate Culture*

Get the masses involved. Drive the culture change down to the grass roots level. See how rapidly the organization begins to exploit change for competitive advantage. This handbook provides an entirely new mindset for your staff, quickly transforming behavior throughout the entire organization to create a more flexible, adaptable culture that thrives on change.

---

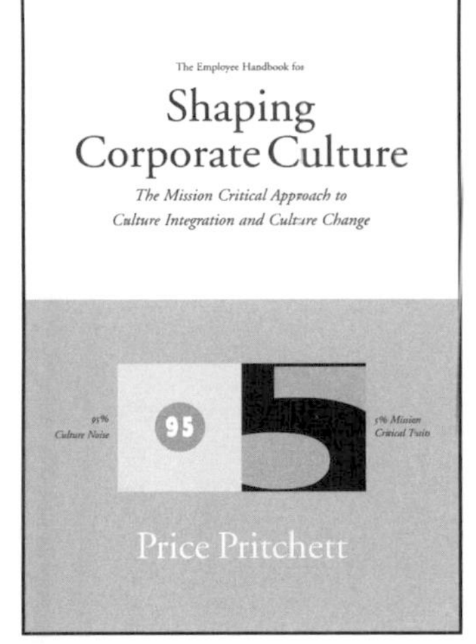


### *The Employee Handbook for Shaping Corporate Culture: The Mission Critical Approach to Culture Integration and Culture Change*

Delivers a crucial all-employee message on the "how-to's" of culture integration and change while distributing accountability for the change effort throughout the organization. This handbook will help your entire workfoce focus on the *mission critical 5 percent.*

# Books by PRITCHETT, LP

## Change Management

- *The 4th Level of Change: 10 Practices for Top Performance During Global Uncertainty*
- *Business As UnUsual: The Handbook for Managing and Supervising Organizational Change*
- *The Comeback*
- *Deep Strengths: Getting to the Heart of High Performance*
- *The Employee Handbook for Organizational Change*
- *The Employee Handbook of New Work Habits for a Radically Changing World: 13 Ground Rules for Job Success*
- *Firing Up Commitment During Organizational Change*
- *Hard Optimism: How to Succeed in a World Where Positive Wins*
- *MindShift: The Employee Handbook for Understanding the Changing World of Work*
- *Resistance: Moving Beyond the Barriers to Change*
- *A Survival Guide to the Stress of Organizational Change*
- *The Unfolding: A Handbook for Living Strong, Being Effective, and Knowing Happiness During Uncertain Times*
- *What's Next? The Hard Core Truth About How to Get Hired*

## Leadership & Teamwork

- *Carpe Mañana: 10 Critical Leadership Practices for Managing Toward the Future*
- *The Leadership Engine Handbook: Building Leaders at Every Level*
- *Team ReConstruction: Building a High Performance Work Group During Change*
- *Teamwork: The Team Member Handbook*

## Growth & Innovation

- *The Breakthrough Principle of 16x: Real Simple Innovation for 16 Times Better Results*
- *Fast Growth: A Career Acceleration Strategy*
- *The Mars Pathfinder Approach to "Faster-Better-Cheaper"*
- *The Quantum Leap Strategy*

*um Leaps*

## Mergers & Acquisitions

- *After the Merger: The Authoritative Guide for Integration Success*
- *The Employee Guide to Mergers and Acquisitions*
- *Making Mergers Work: A Guide to Managing Mergers and Acquisitions*
- *Mergers: Growth in the Fast Lane*
- *Smart Moves: A Crash Course on Merger Integration Management*

## Corporate Culture

- *Culture Shift: The Employee Handbook for Changing Corporate Culture*
- *The Employee Handbook for Shaping Corporate Culture: The Mission Critical Approach to Culture Integration and Culture Change*
- *High-Velocity Culture Change: A Handbook for Managers*

## Other

- *The Ethics of Excellence*
- *Improving Performance: How to Manage the White Space on the Organizational Chart*
- *Managing Sideways: Using the Rummler-Brache Process Improvement Approach to Achieve Performance Breakthrough*
- *Service Excellence!*
- *Solution #1: The Handbook for Workplace Fitness and Health*
- *Topgrading: How to Hire, Coach and Keep A Players*

## Price Pritchett

Price Pritchett is Chairman & CEO of PRITCHETT. For over 30 years he has been advising CEOs, presidents, and other senior executives on a wide range of strategic matters relating to merger integration and major organizational change. His consulting assignments have taken him to the Far East, Europe, the United Kingdom, and all across the Americas. He has been quoted in *Fortune, Business Week, The Wall Street Journal, USA Today,* most major U. S. city newspapers, and interviewed on CNN, CNBC, and numerous corporate cable channels. Over 20 million copies of Dr. Pritchett's books and handbooks are in print, making him one of the best-selling business authors in the U.S.

## Ron Pound

Ron Pound, Ph.D., co-authored six books on organizational change and played a key role in the design and implementation of major change initiatives for a broad range of organizations, both domestically and internationally.

---

## Praise for *Comfort Food*

"Kate Jacobs's breezy follow-up to her bestselling *The Friday Night Knitting Club* is a satisfying read that showcases Jacobs's skill in creating endearingly flawed characters . . . The kind of book you rush home to finish."

—*USA Today*

"Gus and the show's cast, with their humor, moods, and romance, are the sparks that bring this warm and irresistible story to life. Highly recommended."

—*Library Journal*

"Lighthearted."

—*Kirkus Reviews*

"Jacobs delivers amusing characters set against the backdrop of the television culinary world. Add to the mix good, strong storytelling, witty dialogue, and a sympathetic heroine, and you've got a delectable tale and a truly fun read."

—*Romantic Times*

"Meeting the heroine of Kate Jacobs's new novel *Comfort Food* is not unlike breaking bread—or perhaps organic blackberry scones—with an old foodie friend . . . Jacobs has once again crafted a luxuriant yarn of a story . . . *Comfort Food* is good for the heart and the soul, serving up a rich pastiche of friendship and motherhood, with a savory side of romance, too."

—*BookPage*

"Real comfort food makes us feel safe and warm inside. It brings together family and friends by blending years, memories, and tastes. The novel *Comfort Food* by Kate Jacobs brings all these elements to the table."

—*The Paper Palate*

*continued . . .*

## *Knit Two*

"Jacobs stitches together another winning tale of the New York City knitting circle . . . This sequel is as comforting, enveloping, and warm as a well-crafted afghan." —*Publishers Weekly*

"Fans [will] eagerly snuggle in to see how the friends piece together their knitting projects while finding solace in one another's company." —*People*

"As [the women who make Walker and Daughter yarn shop their second home] turn out afghans and booties, [they] also knit the pattern of their own lives in a plot that travels as far as Rome before returning, of course, to 77th and Broadway." —*The New York Times*

"Reading Jacobs's second knitting novel is as warming and cheering as visiting old friends." —*Booklist*

"Readers are left with a sense of how the craft has calmed these souls as they journey through their individual stories of acceptance and personal growth. Fans of Debbie Macomber's Blossom Street series will find much to enjoy here." —*Library Journal*

"As the story presets the challenges that each woman faces, it becomes a beautiful celebration of life, friendship, knitting, and the bonds that tie us together. A delight to read." —*Romantic Times*

"Kate Jacobs's warmhearted sequel, *Knit Two*, is certain to be a cozy companion on a blustery winter night." —*BookPage*

"[*Knit Two*] reflects the relationships among women in real life—their willingness to help each other, their caring attitudes, their discretion when needed, their openness, and their lack of pretense in an emergency." —*The Omaha World-Herald*

## *The Friday Night Knitting Club*

"An absolutely beautiful, deeply moving portrait of female friendship. You'll laugh and cry along with these characters, and if you're like me, you'll wish you knew how to knit." —Kristin Hannah, author of *Comfort and Joy*

"Like *Steel Magnolias* set in Manhattan. If you are looking for an inviting group of gals to spend a few winter evenings with, pull up your afghan and snuggle in with *The Friday Night Knitting Club* . . . [It] makes you yearn for yarn, even if you're not a knitter." —*USA Today*

"Knitters will enjoy seeing the healing power of stitching put into words. Its simplicity and soothing repetition leave room for conversation, laughter, revelations, and friendship—just like the beauty shop in *Steel Magnolias*." —*Detroit Free Press*

"[A] winning first novel . . . impossible to put down." —*Booklist*

"This book's great—worth reading *now*." —*Glamour*

"If you like to write or read or knit, your first reaction to *The Friday Night Knitting Club* may be pure jealousy . . . Readers will come to root for nearly everyone in the sweetly diverse cast of characters." —*Concord (NH) Monitor*

*continued . . .*

"What begins as an unlikely hodgepodge of women soon evolves into an unbreakable sisterhood as the characters learn from each other's differences and bond over their love of knitting." —*Vogue Knitting*

"A *Steel Magnolias* for the twenty-first century." —*Kirkus Reviews*

"Poignant twists propel the plot and help the pacing find a pleasant rhythm." —*Publishers Weekly*

"A really great story." —*Marie Claire*

"Celebrates the power of women's independence and is essentially an urban counterpart to *How to Make an American Quilt*." —*New Statesman*

TITLES BY KATE JACOBS

*The Friday Night Knitting Club*
*Comfort Food*
*Knit Two*

# comfort food

KATE JACOBS

BERKLEY BOOKS, NEW YORK

**THE BERKLEY PUBLISHING GROUP**
**Published by the Penguin Group**
**Penguin Group (USA) Inc.**
**375 Hudson Street, New York, New York 10014, USA**
Penguin Group (Canada), 90 Eglinton Avenue East, Suite 700, Toronto, Ontario M4P 2Y3, Canada
(a division of Pearson Penguin Canada Inc.)
Penguin Books Ltd., 80 Strand, London WC2R 0RL, England
Penguin Group Ireland, 25 St. Stephen's Green, Dublin 2, Ireland
(a division of Penguin Books Ltd.)
Penguin Group (Australia), 250 Camberwell Road, Camberwell, Victoria 3124, Australia
(a division of Pearson Australia Group Pty. Ltd.)
Penguin Books India Pvt. Ltd., 11 Community Centre, Panchsheel Park, New Delhi—110 017, India
Penguin Group (NZ), 67 Apollo Drive, Rosedale, North Shore 0632, New Zealand
(a division of Pearson New Zealand Ltd.)
Penguin Books (South Africa) (Pty.) Ltd., 24 Sturdee Avenue, Rosebank, Johannesburg 2196,
South Africa

Penguin Books Ltd., Registered Offices: 80 Strand, London WC2R 0RL, England



PRINTING HISTORY
G. P. Putnam's Sons hardcover edition / May 2008
Berkley trade paperback edition / April 2009
Scholastic Book Fair edition / April 2009

Scholastic edition ISBN: 978-0-425-23089-3

The Library of Congress has cataloged the G.P. Putnam's Sons edition as follows:

Jacobs, Kate, date.
Comfort food / Kate Jacobs.
p. cm.
ISBN 978-0-399-15465-2
1. Woman cooks—Fiction. 2. Cookery—Fiction. 3. Television programs—Fiction. I. Title.
PR9199.4.J336C66 2008 2008005811

PRINTED IN THE UNITED STATES OF AMERICA

10 9 8 7 6 5 4 3 2 1

# bread and butter

# 1

FEBRUARY 2006

Gus Simpson adored birthday cake.

Chocolate, coconut, lemon, strawberry, vanilla—she had a particular fondness for the classics. Even though she experimented with new flavors and frostings, drizzling with syrups and artfully arranging hibiscus petals, Gus more often took the retro route with piped-on flowers or a flash of candy sprinkles across the iced top. Because birthday cake was really about nostalgia, she knew, about reaching in and using the senses to remember one perfect childhood moment.

After twelve years as a host on the CookingChannel—and with three successful shows to her credit—Gus had made many desserts in her kitchen studios, from her creamy white chocolate mousse to her luscious peach torte, her gooey caramel apple cobbler and her decadent bourbon pecan pie. A "home cook" without culinary school training, she aimed to be warmly elegant without veering into the homespun: she strived to make her dishes feel complete without being complicated.

Still, birthday cake was something altogether different: one sweet slice fed the spirit as much as the stomach. And Gus relished that perfect triumph.

She loved celebrating so much that she threw birthday parties for her grown daughters, Aimee and Sabrina, for her neighbor and good friend Hannah, for her executive producer (and CookingChannel veep) Porter, and for her longtime culinary assistant who'd recently retired and moved to California.

But Gus didn't stop there. She always made a big ta-da for the nation's anniversary, which wasn't so out of the ordinary for an American, and for December 25, which, again, wasn't all that unusual for someone who'd been raised Catholic. Then she also made a fuss for saints Valentine and Patrick, for Lincoln, for Julia Child (culinary genius; August 15), Henry Fowle Durant (founder of her alma mater, Wellesley; February 22), and Isabella Mary Beeton (author of the famous *Mrs. Beeton's Book of Household Management*; March 12). No matter that those guests of honor were quite unavailable to attend, being dead and all.

Some hostesses love parties because they relish being the center of attention. Gus, on the other hand, found her greatest pleasure in creating a party world with a place for everyone and where she believed everyone would be made to feel special.

"Let me fix a little something," Gus said to her daughters, their friends, her colleagues, her viewers. She truly loved the idea of taking care, of nurturing and nourishing. Especially those guests who found it hard to make their way in the crowd: Gus always looked out for those ones the most.

There was only one birthday that Gus was getting tired of organizing. Tired, really, of celebrating at all. Her own. Because in short order—March 25—Augusta Adelaide Simpson was turning fifty.

The problem, of course, was that she didn't feel as old as all that. No, she felt more like a twenty-five-year-old (ignoring, as she often did, the logistical problem that her older daughter, Aimee, was twenty-seven and her younger, Sabrina, was twenty-five). And, as such, she found herself completely caught off guard—genuinely surprised to add up the years—to find that she'd arrived at the half century mark.

A half century of Gus.

"You'll want to use the best sherry you can afford when making a vinaigrette," she had said on a recent show, before realizing the sherry was almost as old as she was.

"I could be bottled up and put on the shelf," she'd said, laughing.

But a nagging dread had snuck up on her, and she resented it. Forty-six, forty-seven, forty-eight, even forty-nine—all those parties had been smashing. When she blew out her candles on last year's cake—a carrot ginger with cinnamon cream cheese icing—and her producer, Porter, had shouted out, "Next year's the big one!" she had laughed along with the crowd. And she felt fine about it. She really, really did. No, really. She did. She hadn't scheduled a session of Botox, hadn't begun wearing scarves to hide her neck. Fifty, she told herself, was no big deal. Until she woke up one morning and realized she hadn't done a thing to plan. She, who never missed a chance to have a party. And that's when she realized that she didn't want to do anything about celebrating, either.

The problem, she reflected one morning while washing her tawny brown hair with color-enhancing shampoo, developed somewhere between working on the show schedule for the upcoming year and learning that the CookingChannel was slashing the budget and ordering fewer episodes than usual.

"All the cable channels are losing market share," Porter had explained. "We just have to ride it out." He'd been in the TV business a long time, longer than Gus, and was enviably successful, a black man in the very white world of food TV. There were rumblings he was even going to be named head of programming. Gus's trust in Porter was absolute.

Then the CookingChannel had hired a style consultant who informed Gus that "after a certain age" some ladies do well to add a few pounds to smooth out the face. ("You're wonderfully slender but it wouldn't hurt to fill in the lines, you know," the stylist had said, not unkindly. "Good lighting can only work for so long.") Finally, she'd met Sabrina for dinner one night and admired the couple at the table across from them, a gorgeous black-haired young woman in a bubble-gum-pink dress accompanied by a frowning older woman clad in an oatmeal linen pantsuit, her hair in a medium-length swingy bob. She was startled to realize the wall across from her was mirrored and the grumpy-faced diner was herself. "Are you okay, Mom?" Sabrina had said, signaling the waiter for more water. "You look as though you're a little ill."

Gus wasn't young anymore.

At first she'd tucked this awareness away with her white shoes after Labor Day. But the truth refused to stay hidden, revealing itself when she spotted a wrinkle she'd never noticed or heard a crackle in her knees when she bent over to pull out a saucepan. Or when her longtime sous chef announced, in what seemed like out-of-the-blue fashion, that she was retiring. Which meant she'd reached retirement age. Alarming when you considered that it meant twelve long years had gone by since Gus had had her first CookingChannel show, *The Lunch Bunch*, in 1994. That the young mom who'd twisted her shimmering butterscotch locks into a loose updo, tendrils escaping, had eschewed aprons and whipped up easy, delicious dishes was now a parent of girls with jobs and lives and kitchens of their own. Girls who had, sort of, become women.

They weren't really grown-up. Not in the real sense. After all, she'd had two children by the time she was Sabrina's age—and that was in addition to a husband, and a year of adventure in the Peace Corps. Aimee and Sabrina, on the other hand, were far from self-sufficient. Aimee seemed never to have anyone serious in her life, and Sabrina changed boyfriends with the seasons. It was funny, really, how today's twelve-year-olds were far more sophisticated than any middle schoolers Gus remembered, and yet the twenty-five-year-olds existed in a state of suspended adolescence. She spent more time worrying about them now than she probably ever had.

So it was easy enough to pop along with the day-to-day of life and not really think about aging in a personal way. But then small things—a word from a stranger, a glance in the mirror—startled her fantasy image. Suddenly, reluctantly, one fact became clear.

Gus Simpson *was* going to be fifty.

Not, in and of itself, a remarkable event. It happened to other people every day. Surely. But Gus had blithely assumed getting older wouldn't quite happen to her. After all, she was slim (if not exactly a devotee of exercise), had a thriving career, a chunk of money in the bank (well managed by David Fazio, a top financial adviser Alan Holt had recommended years ago), a closet bursting with pricey clothes—Gus's signature look was a comfortably elegant collarless silk duster, layered over a smooth shell, with wide-legged silk georgette trousers—and a convertible in her garage, dammit. She listened to Top 40. She used a digital camera. She had an incredibly tiny cell phone. She knew how to send text messages. She still dressed up at Halloween to give out candy. Wasn't all that enough to keep maturity at bay?

Turning forty-nine had had a jaunty ring to it; fifty felt like she ought to buy a pair of orthopedic shoes.

"It's quite impossible to figure out how to act these days," she told her producer, Porter, who had several years on her. "My mother had settled into being a grandmother at this age. But today some women are still having babies at fifty—babies, Porter!"

"Do you want a baby, Gus?" he'd asked, joking.

"No! What I want is to figure out this disconnect between a number on a piece of paper and how I feel inside," said Gus. "Do you know that the women from *Thirtysomething* are now fiftysomething? And they're still young. What about Michelle Pfeiffer? Meryl Streep? Jane Seymour? Oprah? They say fifty is the new thirty."

"So it should be no problem then," reasoned Porter. "You look great."

"And yet it is an issue," admitted Gus. "I have wrinkles. Real wrinkles, not those little crinkles I used to moan about when I turned forty. Porter, I think fondly about turning forty! I mean, I just can't stop wondering, How did I get here?"

"Where did the time go?"

"Yes, really. Where *did* the time go?" asked Gus. "And when do I get to hit 'pause'?"

And so, she reasoned to herself, it had been natural to fall behind on planning her birthday party. It had been easy to just put it off. Any other year she'd have begun organizing her birthday party immediately after Thanksgiving, deciding first on her cake flavor, arranging the food, sending formal invitations in the mail. (No, Gus Simpson simply did not appreciate the informality of Evite, thank you very much. The little details were what made guests feel most welcome, she knew.) She could have picked one item or concept—a pomegranate, an orchid, the color puce—and built the entire festivities around it as a theme. Her ability to decorate and entertain was so innate that she simply assumed anyone could throw parsley on a dish and make it look better than a haphazard explosion of green.

But not this time; not this year. Suddenly it felt like too much effort: Gus Simpson, one of the most popular entertaining gurus on television, didn't want to throw a party. In fact, she'd have preferred canceling her birthday altogether.

She poured a stream of rich hazelnut-scented coffee from her large French press into an oversized blue-and-white-striped pottery mug. With care she carried her drink to the speckled gray-and-black granite breakfast bar, perching herself on the counter-height navy chair. Gus took a sip, just a little almost slurp (since no one else was around) so as not to burn her tongue, and flipped through the *New York Times*, trying to jolly herself out of her gloomy mood. But her natural habit—it was Monday, which meant the weekly Media section, and she loved to follow her industry—led her to a large article above the fold of the paper.

"The New Faces of Food TV," Gus read to herself, feeling a whoosh of anxiety in her chest. "Food is the new fashion and the latest crop of program hosts look as delicious as their culinary creations."

Gus tapped her teeth against each other as she always did when she was tense and scanned the large photo with all the up-and-coming hotshots in cooking television: there was that *young* surfer chef who always wore shorts and looked barely old enough to be in college, the *young* Midwestern housewife who only made dishes that took up to six ingredients, and the *young* Miss Spain who had turned a gig promoting her country's olives into an Internet cult following on YouTube. From there, Gus read how Miss Spain had created her own ten-minute Web show, *FlavorBoom*, which was also downloadable to TiVo, and had edited a small cookbook that had just come out at the holidays a few weeks before. It had already been a top seller online. The story continued on page two of the section, where there was a glamour shot of the gorgeous, black-haired Miss Spain in her crown and far too much mascara, with a large caption underneath: "Carmen Vega: From Beauty Queen to Foodie Queen."

"I bet she can't even cook," Gus announced to her coffee mug, quite ready to close the paper in disgust. But then a familiar line caught her attention, and she found herself scanning the words carefully.

*"Imagine there are only a certain set of ingredients and that's all there*

*is to use," says Gus Simpson, the CookingChannel's ubiquitous program host and star of the well-known* Cooking with Gusto! *in a recent interview in* Every Day with Rachael Ray. *"But we don't all create the same thing. So it's not really about what you put in a dish—it's about how you make that meal taste. It's not about how you make it but about how eating it makes you feel. Cooking, like life, stays interesting when you keep the experience fresh."*

*And fresh new hosts seem to be how cable is hoping to hold on to viewers, as ratings continue to decline on all channels . . .*

Blah, blah, blah went the article. On and on about these exciting new voices in the world of food television, all seemingly sanctioned, via the clever use of already reported quotes, by none other than Gus Simpson. Oh, how she hated that! Being interviewed for one article—which had been published over a year ago—and then finding those same words popping up in every other journalist's food story.

The lesson she'd learned: don't ever say anything, cutesy or cutting, that you don't want to hear parroted back to you for the rest of your life.

Gus thought about crumpling up the paper and tossing it in the bin, but there was no one around to see her dramatics and she always felt that grand behavior wasn't really worth the energy when there was no one to witness it. Television had trained her well. Instead, she sighed and left her spot at the breakfast bar for more comfortable surroundings. She shooed her white cat, Salt, out of an overstuffed wing chair in the bay window and watched her pad her way over to lie in a ray of sun with Pepper, who was black and had a somewhat pungent attitude.

Then, coffee in hand, she settled herself down on the sturdy white twill (for Gus had strong faith in her guests' ability to not spill and in the power of Scotchgard if they did). The large kitchen was a space in which Gus keenly felt a sense of home and was where she did all her important thinking, be it coming up with new recipes or sorting out the endlessly complicated lives of her daughters. The wing chair closest to the French doors, long ago dubbed her "thinking spot" by Aimee, was perfectly positioned to lend a view of the flagstone patio. She could enjoy the color of her divine garden come spring—currently a bit of leftover snow and slushiness from a Westchester winter—as well as have full range of her gleaming kitchen. Sitting in this chair provided what she always called the "viewer's-eye view" because it was how her home appeared on television.

Hers was a dream kitchen, with a deep blue Aga stove, a marble-topped baking area, those granite counters, a deep and divided white farmer's sink, the artfully mismatched cabinets designed to look as though they were pieces of furniture added over time (assuming every flea market and antique shop would miraculously contain wood pieces with precisely the same bun feet and crown molding), and a bank of Sub-Zero freezers and refrigerators along one wall. The pièce de résistance? The substantial rectangular island, with eight-burner cooktop and raised backsplash, ample counter space, and breakfast bar to one side (though not immediately in front of the cooktop, of course, where it might ruin the camera shot). The island was the part of her kitchen most familiar to her viewers.

What a great idea it had been to suggest filming at her home when she began her third CookingChannel program, *Cooking with Gusto!*, in 1999. It certainly cut down commute time and, much more important, had turned the reno into something she could write off. And Gus, for all her professional success, was a devotee of socking away money. For a rainy day. For her retirement. Which had always seemed way, way off, on account of the fact that she was so tremendously, eternally, divinely young. A someday worth planning for but nothing that seemed as though it was about to arrive soon. She was too busy.

In the early years when she first started on television, long before the plump paychecks and the merchandising deals, Gus hosted a half-hour program called *The Lunch Bunch* based on her menu at her gourmet spot The Luncheonette. It filmed in a studio in Manhattan and she took the train home to the small two-bedroom house she shared with Aimee and Sabrina. It was the same compact Westchester bungalow that she had initially moved into with Christopher, after they'd returned from their overseas Peace Corps stint and had given up living in Manhattan, back when they were barely married. When he'd raved about every dinner she burned and she made him brown-bag lunches, with sexy little notes tucked inside. When they were too new at life and marriage to comprehend the bad that could come. Would come.

The tiny place had been home with their two little girls, and Gus had tried out a variety of careers—taking photographs for the local paper, doing part-time camera work for the local cable station, and making a line of homemade candles—while baking cupcakes for Sabrina and Aimee's school and carpooling the neighborhood kids. Still enjoying the luxury of figuring out what she wanted to do.

Christopher's accident had changed things, of course, spurred her to open The Luncheonette, which attracted the attention of Alan Holt and his cable network. Gus's little restaurant, in Westchester County, just north of New York City, specialized in quick bites and tea parties and the like. She was close enough to the station that commuters popped in for beverages and snacks before catching a train. The decor—bright and light with distressed off-white tables and comfy Parsons chairs upholstered in a wide red-and-cream stripe—had been spruced up to lure in the soccer moms with time between errands and school's end. The small but thoughtful selection of gourmet groceries was selected to entice the adventurous home cooks, both the commuter and soccer mom variety.

It had been a gamble when she opened, a chunk of her late husband's life insurance money dwindling in a bank account and her two young daughters. It seemed as though running her own business would provide her the type of flexibility she needed with two young girls, and she'd always loved to cook. Loved to experiment with flavors and cuisines and making things look pretty. Her friends, though well meaning, disapproved, encouraging her instead to invest and live off the interest. But there wasn't really enough to quite do that, and besides, Gus had wanted the risk. She needed the jolt.

However, taking chances did not translate into being sloppy. No, indeed. And meeting with Alan Holt was a tremendous opportunity she couldn't afford to screw up. She had, in fact, served him several pastries and more than a few sandwiches, never knowing him as more than a regular customer. Until the day he handed her his card and suggested he wouldn't be averse to a home-cooked meal over which they could discuss a business proposal. Gus's fervent hope had been that he was interested in showcasing The Luncheonette in an episode or two.

She remembered vividly when Alan came for dinner in the spring of 1994, when Aimee and Sabrina were both young teens and she was a harried single mom, still keenly missing Christopher though he'd been gone six years by then. It was as though she'd hit the "hold" button on her life when he died, waiting for something she couldn't quite place her finger on that might make it somewhat better, and had instead filled up her days with working and organizing her girls. She hadn't much energy left over, which had been her intention. Just enough to wish for the ability to provide her daughters with the life their father would have wanted for them.

All Gus had asked the day Alan Holt came for dinner was to be left alone in the kitchen and for her girls to go out and cut some flowers. Something bright and cheery they could bring to her so she could do up a vase. Her oldest daughter, Aimee, had promptly walked outside to the back patio and flopped into a wicker chair, arms crossed, while Sabrina slowly wandered off through the front door, with a look Gus couldn't discern between sulking and concentration.

In fact, Gus had been quite prepared for the girls to come back empty-handed from the garden and had put together her own centerpiece hours earlier, working efficiently while her just-turned-into-teenagers slept away a gorgeous sunny Saturday morning. She'd tucked her arrangement onto a shelf above the washing machine, knowing her girls were hardly about to go near anything that seemed like a chore. Her request about gathering flowers had really been a mother's trick to get the kids out of her way while she seasoned and sampled in the kitchen.

And then she saw it: seven stones and one feather.

That's what Sabrina had placed on the center of the polished rosewood table.

"What do you think, Mom?" asked the thirteen-year-old, brushing her glossy black bangs out of her eyes as she gestured to a lineup of polished river rocks arranged by size and a random piece of gray fluff that looked, at a distance, more similar to dryer lint than to something that once winged through the sky.

Gus Simpson had chewed her lip as she pondered her younger daughter's contribution that day and cast her eyes down the length of her table, covered with her good ivory linen place mats, clean and crisp, her collection of quality china—the artistically mismatched pieces of creamware she'd collected at estate sales and flea markets and the occasional full-price purchase at a department store—and the genuine crystal goblets and glasses she'd brought back from Ireland years ago. Red, white, water. They'd cost more than three months' worth of mortgage when she'd made the splurge and Gus felt both guilty and exhilarated every time she saw them. Every mouthful—even plain old tap water—tasted better, too.

The Ireland trip had been her last vacation with Christopher, a romantic trip without the girls and filled with night after night in which they turned in early, eager to be alone. They'd laughed as they steered awkwardly around the jaw-droppingly beautiful coast, neither of them quite comfortable driving a stick shift on the other side of the road. But they'd managed it just fine, thank you very much. This made the accident all the more incomprehensible: Christopher had driven the Hutchinson River Parkway every day. Every single day. And then he made a mistake. That's what happened when you let your guard down.

Gus Simpson kept a vigilant watch: she knew that every moment, every detail mattered. Even the table setting.

The just-polished silver had gleamed as it lay on the linen place mats; the sixteen settings had been her great-grandmother's. Every clan has its own version of mythmaking—the hard winter everyone barely survived, the long and impossible transatlantic voyage from the Old World—and Gus's family had their own, of course. It was The Quest for Fine Things. And so the silver service (much more ornate than current fashion) had been purchased, at great sacrifice, as a setting a year from Tiffany & Co. and used only for the big three—Christmas, Easter, and Thanksgiving—in later generations. Sometimes, the story went, a spoon was all that could be afforded, the knives and forks left waiting for a fatter year. And so the set had made its way—though not without causing tension within the family—from mother to oldest daughter to daughter's daughter and finally to Gus, where the flatware had been put to more cutting and eating than ever before. No doubt her grandmothers would have thought it frivolous the way Gus delighted in her good plates and knives, and frowned upon their frequent use. Save, save, save it for later. That had been their motto. Tuck away the good to use only when you really need it. The thing was, Gus always felt as if she really needed it.

Though the night Alan Holt came to dinner, surely, even her grandmothers would have approved Gus setting such a grand table, all ready for the gorgeous meal simmering and roasting away in the kitchen. Cream of asparagus soup. Rack of lamb with herb jus. Gently roasted baby potatoes. Fresh, crusty bread she'd made from scratch, using a wet brick in her oven to generate steam (thanks to the advice of Julia Child in a well-worn copy of *Mastering the Art of French Cooking, Vol. 2*). All followed by a rich, buttery financière with homemade raspberry sorbet.

She'd wanted the meal to be delicious. Homey. Welcoming. After all, it wasn't every day that the president of the CookingChannel came over for Sunday dinner and the prospect of a different future hovered.

"Mom? The table?" her daughter had said.

Ah, yes, the table. Sabrina's display had been the one element of discord in a perfectly arranged tableau: it was clearly unacceptable.

Gus had opened her mouth to tell Sabrina to clean up the mess she'd created. To go upstairs, change out of the clothes she was wearing and put on something decent. To go find her sister and tell her to get ready.

The words had been all ready to tumble out. Even without seeing herself she could feel the frown, her furrowed brow. How many times had Gus criticized Sabrina and Aimee? Change your clothes, turn down that music, tidy up your room, don't leave wet towels on the floor. She, like all mothers of teenagers, had keenly felt her transformation into a walking cliché, as so many of the little issues that had seemed trivial and fuddy-duddy when she was young had stretched to matters of tremendous importance. A widow with two daughters, no less. Turning lights out when she left a room. Wearing a sweater instead of turning up the heat. Using a coaster on the coffee table. Eating leftovers. It was paying the bills that did it. Changed her perspective. Suddenly everything had mattered.

Every *thing* mattered. Even the table setting. She knew it had to be fixed.

But then she had caught the look of anticipation on her youngest daughter's face. The wide eyes, the mouth slightly open, just enough to catch the glimmer of her metal braces. Her heart caught in her throat: Gus had assumed the sad little decoration on her table was a way for Sabrina to make clear how little she cared about Gus's career. But could her daughter have been trying to help? she'd wondered.

At precisely that moment, Aimee had slouched into the room, alerted, no doubt, by the radar all kids have when they sense—

hope—their sibling is about to get in trouble. What is it about family that makes them close ranks to outsiders but attack one another with impunity in private? Thinner and two inches taller than Sabrina, her light brown bangs dyed pink from Kool-Aid, fifteen-year-old Aimee grinned slyly as she saw her mother frowning at the table.

"Nice!" Aimee said, catching her sister's eye, gesturing toward the stone-feather combo. "Mom's totally going to throw that away. It's not perfect. And Gus Simpson doesn't do anything that's not perfect. Right, Mom?" Then Aimee shifted all her weight to one hip, as though standing up straight would take too much effort. She waited.

Sabrina waited.

Gus hesitated as her mom side duked it out with her career side.

"I think Sabrina's arrangement is lovely," Gus declared. "It's very modern, very sleek. It stays on the table."

Aimee rolled her eyes.

"Shut up, Aimee, it's a very karma design," shouted Sabrina.

"I think you mean Zen, dear." Gus smiled, recalling Sabrina's huge ear-to-ear smile, the silver braces gleaming on her teeth, her sweet blue eyes wide and shining. It was the right choice, even though she'd felt a twist in her stomach when Mr. Holt, the CookingChannel president, had looked questioningly at the table as he sat down. But Gus had made no apologies, aware of Sabrina hanging on her every word, and in fact praised her daughter's creativity.

"Part of being a good host is to let everyone feel they've played a part," she'd told him with confidence that spring day long ago.

Mr. Holt, a divorced father, had nodded thoughtfully. "You're just the type of person I'm looking for," he announced. And by the end of cake, Gus Simpson—an unknown gourmet-shop owner without a cookbook to her name—had been asked to host a few episodes on the fledgling cable channel.

Sabrina's display, it turned out, had been karma after all.

And voilà! A few years on TV's CookingChannel and she

became an overnight sensation. That was the thing with all that "overnight" business: it typically took a lot of work beforehand.

And now here she was in 2006, the very heart of food television, The Luncheonette long since sold away. She lived in a stunning manor house in Rye, New York, precisely the style of house that Christopher would have loved: a three-story structure, white with black shutters, with a large formal dining room to the left of the foyer, a conservatory, a small parlor that Gus had converted to her private den, a wood-paneled library, a glassed-in breakfast room, and a cozy sitting room off the kitchen. Plus all the requisite space for her camera crews. There was a spacious patio immediately through the French doors from the kitchen, and a lush back lawn, edged in flowers, that was crowned with a decorative pond and waterfall that gurgled soothingly when she was out among the rosebushes.

There were far too many bedrooms in the manor house for a single woman—her children had been practically packing for college when she signed the deed but she forged ahead anyway—and there were definitely not enough bathrooms for a modern home. It was her plan to update the upper floors, though she'd been too busy over the years to do that just yet.

The house was the proof of her professional success. It appealed to her not only because of its magnificence but also because of its imperfections. It had a history that left it a little worn in places.

And so Gus had purchased the home when she was developing her most popular program, *Cooking with Gusto!* It was her third program for the network and the most well reviewed. Every week she hosted a brilliant chef in the manor house's amazing kitchen (renovated twice since the program had started), and she and her guest drank good wine and chatted as together they prepared an incredible meal, discussing amusing stories from the world of professional restaurant kitchens and doing their sincere best to convince the viewer at home that she, too, could make the scrumptious dishes they were preparing.

Gus Simpson had always been a good home cook. But she was no chef and she knew it: she'd been a photography major at Wellesley and possessed a great eye for visuals, and she'd had an idea ripe for its moment with The Luncheonette. Still, her gift—and it was a gift—had always been about creating an amazing experience. She was a true entertainer: Gus made her guests feel alive—even when her guests were on the other side of a TV screen—and her joie de vivre made every mouthful look and taste refreshing. Gus's main product was Gus, and she sold herself well: she was mother, daughter, best friend, life of the party. And she was good-looking to boot. Not so gorgeous that a viewer simply couldn't stand her, but undeniably attractive with her big brown eyes and her wide, toothy smile.

Gus Simpson was eminently watchable. Her viewers—and therefore her producers—loved her.

Her friends, her daughters, her colleagues: everyone wanted to be around Gus. And Gus, in turn, had been enchanted by the idea of looking after all of them.

Yet now it felt as though the spell was lifting.

So, okay, she didn't want to plan her own party. Who said she had to have one? Gus began pacing about the kitchen, ticking off a list on her fingers of all the people who would be disappointed if she didn't put something together, her frustration rising with every step. She was always doing, doing, doing.

Maybe turning fifty simply meant it was time to shake things up.

"Knock knock?" Shuffling open the white French door from her garden patio was Hannah Levine, her dear friend and neighbor. The two of them had shared an easy intimacy over the seven years they'd been friends. It hadn't been quite that way when they first met, on the very Sunday Gus moved into the manor house during the summer of '99. Gus had walked over to each of her neighbors' homes and presented a freshly baked raspberry pie, expressing how thrilled she was to be in the neighborhood. It was a brilliant touch, of course—pure Gus—and reciprocated by several dinner invitations and the beginning of many warm acquaintanceships. And then there had been Hannah, who lived immediately adjacent in a crisply painted white cottage, converted from what had once been the carriage house to Gus's stately home. Hannah had come to the door in faded gray pajamas, her medium-length red hair pulled back into a low ponytail. Her skin was pale and free of makeup, and she eyed Gus suspiciously through thick black glasses.

"What kind is it?" Hannah had asked, gesturing toward the pie, her body partially hidden by her wide mahogany door. She was even thinner back then, all sharp clavicle and bony wrist. And nervous, tremendously nervous. Of course, Gus was immediately smitten: she simply had to add Hannah to her collection of darlings. To the ones she wanted to nurture and nourish. Her girls, their pals, her coworkers: everyone was clay that Gus was eager to mold. She made a pest of herself that summer, dropping over next door with all manner of muffins and cookie bars, her resolve to befriend her neighbor only heightened by the fact that no one else seemed to visit the gentle, wary woman in pajamas. Certainly Hannah, already in her thirties then, was far too old to be a surrogate daughter; Gus imagined she would become like a little sister. But what happened instead was far more welcome: the two women found they had much in common—a shared love of gardening, an unconventional work schedule, a devotion to finding the perfect chocolate chip cookie, and a love of rising early—from which a true friendship sprang.

When the body wakes up before dawn, as Gus's typically did, there can be several hours when it seems as though there is no one else in the world. A peaceful time for some. Not Gus: she found these early moments, the house dark, the girls' rooms empty, the cats snoozing in far corners, to be tremendously lonely.

Fortunately, Hannah was quite likely to be on her way over by 7 AM, crossing the unfenced property line between their two homes.

Because once it became clear that Gus was going to be persistent, Hannah accepted her friendship as the most natural thing. From early on, she had the peculiar habit of never tapping on the door when she came by, always calling out and making her way inside. With anyone else Gus would have found such a gesture intrusive; with Hannah it seemed perfectly normal. The two of them spent many an early morning sitting in Gus's bay window, on those overstuffed chairs, dipping biscotti into their cappuccino and having the very same conversation they'd had the day before. That was the thing about their friendship: it was all about the being together, never about doing anything. As such it made few demands. Theirs was an easy intimacy.

It was also precious: Hannah was the first real friend Gus had made after becoming well known. There was no handbook for becoming semi-famous. (Or at least nothing that had been handed to Gus by the CookingChannel.) In a society thirsting for celebrity, it didn't take much for people to elevate a widowed mother with a knack for entertaining into a culinary guru. And so even by the late nineties, Gus had developed quite a following, with the requisite cookbooks and calendars, too. It was great; it put Sabrina and Aimee through some good schools. But her sort-of-but-not-quite fame also made it a hurdle to connect—people already "knew" her from TV and therefore it could be a tremendous disappointment to them if Gus turned out, for example, to be even slightly different than they envisioned. To be plain, it had been difficult to make friends. Oh, easy enough to meet people who wanted to say they were chummy with the host of *Cooking with Gusto!* More challenging to get to know individuals who wanted to know Gus.

Hannah Levine had been entirely different.

For one thing, she didn't watch television. Well, not exactly. Hannah watched multiple channels nonstop: CNN, MSNBC, and CourtTV. But dramas, comedies, home decor or cooking shows? Hannah didn't watch any of it. Instead, she holed up in her home office—with its built-in bookcases and large television—and wrote article after article for women's magazines. Sometimes in jeans but most typically in pajamas, with fuzzy slippers on her feet, and a bowl of M&M's nearby. Hannah was a busy freelance journalist, and her area of expertise was health, which pushed her slightly in the direction of obsessing over whatever she'd written about most recently. But she obsessed in a rather benign, almost kindly variety, as concerned for a stranger's odd throat clearing—could it be whooping cough?—as for her own potential ailments. Having the Internet as her main companion all day merely encouraged her cyberchondria.

That was one reason Hannah had been wary of the pie that first summer, having just written an article about an epidemic of *E. coli* on fresh berries, but seemed rather unfazed to learn about Gus's career. And frankly, in all the time since, she seemed yet to have watched one of her programs. Gus absolutely adored her for that.

Now she waved Hannah inside, though of course her friend was already halfway to the coffee. Gus had already left a mug on the counter, spoon on a napkin, and a few slices of fresh banana loaf arranged on a plate.

"I just finished a piece on the dangers of ignoring sore feet last night," Hannah told Gus after swallowing her first mouthful of hot coffee. "Do you stand for the entire time you're on TV, Gus? Because I've got a few ideas to make it a little easier—"

"Don't worry—from now on I think I'll be doing my show from a wheelchair," Gus said, shaking her head at Hannah's worried expression and reaching to show her the section of the *New York Times*. "Apparently I'm over the hill."

Hannah scanned the article. "Look, at least you're in it. You know you're still important when a journalist declares it so." She pulled a face at Gus to show she was joking.

"I'm just feeling a bit of I-don't-know, you know?"

"Is that why I haven't received my invitation to your birthday party?" said Hannah. "If it was anyone else I'd assume I was off the list. With you, I've been worried something's wrong. Your birthday is a few weeks away and I still have to plan my outfit."

Now it was Gus's turn to smile. "Why don't you wear your gray coat dress?" she suggested. That was the same outfit Hannah wore every year, purchased on a rare shopping trip with Gus. Hannah hated to leave her comfort zone of home. Hated to wear anything other than casual, loungy clothes.

"I think I'll just do that," Hannah said, nodding. She didn't mind being teased by Gus.

The two of them settled into a kind of cozy silence, munching on banana loaf and sipping coffee and intently dawdling to avoid the day's work. It was what they did every morning and they loved it.

The phone rang. It was only 7:08 AM.

"Who could that be?" Gus knew she wasn't needed in the studio for a meeting, and the TV crew filmed at her house on Wednesdays. Maybe something was up with Sabrina? Aimee was certainly still asleep at this early hour.

She picked up the cordless and said hello.

"Of course, of course, yes, definitely," she said, jumping up and almost spilling coffee on her white chair. She hung up the phone.

"Well, thank goodness," Gus said, drawing out every syllable for Hannah's benefit. "That was my exec producer. The bad news is that I have to be in the city and ready to be on air in less than two hours. The good news is that Gus Simpson isn't quite yesterday's leftovers."

# 2

From her bedroom window, Gus could see the black sedan coming up the driveway through the snow. It was right on time. She hastily grabbed her makeup bag and a selection of silk scarves—just in case she wanted to change her look—and went out to meet the driver. He was a short man, with closely cropped gray hair, and he wore a red tie.

"Hello!" she said, fairly bursting with excitement. "We've got to make good time."

"Ma'am," he said pleasantly, as he helped Gus into the back. "I've got the directions. Buckle up, now."

She waved him off. The truth was that she was a bad one for riding in cabs and cars without a seat belt, a fact she hid from her daughters and her producers. It's just that she hated the sensation of being squished in, hated the feel of the strap on her neck.

The driver put on his own seat belt, then turned and looked at her expectantly.

"I'm liable if you don't put it on, and we can't have that now, can we?" he asked, waiting, still smiling.

Christopher had worn a seat belt. That's what she'd been told by the police. There had been no indicators on that particular day in 1988, no sense of dread in the air, no feeling that anything remarkable was going to happen. Later she'd wondered if she missed some vital clue, if there was some moment of portent she had ignored. But try as she might, she could never discover any such memory. On a normal, routine day, Christopher left for the office, and then, later, as she put together a mushroom lasagna, a police officer came to the door. That was all. She wondered if cops still did that, came to the front door and knocked, bad news to deliver. She couldn't ever remember *exactly* what the policeman had said to her. Gus recalled the detail of Christopher's seat-belt-wearing and the somber look on the man's face. Her neighbor, Mrs. Clarkson, three doors down, had come over to stay with the girls; they hadn't known each other well but she hadn't hesitated when Gus asked. That was a kindness. And then Gus found herself at the hospital where Christopher had been a jagged, swollen mess and the doctors were saying things that made no sense. Like brain dead.

"What are you, brain dead?" Gus had said that to Christopher on more than one occasion when the girls were small and she was angry with his insistence that no, he didn't know how to pick out their clothes and couldn't she just do it because she was really so much better at it anyway? And she'd dress them and get them off to school and punish him with snappishness. He would reciprocate in kind. Theirs had not been a perfect marriage. No, indeed.

But they had loved each other deeply, with the kind of intensity that sprang from great passion and an unconditional trust that grew out of deep friendship. They'd seen a lot of despair when they were in the Peace Corps together and remembered enough to appreciate each other before getting carried away with petty annoyances. Never, not once, had she ever worried that their joint frustrations with the day-to-day grind would lead to any permanent damage. Even at her crankiest and most tired, when the girls were small and she was hopping mad every time he got to go out for lunch because of his job (while she had to stay home watching *Sesame Street*). Later, he'd make it up to her—even though there was nothing really to make up for—and he'd take Aimee and Sabrina to the park early on a Saturday so that Gus could sleep in.

"I'll lock you in the bedroom so you take a nap," he'd say. "Don't you dare get up before we get back."

And many nights they'd lain awake in that very same bed, sometimes tired from making love, sometimes tired from running after two rambunctious little girls, whispering animatedly to each other.

"Bring those Popsicles over here," Christopher would say, fake-moaning in horror as Gus tucked her always cold feet under his knees. They'd snuggle up to talk about all the places they wanted to take Sabrina and Aimee and all the ways they wanted to fix up their home and what Christopher's next career move should be and what was it, really, that Gus wanted to do? Their future, to them, was endlessly fascinating and exciting, a mysterious gift they had all the time in the world to unwrap.

The doctor on call had insisted he was feeling no pain, which had seemed odd, given the bruising. But then Gus had felt strangely numb herself, those first few hours with all the decisions and later all through the casseroles and the well-wishers. Through the nodding looks of approval at how well she was holding up.

"I can always tell when someone has suffered," said a woman—a stranger—at the book signing for her first cookbook in the mid-nineties. "You're cheery on television but I can see auras. And sadness floats about you like a cloud. I just wish I could give you a hug."

Gus had demurred, thanking the fan for her concern.

Privately, she worried others could see that far inside.

"The seat belt, please?" The black car hadn't moved from her driveway.

Gus nodded at the driver and reached behind her for the shoulder strap.

"Right, sorry, I was just distracted for a moment," she said, giving a thin facsimile of a smile. That was one thing she liked about riding in cars—sitting alone with her thoughts. Because her travel time was finite, she never had to worry about things becoming too dark in her mind. Not like at home, where she preferred to do something with her hands rather than risk becoming morose. It had been easier when the girls were younger and had been noising up the place, fighting and slamming doors. They'd always provided quite the distraction. Now Sabrina and Aimee still took up inordinate amounts of her brainpower without even the relief or peace of mind that came from knowing they were tucked in at night. It was funny, in a way, how she fretted about them even more since they'd left home.

Aimee was always the more solid of the two, serious-minded and capable. Even when she went through the sulky phase, as all teens did, it was short-lived. More an experiment before she settled into her role. One could always count on Aimee: a clever student, treasurer of the student council, then on to studying economics. She was a brain, that girl. Not to mention she'd been a great help in the AC days. After Christopher. When all Gus had wanted was to lie in bed—day and night—and think think think about the day he'd gone and come up with a plan of how to save him. She could convince Christopher to call in sick, thereby getting him off the road, or she could suggest he take the train instead of the car. Yes, that's what she'd do. Instead of the policeman coming to her door, it would have been Christopher, knocking because he'd dropped his keys and famished for her mushroom lasagna. Only once she had determined how she could have saved him—soothing herself by endlessly reliving and analyzing and changing the day's events to a better outcome—could she feel any moment of relief. A very brief respite before the reality of

Christopher's death kicked at her consciousness and the shock and trauma started all again.

And then there had been Aimee, waiting for Gus on the stairs in her pajamas when she returned from the hospital. Coming into her bedroom late at night, before Gus took to crying in the shower to muffle the sound, wide-eyed and watchful.

"It's okay," she'd said. "I covered Sabrina's ears."

Gus had had to get up. There was no other choice, was there? She would deal with herself some other time. Later. She wasn't about to let Christopher down, and what mattered most, she realized then, were their daughters.

And yet she felt more distant than ever now. Aimee rarely called, and when the two of them met, Gus found herself struggling to connect with her increasingly prickly daughter. It was as though that girl felt she had the weight of the world on her shoulders.

Sabrina, on the other hand, had always been rather scattered. A bit of a flake, that one. Popular but naive; Gus wouldn't have been surprised if she called home to say she'd sent money to Nigeria in an Internet scam. Trusting. Too trusting. She jumped into everything without looking and then came to Gus in pieces.

When Sabrina had left for college—the first college, there had been two—Gus had awakened in the middle of the night, sweating and pulling at the sheets, having dreamed that a group of kidnappers had stolen her little girl and tried to drown her in a toilet.

She still had that dream sometimes.

"Nervous about going into the city, are you?" asked the driver, turning on the radio for a little music.

Gus looked up, could feel her face tight from frowning.

"No, I go there often." She spoke a bit curtly, trying to dissuade the man from wanting to carry on a conversation. Alas, no luck.

"It's a fine house you have there," he said.

"Yes."

"Have you lived there a long time then?"

"Yes," she said. Then, not wanting to seem rude, added: "Seven years."

"How many rooms do you have?"

"Nineteen."

"That's too darn much!"

Gus stared at the man, intending to do her best and most believable haughty attitude. Instead, she looked into the rearview mirror, saw his broad grin, and then burst out laughing.

"You're right—it is," she said. "I used to live in a much smaller place, in fact. What's with the game of twenty questions?"

"I knew it," the man replied.

"Knew what?"

"You just need a little coaxing. I like to talk when I drive, and I've a good read on people," he said. "I guessed you were a happy sort underneath."

"Well, I'm not. I'm a professional pessimist."

"Me, too. The world's coming to a bad end," the driver said merrily, navigating a merge onto the expressway. A red SUV slowed down just as he tried to change lanes. "And that car is proof of it. But no reason not to have a laugh now and again."

He whistled as they crept closer to the cars all bumped up together in traffic.

"This is what I get for being a driver," he said, looking in the rearview mirror. "Hours in exhaust fumes all day. So what do you do?"

"I cook."

"You have a restaurant, then?"

"No, I just cook."

"You mean you're a housewife! Oh, that's a clever way to put it," he said.

"Umm, no. Well, yes, sort of. I am, or at least I used to be. But I get paid to cook, as well. I'm good at throwing parties." Gus leaned forward as best she could with her belt on and took a deep breath. "Do you know who I am?" It was a ridiculous question, and she felt silly asking it. But she wondered.

The driver glanced back at her for a moment; the expressway might as well have been a parking lot for how fast they were going.

"I haven't a damn idea," he said. "I hope you don't take offense. I don't know all of my passengers. But I drove for Angelina Jolie last week, and Derek Jeter before that. Not together, I don't mean. I'm not suggesting anything."

"Of course not," said Gus, relaxing. It had been a long time since she'd had a chat where she was just a stranger. She could tell this man she was an astronaut and he wouldn't care. It had been a strange and unexpected transition over the past decade, from being just a regular person to being someone who had to worry about what she said, concerned that a comment gone awry would show up in a tabloid. (The headline GUS SIMPSON HATES PEAS! had resulted in all sorts of calls from the pea lobby—who knew?—to Alan, producer's notes from Porter, and an official mea culpa that culminated in a show on pea soup. And all because she'd requested they leave them off her salad at Jean-Georges.)

"I hate peas," she said impulsively.

The gray-haired driver seemed to take her declaration as the most natural thing in the world.

"I'm reluctant to eat asparagus myself but the wife loves 'em," he said. "Too mushy, I find."

"Oh, no, you should just steam them quickly," said Gus. "Put a little water in the bottom of a sauté pan, cover for just a few minutes, drain, then put it back on the flame and toss with a bit of lemon and pepper."

"You are the cook, then," he said. "So what's your name, then, if you're so famous. I'm Joe."

She hesitated. "Augusta," she said. Then, feeling a bit sneaky, she came clean. "I'm called Gus. I've always been a Gus."

"Gus! Now that's a name for a big greasy mechanic, not a pretty lady."

"My cousin called me that, after the fat mouse in Cinderella," said Gus, wondering why on earth she simply didn't shut up. But it felt good to just talk. "You know, the cartoon? My mother didn't like it but my father thought it was cute. I guess it stuck."

"You're not fat now," said the man appreciatively. "If you don't mind my saying."

Gus blushed. She'd never done all that well with men after Christopher. Even innocuous little comments like the driver's. Finding her way around the clever pickup lines had been impossible before she met Christopher, and after the accident, well, there just hadn't been time. And it hadn't been the right time. She could count on one hand the number of times she'd been in a bar when she was in college. She'd always thought she was terrible at flirting. Gus could whip up a chicken Francese in a heartbeat, could host a party for one hundred with a day of planning, but she could rarely keep up her end of a little playful exchange unless she had a week to think on it. ("Mind?" she'd later think of how she could have replied to the driver. "Compliments have no calories." And then remember to toss her rich butterscotch-colored hair and laugh. Ha ha ha ha.)

The closest she ever came to flirting was the occasional sweet comment from Porter, who was happily married. She sometimes suspected his wife encouraged him to tell Gus how nice she looked. The two of them had been good friends to her for years now.

"I was chubby-cute, I like to think," she continued. "I tried calling myself 'Augusta' in college but it felt as though I was trying on clothes a size too big."

Joe gave the accelerator a bit of gas, careful not to go too fast with the snow. "Don't worry; we'll get there in time. I know a few side streets that'll speed things up."

"Do you like your job?" she asked suddenly.

"I get tired of the driving, no question," he said. "People think it's easy, no brains, but there's no job like that. We all have stress, you know. And my back gets sore from the sitting."

"You could get out and stretch after every run," Gus said, as the man shook his head no, explaining how he was on the clock.

"I see how it is with you, Augusta called Gus," said Joe. "You're the type who's always giving out the advice, too."

"Yes, I am," Gus admitted. She hesitated, then continued. "It's like I can't help it. I see something wrong and I have to zap it!"

"I'm married to one like that. She always wants to talk talk talk. Right when I want to watch the TV." The driver smoothly turned off the FDR drive at Ninety-seventh Street and stopped at a red light.

"I hate it when other people make mistakes," she said. "It really pains me. Maybe it's like that for your wife."

"Well, surely you've made a mistake or two."

"Too many, I think," said Gus. "It's how I know what to do now."

They fell into a few moments of silence as the car made its way down Second Avenue. Gus saw the dry cleaning shop, the gym, the florist, as the car rolled down the street.

"I used to live here," she told the driver, who nodded. "Back when it was called Yorkville. My husband and I."

"Before you made it big, eh?"

The realtors dubbed it Carnegie Hill when the real estate values went up in the late nineties. But back when she and Christopher were not that long out of school and just back from their year digging wells in Africa, they had rented a small studio in the building on Ninety-fifth and Madison. They were too far north then to be in any way fashionable. But it was beyond thrilling to share a home, to brighten a room by putting cheap glass vases in the window, filled with water that she'd dyed green, red, and blue. Their bed had been a pullout sofa, but it was far more comfortable than what they'd slept on overseas. Christopher had hoped to get into journalism in those days and wrote for anyone who would publish him, Gus proofing his articles and staying up with him late into the night to make coffee and offer feedback. But excitement and possibility didn't pay the bills.

Eventually, he went to work for his father, selling surgical instruments, and they moved up to Westchester to be closer to his sales territory. And closer to her family: she needed the help when Aimee and Sabrina arrived in fairly rapid succession. Gus hadn't expected it would all be so hard.

She looked down at the thin gold band she wore on the little finger of her right hand. It was her mother's wedding ring and she'd had it resized a few years before, after her mother died. Her father had been gone by then, too. I'm officially an orphan, Gus thought, an orphan and a widow. A twofer.

Outside her window she saw the Food Emporium, the Barnes & Noble, the Heidelberg restaurant, and the German bakery, the only remnants of a neighborhood that had once been Germantown. Yorkville, then Germantown—every handful of blocks meant a different feel in the city, a different community, a different cuisine.

"Everything changes," she said.

"That's good, in its way," he replied.

"I used to like change," Gus said, in a quick rush of words as though confessing. "But lately it's made me nervous. I feel a bit stuck." She hadn't been in a church in years, had stopped going when she decided that God didn't need yet another foul-weather friend, someone who only came pleading for help when things turned ugly. Besides, she mostly suspected God wasn't around at all. It was easier that way. And now she was suddenly pouring her heart out to the good-natured driver of a Lincoln Town Car.

"People must tell you the craziest things," she added, feeling a bit embarrassed.

"They do," he replied with a grin. "They also do some crazy things in the back but the relationship between a driver and a passenger is one of complete confidentiality. So I can't go telling you about that stuff." He chuckled, maneuvering the car westward toward Rockefeller Center.

Gus glanced at the crowded midtown streets, watching the men and women rush to get to their destinations. That's what had been fun about the city: the energy. The excitement in the air. Perhaps, she thought, what she needed was to recapture that energy. Maybe what she needed was to give her loved ones the ingredients to put together successful lives of their own so she could finally do some reinventing herself. She'd done it before, found her way to an entirely new life and career.

"Almost there," said Joe. "But now you're frowning again."

"It's a habit."

"Habits are made to be broke, I always say."

"Not the good ones," she replied.

"Gus, I wish you a very good day," said Joe. They were pulling up to their destination. "But I must say, you seem like a worrywart."

"Of course," she replied as she gathered up her things. "I have two daughters."

# 3

Aimee wearily checked her clock. She'd set her alarm a full fifty-five minutes earlier than usual, with a plan of going to the gym. Although she'd decided to start a new fitness plan last Thursday, she had, of course, waited until a Monday to get going. She glanced quickly toward the unadorned window—no shade, no curtains, not even a valance—before peeling out of the warmth of her amber-colored cotton sheets (Macy's January White Sale, 25% off plus an extra $10 savings with coupon) and realized she couldn't even make out the shape of the high-rise across the street. All she could see was white. Hah! It was snowing. And, as everyone knows, it's practically a commandment that a girl does not have to go to the gym in the snow. Sometimes, thought Aimee, there were wonderful benefits to living in New York in February.

She pulled her fluffy duvet up and over her thick, short sandy hair sticking out every which way, and pretended the alarm had never gone off. But just as Aimee was drifting back to much-desired sleep, the loud banging from the hall brought her to wakefulness abruptly.

Sabrina. It had to be Sabrina.

Aimee padded out of her bedroom to see her black-haired younger sister scooping up illustrated sketches from atop the dining room table and trying to stack them in a neat pile. As usual, Sabrina was impeccably dressed, this morning in a lilac suit with a fluted skirt, a sharp contrast to Aimee's stretched-out and faded pajamas.

"I thought you stayed over at Billy's last night," Aimee said, her face in a practiced neutral expression, as she leaned in her doorway. The best thing about sharing an apartment with a sister who was always playing house with her boyfriend-of-the-moment was that it was almost as though she had a place of her very own. Right now she could feel the tug of her bed, empty but warm, so warm, encouraging her by its very fluffiness to lie down again. Her pillow still had the dent from where her head had been.

"I did. But I've got a meeting in a half hour and I had to come all this way downtown because I forgot my drawings!" Sabrina stopped moving for a millisecond and scowled. "Think you could help me here?"

"Uh, no," drawled Aimee. "I'm in economics, remember? More into averting global disaster, not so much the individual issues."

"Aimee! If I don't get this job I'm not going to come up with my share of the rent." Sabrina didn't move, confident in the knowledge that money—or lack thereof—always spurred Aimee into action.

"Do you want some tips about getting it together, little sis?"

"No, I don't need you to tell me how to live, Aimee. I need you to help me, right now, for half a minute, to find my design board."

"Right."

"Have you seen it?"

"Yes. I left you a message last night telling you it had been abandoned on the living room sofa and that I was going to throw it away."

"What?! I haven't had time to dial my voice mail," screeched Sabrina. "I can't believe you chucked my presentation!"

Once, a long time ago, in the hazy time after their father had passed away and before their mother had a television program, Aimee became so enraged with Sabrina's side of the room being messy that she stuffed her sister's European history report down the garbage disposal and turned it on. Bye-bye, Queen Isabella of Spain. Some manner of punishment had resulted—a grounding, or a week without television. Nothing that made the destruction any less worth it, that was for sure.

Aimee later wondered why it hadn't occurred to Gus to penalize her where it would have counted. To mess up her tidy side or prevent her from eating her vegetables in alphabetical order. Something that would have had an impact.

At any rate, the mulching of the paper was one of those instances that immediately became a core family story. The kind that lived on in frequent telling, getting bigger over time, establishing Aimee as the cool cucumber and Sabrina as . . . what? The easily crushed tomato? Something that needed special care and attention. A peach.

Yes, that was Sabrina. A peach.

Now Aimee watched her sister with an air of detachment, but in her heart she was thoroughly enjoying herself. It doesn't matter how old one becomes—there remains something splendidly fun about tormenting a sibling. A certain inexplicable rush of power. Enhanced, to be sure, when a parent is nearby, but satisfying all the same. "You should really take better care of your things," drawled Aimee, walking back into her bedroom as Sabrina worked herself into a frenzy.

"Oh, go save someone who wants it," yelled Sabrina, following Aimee into her room to continue their fight.

With a sigh of exasperation, Aimee pointed to her closet. Sabrina turned her head; there, against the open door, lay her black microfiber portfolio case. Aimee nodded. Quickly Sabrina picked up the case by the handles and walked out of the room, then made a concerted effort to slam the apartment door. Nearly impossible with a door that had a hydraulic cylinder but Aimee gave her mental points for effort.

She waited until the door had closed, locked it, then headed to the bathroom mirror.

"You're kinda rotten as a big sister, you know that?" Aimee told herself. Her reflection stuck out its tongue in reply.

It had been a miracle to get a cab and Sabrina knew it. As soon as a few drops of rain or snow fell, New Yorkers rushed to hail the nearest yellow taxi and gloat through their car windows at the suckers still on the street. And that morning's sprinkling of snow had resulted in a veritable cab desert. But Sabrina lucked out when a patron pulled up to her regular corner. A lot of New Yorkers work the corners, of course, sticking day to day with a location they believed, based mainly on gut instinct and experience, worked best to get a taxi. And if Sabrina had a religion, its main belief was to avoid public transportation at all costs. ("I don't believe in being underground," she'd explained to Aimee about a thousand times.) On the mornings she woke up at the Tudor City apartment she shared with Aimee, she walked up three blocks and crossed the street to her lucky corner. If she found herself at Billy's Upper East Side condo, then she went to Ninety-sixth and Second; the year before, when she'd been dating Troy, she would stroll over from his NoLita walk-up to flag at Mercer and Houston. That had been a good spot, near Troy's place.

Taking taxis was one of the reasons she shared an apartment with Aimee instead of getting a studio of her own: Sabrina needed the disposable income to make sure she had cab money. After all, in the first few years after college, when she was interning and working as an assistant, there had been barely enough money for her MetroCard. But there was no going back once she'd landed a few interior design gigs of her own and savored how good it could be to be driven around. Her not-so-secret goal was to eventually work her way to having her own car and driver. A lofty ambition, to be sure, but one well worth the hours she was putting in. Her boyfriend of four months, Billy, had been complaining about how much she worked, in fact. Sabrina could just imagine Aimee's reaction.

"You?" Aimee would say. "Someone thinks you're working too much?" And she'd laugh in that superior way of hers.

Had it always been like this? She had a memory, more a gut feeling than anything else, of happier days. And certainly her mother, Gus, insisted there had been a time when the two of them were as thick as thieves. Generally, though, Sabrina could only remember arguments and hair pulling and being ignored at school. Even though she'd had a large circle of friends, it bothered her then—and it bothered her now—that Aimee seemed to find it a burden to be around her when other people were present. The simplest thing could set her off on a tear, such as the time Aimee mulched her history paper in the garbage disposal. Queen Isabella of Spain down the drain. That's what Aimee had said: Queen Isabella of Spain down the drain.

Their mother hadn't done anything about it, either. Just tried to smooth it over as she always did. Making things just so was very important to Gus. She expected a lot from her girls.

Sabrina quickly unzipped her portfolio case, just to reassure herself that it was all there. That Aimee hadn't actually thrown away her work or tried to put it in the blender or the oven. She felt around with her fingers, peeled back the cover a few inches. Everything was in its right place. With a few extra pens tucked into a pocket that had been empty the day before and—what was this? A granola bar and a small bag of Cheerios.

From Aimee, of course.

From Aimee.

The secret to delicious scrambled eggs was to cook them in a saucepan with bubbling butter and stir them constantly with a wooden spoon. Keep the heat medium-low. Resist the temptation to turn up the gas and cook the damn thing in two seconds. Only patience would allow the eggs to come together soft and fluffy and very, very light, Aimee thought to herself as she made little figure eights through the liquidy mixture, careful not to spill on her work clothes. Her plate, with a small dollop of ketchup, stood ready next to the stove, a fork resting on a folded napkin. A slice of bread browned in the stainless toaster.

"Stir, stir, stir," she said aloud, repeating what her mother, Gus, had always said when she insisted Aimee help out with breakfast. "Stir..."

"...and you won't be sorry," cried out Gus cheerily.

Aimee whirled around, nearly causing the saucepan to fall off the stove.

"Mom?"

Silence.

Oh, funny how it can sneak up on you: the moment of madness. It was one thing to repeat little phrases but now she was actually hearing her mother's voice *outside* her head. What's the standard procedure for losing one's mind, anyway? Do you call in sick? Check yourself into a hospital? Aimee waited a second before she continued to stir, reassured that it was just one of those moments when the background noises come together to sound like something familiar. A fluke.

Then she heard it again. Gus, talking slowly and clearly. Oh, dear God, had Gus died in the night? Was she haunting Aimee? She'd seen that in a movie once, though the parent was trying to convey an important secret that would save the family from a curse.

"Mom, if that's you, say something else."

"I'd never dream of using ketchup on eggs!" came Gus's voice in reply. And then a spurt of laughter. From the bedroom.

Spoon in hand, Aimee left the eggs and walked apprehensively, heart beating, into her bedroom. And that's when she saw Gus. In a turquoise linen shirt and khaki pants, her signature navy spatula in hand.

On the TV.

Gus was on television, cooking breakfast for the hosts of the *Today* show, who were eating and laughing.

"So aren't you the longest-running host on the Cooking-Channel?" asked Matt Lauer with a grin, knowing the answer already, thanks to his research department.

Gus smiled wanly.

"Yes, I just read that you're considered the grande dame of food television with all those young upstarts coming around," piped in Ann Curry before changing topics. "This crème brûlée French toast is amazing. Are we putting the recipe on our website? Fantastic."

And the chatter went on and on and on; Aimee held the remote in her hand, finger on the power button, but didn't press. Like everyone else, she found the host of *Cooking with Gusto!* engaging. Watchable. Likable. Unlike everyone else, Gus Simpson was *her* mother. It was, well, weird. Always had been. Though you had to admire her.

With no professional culinary education, Gus had managed to turn an interest in food and a knack for timing into a mega career. She could cook, she could throw a damn good party, and she never tired of talking, thought Aimee. Between Gus and Sabrina, it was always rather impossible to get in a word at the Simpson household.

"You're so different than I remember," her mother's longtime producer, Porter Watson, had said to her at Gus's holiday party in December, just over two months ago now. The two of them had waded through a standard, awkward nice-to-see-you commentary at the punch bowl and arrived, thanks to an offhand line about charity, at a discussion of Aimee's work at the UN. Porter seemed genuinely intrigued and said so.

"I don't think we've ever really spoken until now," Aimee replied quietly.

He'd looked at her with seriousness, as though he wanted to reply, when Gus motioned him over. She was standing partway up the staircase, admiring Sabrina's sage-and-cherry ribbon garlands on the banisters. "It's a far cry from seven stones on a table," Gus laughed. Alan Holt's first dinner meeting with Gus, and Sabrina's pitiful little centerpiece, was a well-worn anecdote. Gus had raised her glass and her partygoers did the same.

Then it was time for toasts and cake—always cake!—and Aimee had slipped out onto the patio and the garden beyond, cold just as a Westchester December should be, to huddle until making her exit wouldn't seem rude. From time to time she would glance toward a window, quickly so she didn't even have to admit to herself she was looking, hoping to catch sight of her mother looking for her.

The volume on the television grew louder as the *Today* show cut to commercial, jolting her back to her own breakfast in the kitchen. Aimee went back to look at her eggs. Not quite the perfection she'd hoped for. She scraped the rubbery mess into the garbage, rinsed off her plate and put it into the dishwasher, and took a bite of the dry, cold toast, then tossed that into the bin as well before leaving for the day.

Sabrina stepped out of the cab on Forty-ninth Street and Sixth and right into a puddle of melting snow. Thank God the fashion world had gotten over the open-toed-shoes-in-winter thing, she thought, grateful for her tall brown leather boots and her warm cashmere coat. She stepped up onto the curb, shifted her portfolio from one hand to the other while she pulled on her gloves, and then hustled eastward from Sixth to Rock Center. Her potential new client—and a steaming cup of mocha—was waiting for her at the Dean & DeLuca gourmet food shop and Sabrina was eager to see both of them. There was a crowd of onlookers standing in front of the *Today* show studio just ahead of the shop and she gave a quick look to assess jaywalking into the street, but a slew of black town cars and yellow cabs were clogging things up. Argh! Resigned to fighting through the crowd, Sabrina picked her way through the tourists who were gushing and cooing about whichever celebrity was being interviewed.

"I love her!"

"She's so real, you know?"

"I just wish she'd come to my house and make dinner!"

At that last comment Sabrina swiveled her black head involuntarily toward the glass-fronted studio and felt her stomach drop.

Through the window. On the monitors. Smiling and laughing and playing to the crowd. Just as she always did. Just as Sabrina was about to meet this client, the first one she'd set up on her very own. There she was.

Gus.

There was always Gus.

# 4

Carmen Vega scratched her arms—and her legs—and stared at her mini-television in the carefully refurbished galley kitchen of her overpriced Tribeca studio. What she saw on screen almost made her forget how much her skin itched. Because there, in her spot—the one her publicist had worked so hard to land, to coincide with the article in the *New York Times* that heralded her emergence as a full-fledged Foodie Queen—was Gus Simpson. It was simply infuriating! Gus Simpson was everywhere, with her own brand of knives, her own brand of spices, her mega-selling cookbooks, and all those *Cooking with Gusto!* episodes that ran daily on the CookingChannel—not to mention additional repeats of her 1990s programs *The Lunch Bunch* and *Entertaining Eats*. (Why on earth anyone watched those episodes of

Simpson in colored jeans and brocaded vests was beyond Carmen. Nothing ever looks as bad as a bygone trend.)

There was even talk that Gus had been approached to start her own magazine. Carmen already had a name for *her* own magazine and had even bought an online address, if only someone was willing to fund it. Being Miss Spain 1999 might intrigue some of her fans but it did not necessarily cause investors to pony up, unfortunately. She simply hadn't been able to raise enough money. (Though, much to her annoyance, she'd been asked out on several dates by those same investors, male and female alike.) What bothered Carmen the most was that, despite her beauty pageant background, she had a degree from the Culinary Institute of America. Gus Simpson did not.

All Gus was doing on the TV was making a breakfast every person in America already knew how to make, and yet there was Matt Lauer, yakking it up as though he'd never seen an egg.

Damn, a person just couldn't get away from that woman! Carmen had heard, through the culinary grapevine, about Gus being demanding. Which was believable—all the celebrity chefs she'd ever met were far worse than the beauty pageant contestants she'd once known. At least the beauty queens relaxed a bit when the lights went down and the double-stick tape was peeled off their boobs.

Chefs, on the other hand, never put away their knives.

And the thought of having something sharp really appealed right about now: Carmen wiggled, desperate to reach that place on her back that itched more than anywhere else.

"Don't scratch!" her publicist had BlackBerryed the night before. "Chicken pox can leave scars. Think of your face!"

Who gets chicken pox the night before they're supposed to go on the *Today* show? Carmen Vega, that's who, she thought glumly, rubbing her back against the edge of the concrete countertop for a little scratch without letting her eyes leave the television.

If Carmen wanted her magazine, a line of saucepans, and a far fatter bank account, she was going to have to raise her profile. And getting sick before a big TV appearance wasn't going to cut it. She'd wanted to go on anyway—a generous slather of foundation might have done the trick—but her publicist wouldn't risk becoming persona non grata if the *Today* show hosts caught the virus.

Carmen hadn't even known that adults could get chicken pox, and so wasn't highly alarmed when, two weeks ago, she saw several children with scabby little spots during her afternoon stint as a guest teacher in a second-grade classroom. It had been yet another stunt that was the creative brainchild of her increasingly too expensive publicist, and the event had attracted a handful of reporters. It had even garnered her a few meetings with interested executives. But most of the commentary, as usual, came from the ubiquitous foodie-bloggers-turned-journalists. The Internet bloggers were Carmen's mainstay, pumping up her career, coming to her cooking demonstrations in malls, and posting their meet-and-greets on YouTube. And she loved them for it. The Internet fans had made her career by watching her and then talking about how they felt while watching her. It was very postmodern.

And they loved to talk about how she looked as much as what she cooked.

"You're so beautiful!" Eventually, someone would say it. Carmen was one of those lucky few who get more than their fair share of good genes: her olive skin was smooth and glowing, her figure trim, her legs shapely, her black hair glossy and thick, her brown eyes wide and rimmed with dark lashes. But so what? She knew she wasn't as good-looking as her mother and older sister Marisol, who lived quiet lives back home in Seville. But Carmen had the gumption to use those family genes to her professional advantage, first in the world of pageants and briefly as a model. Her original plan had been to get to Hollywood. By the time she flubbed her shot at the Miss Universe title—a wardrobe malfunction with her halter top during the swimsuit competition meant she quickly became one of the more well-known runners-up—led to a role in a blockbuster film spoofing herself, and a tabloid-heavy courtship with the bleached-blond singer from a popular boy band. By early 2002, the crooner was on to a new piece of arm candy, Carmen hadn't landed any additional acting work, and even a fender bender in Beverly Hills hadn't attracted even one paparazzo. Her more-than-fifteen-minutes were all used up: Miss Spain had become Miss Lame.

That's why Carmen, bored, frustrated, and more than a little freaked out, locked herself in her rented guesthouse to hide. To figure out her next move. Sleeping in until noon, with no plans for her afternoons, she made dish after dish that reminded her of home: paella, gazpacho, and fried fish. At night she lay on her sofa and drank glass after glass of wine, full from her cooking and overwhelmed with self-pity, the CookingChannel playing on the television for background noise. Lulled into fitful sleep by the sound of Gus Simpson planning parties on television.

Finally, one day, chopping up vegetables with a mild hangover, the pieces came together in a coherent idea: Carmen wanted a career in front of the cameras and she loved to cook. The next day she awoke before midday for the first time in months and used her cell phone to call for admissions applications to culinary schools all across the country. Carmen Vega was going to cook her way to stardom.

Four years later, she had a steady income as a spokesperson for the top importer of black Spanish empeltres olives, and her live ten-minute Internet show, *FlavorBoom*, was garnering attention. Carmen was on her way to crossing from cult hit to mainstream star.

Though, to be honest, a lot of her fans were as interested in her favorite brand of lip gloss as much as her lip-smacking recipes. And, keeping the universe in balance, she had also attracted a dedicated following of Carmen-haters. Every so often she deigned to check in on the latest ramblings on CarmenVegaSucks.com, the online home of an anonymous blogger who savaged *FlavorBoom* with regularity. She told herself it didn't bother her, though she called her mother after each new update, unable to express her anger as succinctly in English as she could in Spanish.

Reflexively, Carmen reached for the phone—one eye still on Gus Simpson cooking on the *Today* show—and dialed the number she knew so well.

"*¿Mamá? Tengo otro día malo . . .*"

Overcooked instant rice, dry pork chops, canned yellow beans, and wilted iceberg lettuce.

That's what Gus said whenever an interviewer asked how she got into cooking. She recited the dinner menu her mother had cooked most often, typically more than once a week. Sometimes with apple sauce from a jar, sometimes without seasoning at all.

Her mother and father would sit across from each other, Gus in the middle. Pass the salt, pass the pepper. No one talked as they chewed, slowly, swallowing hard to get down each bite.

"Don't believe it when you hear that the fifties and early sixties were all about Suzy Homemaker." Gus repeated the same words to Al Roker that she'd said many times before: "Just like now, a lot of those folks couldn't boil water and hadn't a clue how to make a proper meal. My mother was one of them."

And then Gus launched into her condensed but well-practiced anecdote of using her library card to take out cookbooks, of saving up her allowance to finally buy a copy of Julia Child's *Mastering the Art of French Cooking* for her very own, and of spending her Saturday and Sunday afternoons experimenting and forcing the neighborhood kids to eat her concoctions.

"I just wanted to eat something that tasted good!" she concluded with a laugh.

"Well, this brunch is fantastic," said Ann Curry. "Thanks to Gus Simpson, host of *Cooking with Gusto!*, for sharing these great recipes! We'll see all of you tomorrow."

"And we're out," called out a voice offstage. One of the producers walked onto the set.

"Thanks so much for filling in last minute, Gus," he said. "We were so shocked to find out Carmen Vega has the chicken pox. But you really saved our bacon, pun intended."

With a light touch on her arm, he steered her off set, laughing, as though the two of them were coconspirators, saving the *Today* show from dead air. (Which, after years in television, Gus knew wouldn't have actually happened.)

"Oh, I'm just delighted—delighted," she repeated, a smile pasted on her face as he walked her to a dressing room. Carmen Vega! The young Internet Foodie Queen? Whom Gus had been replacing was one fact, she realized now, that had been conspicuously left out when she had been called as an emergency guest. In fact, she was so thrilled to get the call, she hadn't even thought to ask who had dropped out. The reality was that she hadn't done morning television in almost a year, as the breakfast shows had become more focused on the chef-testants of *Top Chef* and the latest cook with a gimmick. And now Gus understood: she'd morphed, seemingly overnight, from sexy fun guru of entertaining to the reliable old stalwart when they needed someone who would show up. Not someone who was . . . exciting. Not a beauty queen.

And, for God's sake, what had Gus done? She'd gone on the air and scrambled eggs.

"I could have at least done an omelette," she said to no one in particular.

Maybe they were right.

She sat down in front of a mirror and wiped off the heavy TV makeup from her face, dabbing on a little moisturizer and reapplying a neutral lipstick and a swipe of mascara. She glanced down at her blouse quickly, checking to make sure she hadn't rubbed any foundation on her. Then she stood, smoothing out her flat-fronted pants as she did so. "I look just like Gus Simpson," she sighed, noting her golden-brownish hair pinned loosely at the back of her head, the few tendrils of hair pulled loose to soften the look, the flowing style of her clothing, the chunky necklace with a pendant that fell just above her breasts. She was always comfortably elegant. A viewer, a producer: everybody knew what they were getting when they ordered up Gus. Maybe it really was time to think about a makeover. Take a page from Carmen Vega's book.

A quick check of her watch revealed it was just 10:20 AM. Perhaps she wouldn't head back to Westchester immediately, would stroll over the few blocks from the NBC studios to Saks and poke around, buy something fresh.

Gus zipped up her handbag and switched on her cell phone to check in. Her first call was to Porter.

"Hey, Gus. Did you get my message? " He'd been producing her programs ever since her first stint on *The Lunch Bunch*. "Look, since you're in the city, I was wondering if you could come by? Marketing has just brought in the results from a new focus group, and, well, I think we should just put our heads together."

"Oh, Porter, it's bad, isn't it?" Gus was worried. "I know the ratings weren't as strong last fall but—"

"Let's talk face-to-face. See you when you get here." And he was gone.

There went her quiet day of shopping.

# upsetting the apple cart

# 5

It had been Hannah's idea for Gus to call Troy and ask his advice. He was young and smart and he knew how to think on his feet. And Gus needed the help. She hadn't been completely surprised by the news from her producer—that ratings were down again and the focus groups were favoring live shows over taped programs like *Cooking with Gusto!* What she hadn't expected to hear was that her season was going to be cut short or, possibly, pulled completely to make way for a mid-season replacement. Just like that. Twelve years on the CookingChannel and suddenly, just like anyone else, she was being told to put up or shut up.

"I'll call Alan and get this straightened out," she told Porter, with confidence. "He may be the president but you and I have been with him since the beginning. There's been some mistake."

Porter had sat there quietly as Gus borrowed his office phone to place the call. She watched as he tapped his dark-skinned fingers on the desk, pointedly avoiding her gaze. Giving her privacy even though she was mere feet away.

Alan, she'd been told slowly and repeatedly by his administrative assistant, was in a meeting. A meeting that was going to last all week, apparently. Gus held on to the handset long after the assistant had clicked off.

Business can seem so very personal, when you're all friends sitting around a table toasting the latest success. But, in the end, business is just that. It's business.

Gus Simpson could have her show canceled just like anyone else. And it hurt.

Porter, after breaking off a piece of good Swiss chocolate from the stash in his desk and encouraging Gus to nibble, had stripped the situation bare: the *Today* show appearance had been a fluke. Carmen Vega had chicken pox and Rachael Ray, their first choice of replacement, was shooting the world's first all-cooking movie up in Albany. Gus had been close enough to their studio to make it on time. And she was a solid. Dependable. Enough said.

Not to mention, Porter explained, but he'd heard that all the well-known cooking personalities were retooling their programs on all the cable channels: Nigella Lawson was doing a thirteen-episode series devoted to the barbecue, that most un-English of meals, and while wearing designer tankinis, no less. Gus's longtime rival, the incomparable Barefoot Contessa, was turning her program into a musical, sharing recipes set to lyric and score.

"You're joking?"

"Gus, Ina Garten has an amazing range." Porter shrugged his shoulders. "Everyone has a gimmick but you. And good food well prepared is snoring boring. Nobody's tuning in anymore."

"But I have a contract," Gus sputtered.

"Contracts have a way of biting you," Porter replied. "You know that part where it says you get a bonus if the ratings jump by ten percent? It also has a clause that the contract can be canceled if the ratings drop by the same percentage."

"I haven't read the contract since I signed it years ago..." Gus sighed. She never thought things would go this way.

But Porter had saved the best for last: the show's budget was being slashed in half. And Carmen, the gorgeous Beauty Foodie Queen, had been spotted coming out of the president's office at the Cooking-Channel studio the week before. And he wasn't getting a straight answer from anybody.

Gus shot daggers with her eyes, her mouth full of chocolate.

"I figured we had more time to get things on track but it's not looking good—for either of us," Porter said, a wan smile on his face. "Give me something fresh, Gus. It's the only way I can save your show."

Of all the unexpected things to happen since moving from Oregon to Manhattan as a new college grad more than a decade ago, Troy never anticipated that he'd end up being dumped by the girl of his dreams while remaining on stellar terms with her mother. Who does that? It simply wasn't normal. But it was true: Troy Park had a far more loyal friend in Gus Simpson than he'd ever had in her fickle daughter Sabrina. Gorgeous, sexy Sabrina, all glossy black hair and dewy blue eyes, forever dressing in lollipop colors. She was an eye-catching one, that girl, the type of woman who glided into any room and immediately demanded attention without saying a word. There was a certain sweet vulnerability to the young Miss Simpson, a softness that appealed. She was light on her feet and rather cheerful, in fact. Sabrina was unlike any woman he'd ever met.

Which was all the more ironic since Troy had always made it rather a point of honor to roll his eyes whenever a pal confided, over a fifth or sixth beer, about being hit by a thunderbolt. About falling in *love*.

And then it happened to Troy.

He'd just left his advertising job to work full-time on his entrepreneurial venture. It was a little sooner than he'd imagined and he wasn't completely ready. But the timing for the product was right and his father had encouraged him to go for it. It's always better, his father had said, to work for yourself. Then you know that you can always trust the boss.

His parents had worked side by side, growing apples and pears in their acres of orchard. Oregon had good soil, his father said, that's why they moved there after arriving as newlyweds from South Korea, both working in a restaurant operated by another immigrant family until they could finally put a down payment on the land they so desperately wanted. Troy was five when the Park family moved into the compact farmhouse on the property, and his mother's excitement as she unpacked boxes, his sister Alice strapped into her high chair so she couldn't crawl through the dust, remained vivid in his mind. His mother had not stopped smiling even as she washed the floors.

His father had walked him by each and every tree on the Park family farm that very night, carrying him after Troy's stubby five-year-old legs could go no farther.

"Focus on what you want," his father said, "and never lose sight of your goal. Then you must take a chance."

Now Troy had started FarmFresh, a vending company that specialized in supplying custom refrigerated machines with fresh fruit, bottled water, and yogurt. Carrying on the Park family tradition.

And, because he was his mother's son, he wanted to spiff up his offices. There was no denying that he'd been entranced by Sabrina from the moment she walked into his rented office space. He'd heard about her from the new wife of one of those beer buddies—she'd just done over their new apartment—and the newlyweds were ecstatic, driving Troy crazy with their insatiable need to discuss roman shades and the importance of choosing the right hardware for the bathroom vanity. "Sabrina is such a talent and just the right price because she's starting out," he'd been told. "Plus she's the daughter of that entertainer-cook lady on TV. Only Sabrina doesn't do kitchens."

Good enough for Troy as he didn't have a kitchen in his office. But he had enthusiasm: all the eagerness of a young businessman in receipt of his first major influx of cash, ready to outfit his workplace in a style befitting his business philosophy, his hope for the future, his wit. By which he envisioned some combination of Scandinavian design, earth tones, ergonomic chairs, an office dog, and a wall-mounted basketball hoop. Perhaps even a banner of his college team, the Oregon Ducks, placed just so on a wall behind his desk.

"That's absolutely fantastic," Sabrina had said, smiling, as Troy had detailed his wish list in that initial meeting. She had a pedicure of shimmering coral and showed a good amount of smooth leg all the way up to a lime-colored sleeveless tweedy dress, its nubbly texture practically begging him to rub his hands on her. (*Likes green* is what he'd written in his PDA; Troy made a point of noticing the small details when he was interested in a woman.) Then she pulled out a design board with hardwood and carpet samples and some fabric swatches. A much more conservative look. Mature. "What's neat is that we're going with something entirely different from dot-com fabulousness and I can't wait for you to see it," she said, and never stopped smiling the entire time she talked. Sabrina was unlike any other New Yorker he'd ever met: she looked happy instead of seriously determined, and she owned not one stitch of black clothing. Even her walk was upbeat, more of a skip than a stroll. Sabrina made everything seem . . . lighter.

Quite without planning, their meetings had led to dates. (Well, without planning on Sabrina's part, that is. Troy had gone out of his way to set up reasons for them to meet, had feigned interest in desks and carpets and made a point of shopping with her, followed up with coffees and dinners and movies.) And soon enough they were inseparable, the tall, broad-shouldered Asian-American man from Oregon and the bright-eyed, dark-haired smiling girl from New York.

Troy humbly, even happily, accepted his much-deserved ribbing from the chums he'd mocked over the years. He let Sabrina sell his black leather couch on Craigslist and wrote her a check to redecorate his overpriced apartment in the Meatpacking District. He made a point to spend time with the Simpson ladies, enjoying lazy Sundays up at Gus's house in Westchester while she tossed together a sumptuous roast beef dinner, even going so far to ingratiate himself as to set up an ill-fated double date between his business partner and Sabrina's sister. In Troy's mind, Aimee was the anti-Sabrina, all dourness and disgruntlement. To his surprise, his business partner dated Aimee for several weeks before they parted ways amicably. Some people had strange taste, that was for sure.

But all of that was mere detail in Troy's quest to make himself indispensable to Sabrina. He wanted her to need him. But for all of her cheeriness and laughter, Sabrina remained mysteriously unlike any of the girls he'd known before. She was remarkably unperturbed if he failed to call on time, for example. Or he could spend an entire long weekend with her and then not get a reply to his "had a great time with you" email until Wednesday. It was maddening.

Of course, they'd had all the proper conversations in due course—just the nuts-and-bolts sexual history, no need for the hows and how-was-its—and Troy, so convinced of their particular and unique bond, hadn't even been alarmed to learn that Sabrina had been engaged to more than one man in the preceding three years. It made perfect sense when she told Troy that those relationships just didn't feel right and that she'd broken them off; perfect sense, of course, because clearly she'd been waiting for Troy.

So, to his way of thinking, he hadn't had any warning on the day Sabrina called him from Gus's house and said she would be taking the train back to the city and would he meet her at their favorite brunch spot? He remained confused when she told him she'd stopped off at her apartment to collect his toothbrush and his clothes. He felt numb as she handed over a paper Whole Foods bag with his shirts, neatly folded one atop the other, and his toothbrush, wrapped in tissues, sitting on top of the pile. The bag still had a faint scent of fruit. Then she said it.

"You're a great guy, Troy. Let's be friends."

And she didn't stop smiling the entire time.

After that, Troy was more than ready to say goodbye to the whole lot of Simpsons. He'd never, in all his thirty-four years, been dumped before. (Eleni Dicoupolous from eleventh grade did not actually count, in his opinion.) It's not that Troy had been a player; he'd had a number of perfectly nice girlfriends with whom he'd had perfectly nice relationships. They all pretty much ran their course. But with Sabrina it had been completely, inspiringly different. Somehow all those stupidly popular song lyrics finally made some sense.

But there was a teeny little glitch in his quest to cut all ties with Sabrina. Because Gus Simpson believed a fresh fruit vending business—with machines in airports, in schools, in workplaces—was a thing of brilliance. And a few months before the breakup, back when he imagined Sabrina was going to become Mrs. Park soon enough, it hadn't seemed unusual at all when Gus approached him to buy a stake. After all, she'd simply been investing in her daughter's future, and what entrepreneur couldn't use extra funding and the backing of a popular CookingChannel TV host?

Exactly.

Now he was stuck with regular inquiries from Gus—and she was on her way over for yet another visit. He'd never expected her to take such an interest in how things were going. And not merely with his company.

Troy opened his bottom left drawer and pulled out a yellow nerf ball, one of several nesting in his desk. With precision he tossed the ball high into the air, up and on its way across the room, waiting to see it swoosh through the small net. Once Sabrina had taken herself out of the picture, Troy went out the very next morning and put basketball hoops in every office and a pool table in the conference room.

With a wooden board on the top it worked rather well for meetings, in fact.

He kept his eye on the yellow nerf ball as it began its descent . . . and landed right on Gus Simpson's beautifully coiffed head.

"Oof!"

"Oh, Gus, I'm so sorry." Then Troy grinned. "You make a great defense. Game of Twenty-one?"

She walked into his office and put down her handbag, took off her winter coat and shook off a few snowflakes.

"No, thank you," she said, looking him up and down. She continued to stand. "You seem a little thin."

"Just been working on my six-pack abs."

"Uh-huh. Well, the bags under your eyes don't exactly send that 'picture of health' image."

"Been working a lot."

"You should come to dinner soon. Sunday?"

Troy stood up and walked around his desk, then pulled out a chair. Gus finally sat down.

"I'd come by, Gus, but I have a feeling that Sabrina might be invited, just like the last two times."

"Oh, I told you that was a mistake."

"Once is a mistake. Twice is stupid—on my part."

"Well, a mother knows, Troy. The two of you had something special."

The black-haired man crossed his arms and leaned in to Gus, his jaw clenched.

"I'm not in the mood, today, Gus. We're bidding on a major contract and I don't have time to listen to the wild and wacky tales of Sabrina Simpson's romances."

"But, Troy, it's just that she's dating some Billy fellow who's completely wrong for her—"

"Not my problem."

"It is your problem. You're perfect for Sabrina. And you *love* her!"

"I stopped loving your daughter the day she handed me my ass in a paper bag."

Gus looked startled. Then she laughed.

"Troy," she said quietly. "You are a terrible actor." She gazed at him for a few moments in silence. "Now what about dinner?" she asked.

"No."

Sighing, Gus held up her hands in defeat. "Okay, that's enough for today," she said. "I'm actually here for some help."

"Gus!"

"*Not* about Sabrina."

Troy moved around to take his seat behind the desk. "All right then, I'm at your service. What do you need?"

"For you to put on your adman's brain and reinvent my show."

Troy made a hooting sound. "I'm an entrepreneur now. And you're an icon of food television, Mrs. Simpson."

"And about to be booted off the air if I don't make things fresh, according to my producer."

"You're kidding me."

There was none of her daughter's smiliness in Gus's face as she stared directly at Troy. Just worry lines across her forehead. It was clear that the graceful woman in his office was very, very troubled.

He let out a sharp intake of air. Then he opened a drawer on the right side of his desk—mercifully free of nerf balls—and pulled out a yellow legal pad.

"Let's brainstorm. Quick meals?"

"Been done before."

"Rare ingredients?"

"*Iron Chef.*"

"Okay, okay, okay, maybe we don't need to be completely original. Just a new take—a twist on what you've been doing," puffed Troy. "What about a live show, Gus?"

"Emeril's live."

"True. And it's worked for him. He's a guy with a famous catchphrase: Shazam!"

"That was Captain Marvel. Emeril says 'Bam!'"

Troy nodded thoughtfully. "What's your catchphrase?"

Gus appeared displeased.

"I don't have one."

"Methinks perhaps we've isolated our first problem."

"So you think viewers will start tuning in because I'm live and say 'Wham!' instead of 'Bam'?"

He shook his head. "Uh, no. Gus, you've gotta stop taking this all so personally. No one said there's anything wrong with Gus Simpson the person. The issue is Gus Simpson the personality."

Gus looked as if she was about to cry.

"I'm just myself!"

Troy smiled. "No, you're not. You're your best self. You're too damn perfect."

"I'm not understanding what you're suggesting, Troy."

"We need to up the risk. Put you on the spot. See a hair out of place. Add some novelty."

"Novelty? I don't like where this conversation is heading."

"People get bored with the same-old. It happens with work, it happens with entertainment—think of the classic second-season sitcom drop-off—and, at the risk of seeming to mention your youngest, cruelest daughter, it happens with relationships. With boyfriends."

"So..."

"So go back to your producer and tell him you want a show that airs live."

"But I don't want a live show!"

"And no more of these chef guests creating froufrou dishes. Not unless they're on their own reality shows and have Q-ratings."

"I beg your pardon?"

"You want hot guests and cool food," mused Troy. "Or maybe it's cool guests, hot food. Yes... that could be your tagline! *Cooking with*

*Gusto!*: Hot food. Cool guests." He began writing on his yellow pad, had trouble getting the ballpoint to run.

"This doesn't sound like my show at all," insisted Gus.

"Exactly." Troy opened and closed desk drawers quickly, searching for a pen before his slogan fell out of his head. Without thinking he blindly reached into his bottom left-hand drawer and pulled out an orange nerf ball.

"Hey," he said. "What do you think about basketball?"

# 6

Gus grabbed the remote control and settled herself in front of the TV in her large family room, joined by her cats Salt and Pepper. She had never watched a basketball game—nor heard of March Madness—before that afternoon in Troy's office several weeks ago. Well, maybe she was aware of the college basketball championships, in the way she also knew the name of Kelly Clarkson even though she'd never watched *American Idol*. (She was much more of a Beatles fan, maybe with a little late disco thrown in.) The details—of sports, of pop music—floated about in the air somehow, headlines on her Web browser when she went to check her email or magazine covers at the newsstand that she glanced at.

The funny thing was, she'd been fully prepared for Porter to nix Troy's idea when she brought it to him, imagined his response: "You?

And NBA stars making party food on live TV as you get ready to watch college ball together? That's insane!"

Instead, Porter formed a tent with his hands and began tapping his fingertips together.

"Would you wear a cheerleader costume?" he asked, raising one eyebrow.

"Good God, no!" Gus was horrified.

"Just trying." Porter winked.

"I'll tell Ellie you asked me that," Gus said in a fake threatening way. Porter had been happily married for thirty years and had nothing more than a healthy, mostly professional, appreciation of Gus's figure. "Seriously, though..."

Porter spoke slowly, turning his thoughts in his mind. "What I like is that your approach is fairly off-the-wall. A complete departure for Gus Simpson, which should get us some media buzz. We might alienate a few longtime viewers, but we're definitely going to attract a younger crowd, maybe even some men in the eighteen-to-twenty-four range." Porter began nodding vigorously.

"And what appeals to advertisers will appeal to Alan Holt," finished Gus. "Thank you, Mr. Watson."

"Thank you, Mrs. Simpson."

They were hopeful but aware of the urgency. Both of them needed this episode to succeed; there were no plans in the works to tape any more episodes of *Cooking with Gusto!* until this program aired live and the ratings were in.

And the show was going to air on her birthday, no less. Gus couldn't have come up with a more perfect excuse not to throw a party—she simply didn't have room in her schedule to plan, did she? Because all she had time for now was the upcoming live show. Troy had proved invaluable, fielding her calls about free throws and three-pointers. The private surprise of it all was that getting ready for the shoot felt much more like fun than work.

It was energizing to have a new challenge. Tantalizing.

Sure, Gus Simpson had never shied away from difficulty. She didn't crumple (for long) when Christopher passed, and she didn't let a few early hiccups derail The Luncheonette, and she stood by Sabrina's centerpiece when Alan Holt came to dinner in 1994. Although she never would have guessed that Alan would become so cutthroat, with seemingly no regard for loyalty. For example, he could have given her another season to boost ratings. Right? But no: it was the one live episode to prove her worth to the CookingChannel. After twelve years! And the network president wasn't the only person who wouldn't stick with Gus: her culinary producer, Maggie Dennis, had up and quit when she heard the show was having problems.

Even though Porter handled the big picture as exec producer, a top cooking show could not exist without a culinary producer. It was the culinary producer's role to make sure the pantry was well stocked, the kitchen was ready, and to generally be Gus's right hand. Not that she could blame Maggie, a talented chef with bills and a family of her own. Still, thanks to her years on *Gusto!* the woman had lined up another job almost immediately for a cooking-with-kids show. And it would have been no easy task to hire a replacement when all she had to offer was work on one—and possibly the final—episode of *Cooking with Gusto!* But she didn't even have to try: Porter told her the show had been assigned a culinary producer. Just like that. Some guy named Oliver Cooper, who'd graduated a few years earlier from the Institute of Culinary Education in New York and had been working as a sous chef at Eleven Madison Park.

"But I've always chosen who works in the kitchen with me," Gus protested.

"This came down from Alan Holt himself," replied Porter. "And with the budget cuts, he's got to juggle being a combination sous chef, culinary producer, and all-around guy Friday."

And so there it was: a new format, a new culinary producer who lacked television experience, and a new level of pressure.

Hardly surprising, then, that Gus hadn't been able to sleep

much lately. But it wasn't just fear that was keeping her awake. Every night she lay on her smooth crimson sateen sheets, her hair brushed out and fanned around her, and stared at the ceiling as she cooked through all the upcoming dishes in her mind. She racked her brain for quirky slogans and cutesy taglines. Even the hours spent in front of the television watching sports were exciting, getting caught up in the energy of it all. It made sense, too, because suddenly everything around her was about winning and losing. And make no mistake—Gus Simpson was a competitor at heart. Fifty or not.

Please God, she thought now, as she watched yet another team dribble that orange ball up and down the court on her television, zap all the Nielson boxes in America when I'm on the air. Zap them until my ratings go through the roof.

She stayed up late watching ESPN and began polling everyone she knew about their favorite basketball players.

"Quick—ever heard of LeBron James?" Gus asked the bagger at the grocery store when she ran in for some heavy cream, a quiet dinner of gnocchi Gorgonzola in the offing.

The bagger, a sixteen-year-old who hadn't quite grown into his arms and legs, laughed.

"Duh," he responded. "But I prefer Steve Nash."

"Who?" said Gus, making a mental note to write that name down.

She talked b-ball (what little she knew about it!) with everyone from her paperboy to her cleaning lady to her neighbor Hannah (who hadn't been much help) to Troy and her daughters until finally Gus felt she had a handle on who she thought would make charming, gracious guests.

She'd paid careful attention to after-game interviews and profiles in *Sports Illustrated*, of course. The date she'd been given by the CookingChannel coincided with the out-of-town games for the Knicks and the Nets, much to her frustration. Instead, she'd had to go further afield, inviting players from the Trail Blazers and the Rockets and the Pistons.

At her request, the CookingChannel PR team got in touch with sports agents and publicity managers until Gus had herself a willing list of b-ball heroes: Tracy McGrady, Yao Ming, and Rasheed Wallace.

She consulted on the show with Porter and her new culinary producer, Oliver, a strikingly tall man with a shaved head. Oliver was, she'd said privately to Porter, a bit intimidating on first glance. He wasn't the newbie she'd feared—he was clearly in his late thirties—but that also changed the equilibrium, in a way. Still, he had good ideas—such as having viewers upload their own March Madness parties via the CookingChannel website. In the last few minutes of the live *Gusto!*, Gus would introduce some of the clips picked out by Porter and his team.

Together they settled on a March Madness menu perfect for hosting a party to watch the finals of the NCAA championships: salmon cakes (rounded, like mini basketballs), sliced Kobe beef sliders on mini biscuits, and red pepper–garlic fries. Plus they'd promote a selection of handcrafted root beers from around the country.

She'd also invited Troy to come up to the house to meet the players, and he'd agreed enthusiastically, not thinking she'd make a point to get Sabrina there, as well. (Gus was never one to overlook an opportunity.) It was crucial to her that she assemble an "audience"—and she promised Hannah, her girls, and Troy that they would remain off-screen. Remaining off-camera was tremendously important to Hannah, of course, and Gus wouldn't dream of making her uncomfortable. Still, she wanted her best friend to be there for support.

"It's all a ratings game right now," she had explained to Hannah over another 7 AM coffee tête-à-tête. There'd been another snowfall and, from their perch in the bay window, the garden looked a peaceful winter wonderland. "One week they're trying out that surfer chef, another week some Japanese knockoff, then it's our turn."

"At least you've got some breaks in there," Hannah pointed out.

"My frustration is that it's all just temporary—a reprieve from the inevitable. But we're still marching down the same road to cancellation," said Gus. "Porter says whichever show does the best is going to get the Sunday evening time slot all to themselves. Dear Alan, apparently, is even thinking about having viewers call a one-eight-hundred number to make the final selection. Like that celebrity dance show."

"So don't hold back, then. Let the world see the crazy coffee-drinking Gus Simpson I know," said Hannah.

Gus threw her a sharp look.

"That's the problem," she said. "We've been running a few tests. The food makes sense, the guests make sense. The only thing that doesn't work so naturally is the host. Too formal, according to Porter."

"You've gotten a little serious lately," agreed Hannah. "You need to release your inner goofball."

Gus looked doubtful.

"Okay, maybe just a new look." Hannah reached over to pat Gus's hair, one of the only people on the planet, really, who would be so familiar with her. "Why don't you grow out your bob?"

"That much more to color, that's why!"

Gus cracked a grin as Hannah laughed. At thirty-six, Hannah was technically closer in age to Sabrina and Aimee but she seemed worlds older than those two. Part of it, no doubt, was the fact that Hannah had grown up a lot faster than her daughters; Hannah seemed to belong much more to Gus's generation. She had a certain gravitas, a crinkle of sadness about the eyes. Hannah and Gus shared a mutual respect for each other's experiences, and a certain independence, forged from often being alone, from spending so much time in their own thoughts.

"No, the hair stays," Gus said definitively, tossing her hair for effect. "I want to prove to Alan Holt and everyone else that I'm good enough just as I am."

She was more than ready by the morning of the historic live *Cooking with Gusto!* Her outfit—black silk pants, a deep pink shell, and a sheer black shirt jacket—was quintessential Gus and waited, clean and pressed just so, in her closet. With a whoop she bounded out of bed; it was still dark at such an early hour and she padded downstairs to make some hazelnut coffee. The kitchen in Gus's pristine manor house practically radiated cleanliness, ready for the onslaught of producers and guests. Without reaching for a shawl to shield her against the cold, Gus opened the door to her patio and stepped outside, her feet bare, inhaling the air until her lungs hurt. A fresh coat of snow covered the outdoor furniture, the planters, and the trees: the white stuff had clearly fallen all night. Gus looked up at the early morning sky and admired the beauty of the late March snowfall, which seemed to be washing everything clean. It was like a message: she *could* do it. She was going to revive her show, her career, her life. Anything was possible.

Hours later Gus was cursing the snow and snapping at everyone. Porter, Oliver, and the food stylist had arrived many hours behind schedule, rushing around to set up the show. The ingredients were mostly chopped and sliced and off to the side. Oliver and the food stylist had rearranged the inside of the fridge so it looked perfectly believable and yet undeniably perfect, ready for an interior shot or two as Gus reached for cream or butter. The cameras were all ready, the kitchen having been cleverly renovated to simplify setup, and the off-screen audience was on hand, with Aimee and Sabrina and Hannah in one corner, Troy fuming in another.

"Surely you can't be all that surprised that Sabrina's here?" Gus had said to him soon after he arrived, wet and grumpy after a snow-delayed Metro-North train.

But none of that compared to Gus's biggest problem: all of the city's airports had shut down and the city's streets were a soup of slush and ice and taxicabs slipping every which way. Kids throughout the tristate area were glued to their televisions, awaiting confirmations of school cancellations: all of New York was gearing up to savor a snow day. Except for Gus Simpson, that is. She had ninety-seven minutes until she was live on television with her much-hyped show of NBA basketball stars and scrumptious party food.

Only the snow had prevented all her sports celebs from getting there.

*Cooking with Gusto!* was guest-free. And it was going to go out with a whimper.

"Here's where we're at," said Porter, in a hastily assembled war room in Gus's two-story library. He'd just taken another call on his cell. "Alan Holt has left his country house and is being driven here now. And he's bringing his current girlfriend."

Gus was barely paying attention, shocked to have her career melting due to some unexpected precipitation.

"Why don't they just run an old tape at the studio?" she asked with a sigh, her head in her hands.

"Gus? Listen up!" Porter's voice was shrill. "I'm going to draw you a picture. Alan's date is coming with him. Alan has been dating Carmen Vega. And they're on their way over here to do a live program in *your* kitchen."

"What?! In my house? I won't let that woman in the door," shouted Gus.

"Doesn't work like that, kid; you signed a contract that the CookingChannel could film here."

Gus was set to protest or call her lawyer or something—anything—when Oliver poked his bald head in the door.

"It's fifteen minutes to airtime," he reminded Porter. "The camera guys are freaking out."

In an instant Gus was barking orders at Oliver: "Are the platters set out? What about the saucepans? The wine?"

He nodded.

"Porter, I won't sit here and watch that girl lay claim to everything I've worked for simply because she's young and she's sleeping with Alan." Gus was, for the first time in over an hour, completely calm. "We're going live, I am going to host, and I am going to throw a party with my wonderful guests."

"You don't have any guests, kid."

"I have Sabrina, Aimee, Troy, and Hannah," insisted Gus. "And Oliver! And if I can make a party with that motley crew, then any dear viewer can do it."

Porter's phone rang again. "Alan's driver needs directions," he said to Gus.

"Of course, let me write them down," she said loudly enough for the person on the other line to hear. On a sheet of paper she wrote: *Get them lost!*

Her exec producer nodded, then took the pencil from her hand. *Go!* he wrote in reply.

In a flash, Gus ran to her bedroom for a brush and some lipstick, then dashed down the stairs to demand, coax, and beg her friends and family to go on air.

Sabrina was eager, Aimee was reluctant, Hannah was nearly in tears, and Troy was heading for the door.

"You," Gus said to Sabrina, "put on some lipstick and brush your hair. Then do your sister's."

"You," she said to Aimee. "I'm your mother and I put you through college. 'Nuff said."

"You," she said to Hannah. "You can do whatever you want but do I ever need you now."

"And you," she said to Troy, "know exactly why you need to turn around and get on air. And even if you don't, I know all the shareholders of FarmFresh would appreciate the free advertising." Gus turned to Oliver. "Can we add some fresh fruit kebabs to the menu?"

"The pantry is well stocked."

"Then we're set."

"Five minutes," shouted a staffer.

Porter came rushing in. "We've got at least a half hour until you-know-who arrives. The Web is already receiving downloads of people sending images of their parties, and I haven't a clue how we're going to pull this off."

"It's simple," said Gus. "I'm going to do what I've always done. Show my viewers how to entertain with ease. And, just to help them relate, I'll have a few folks here who don't know a damn thing about cooking."

The countdown began and Gus plastered a huge smile on her face.

"Hello and welcome to *Cooking with Gusto!*" she said. "Tonight is an evening of firsts. It's our first live program, the first time we're interacting in real time via our website, the first time I'm going to cook on air with my daughters, and the first time ever that my scheduled guests have been delayed by the weather. But don't worry because we're going to try and get our NBA stars on the phone, and I'm going to teach you how to keep a party going even when it seems as though everything is going wrong."

Porter cued to commercial and then gave a thumbs-up to Gus. "You amaze me, kid."

"Tell me that in fifty-seven minutes," she responded, before instructing Oliver how she wanted to set up Troy, Hannah, Sabrina, and Aimee around the island.

"One of the most challenging things about being a host," Gus said to the camera as the show returned to air, "is that guests typically want to feel as though they're being useful when they're really just—let's admit it—in the way. So the trick is to give them something easy to put together. . . ."

There were snafus, to be sure; Hannah kept looking away every time the camera got too close, and Aimee nearly chopped off her thumb. Troy made snide remarks about Sabrina's boyfriend, and Sabrina flirted with Oliver, who seemed oblivious to everything but the food.

"For years now," Gus was saying to the camera, "I've been on television showing how to throw a perfect party. But in reality my life is filled with this group of folks." She opened her arms wide to point out her guests.

"And since, as usual, they're not listening to me, I can tell you that they're far from perfect—but they sure keep things moving." She kept talking, even as she drizzled the beef with marinade and as Troy dropped a handful of uncooked salmon on the floor and then shouted, "Five-second rule!"

It was absurd, a ridiculous concept for a show: two professional chefs and four neophytes trying to make a party. But the truth was that Gus was having the best time of her life. She couldn't stop smiling.

The snow that Carmen could see outside the car window was spectacular, whitewashing the world.

"Better buckle up—I don't want my new star to get hurt." Alan reached over and patted Carmen's knee. She peeled back her wrap just enough to reveal her seat belt. She was still dressed for dinner, in a turquoise silk shantung suit and lavender cashmere wrap. No time to change, Alan had said, we've got to get over to Gus Simpson's house and save the show! And they'd left in an instant, her feet freezing in ridiculous metallic slingbacks.

It had been a sudden invitation, a weekend at Alan Holt's country house, but her publicist assured her it was important. The president of the CookingChannel liked to get to know his team on a personal level. And Alan had been a gracious host, accommodating all her various concerns. Still. It was awkward.

Carmen's stomach was a mess of butterflies—she knew her moment on television was going to come but she didn't expect it was going to happen before they even got through the canapés.

Alan looked at his watch and then spoke to his driver. "You got the directions, right?"

Although Gus's house was hardly as wired as the studio, Porter had managed to receive call-ins from the NBA stars, stuck at airports in the Midwest. And, thanks to the website, Gus was able to ask viewers' questions directly to the stars, which provided some levity—and, at the very least, meant the show would live up to the hype. (Sort of.) But what amazed Porter was how this seeming train wreck of a cooking program was so eminently watchable. He had never, in twelve years of working with Gus, seen her so relaxed on air. Not just seeming amused, but it was literally like being at a private party with Gus and her goofy family. Gus was, for the first time ever, truly cooking with gusto.

He'd never realized how much better the show could have been until now.

And then Alan arrived, frustrated and cold, with a scared-looking Carmen Vega in tow. Porter almost felt sorry for her.

Almost.

Alan Holt began talking as soon as they cut to commercial; there were twenty minutes left before the end of the hour and he was indescribably angry.

"What the hell has been happening here?" he shouted as he saw the messy kitchen, the spills on the counter, and the haphazard group assembled around the island.

"Some excellent reality TV," Porter said drily.

"I don't know about this show..." said Alan. "But, look, in the spirit of everything but the kitchen sink, you might as well bring in Carmen."

"Why?" asked Hannah, one of the few words she'd uttered all evening, too busy pretending to look into cupboards to avoid being seen on camera.

"Because I said so," replied Alan. "Who is this woman?"

"My friend," said Gus.

"Well, here's a new friend for you, then," Alan said, pushing Carmen into the kitchen area as the commercial break drew to a close.

"Hello," Carmen said simply.

"Your jacket crinkles," responded Gus curtly, touching the silk shantung. Wearing noisy clothes was a real problem with a mike. A pro would know better.

Carmen hesitated, aware she had only a lacy spaghetti strap top underneath.

"And ten...nine...eight..." Porter was counting down.

Carmen hastily unbuttoned her jacket. "How about a little skin?" she said, just as the red light went on above the camera.

"Welcome back, and look who's joined us," Gus said. "Because, just like you, sometimes I get a wonderful surprise guest. And tonight it's Carmen Vega."

"Weren't you Miss Europe?" asked Troy.

"Miss Spain," Carmen said through gritted teeth. "I was Miss Spain."

"Cool. Do you like basketball? Because coming up after our show we're all going to watch the game."

Carmen didn't know a thing about basketball but she hadn't been a beauty queen for nothing. "Oh," she said sweetly. "I think sports are all about the children. Just getting out there to cheer and shout. It's wonderful. What's next on the menu, Gus?"

Gus was just about finished with the chutney for the salmon cakes when Carmen leaned in.

"Let's experiment," she whispered, as Porter cued them back on air.

"Gus and I were just talking and we've decided to mix it up a bit," Carmen said to the camera while Gus used all her energies to prevent a scowl from forming. With a flick of the wrist, Carmen had ramped up the seasonings—a little more cilantro, some cayenne, and finally a touch of mint—and then put a clean spoon in to taste. But instead of bringing it to her own mouth, she held it out to Gus.

"Mmmm," said Gus, in a practiced voice, not actually paying attention. Tasting the food, after all, was the money shot in the world of food television. Then she actually felt the flavors hit her tongue: the heat of the cayenne, the fresh bite of the mint. "This is divine," she exclaimed spontaneously.

And, like a stampede of seven-year-olds waiting for goodies at a birthday party, Troy, Aimee, and Sabrina rushed over immediately.

"Let me try!"

"Oh, this is delicious!"

"I chopped the fruit that went into this, you know. I did it."

Although the plating was a little—okay, a lot—sloppy, the group had set out a buffet of salmon cakes, fries, and Kobe beef sliders on toasty rolls by the end of the program.

"It's about being merry!" shouted Sabrina, a wee bit tipsy.

"That's right," said Gus, looking intently into the camera. Could this be her final parting words to her viewers after twelve long years in food television? She took a deep breath, picked up a salmon cake in her left hand and a glass of deep red wine in her right. "My friends," she said, "eat, drink... and be." She took a bite. And didn't stop smiling until they were off the air.

Goodbye, audience, she thought. Goodbye, career. Hello, fifty. Happy birthday to me.

Gus lay in bed all the next morning, tucked between her sateen sheets, pretending to sleep. She ignored the phone, certain she was going to hear from reporters, from rivals, from Alan Holt. She pulled her heavy down comforter over her head.

"I'm taking a snow day," she yelled, her voice muffled by the fluffy blanket. She popped her head out when she began to feel too hot. Reluctantly she put a hand out to her phone, scrolled through the missed call log. It had been Porter interrupting her all morning. She dialed his number with resignation, waiting to hear the news.

He got straight to the point. *Cooking with Gusto!* was officially dead. Kaput.

Gus felt a lump in her throat.

And then he dropped a bombshell.

The CookingChannel had ordered seven episodes of an all-new, all-live program:

*Eat Drink and Be...*

*Hosted by Gus Simpson.*

*And Carmen Vega.*

# oil and water

# 7

What Gus craved was a week off and a cozy beach cottage near a warm ocean: a chance to relax and savor the ratings victory. And also time to sort out this mess of being forced to have Carmen Vega as a cohost. She'd never had a cohost before, not even when she was a newbie to television and nervously flubbing basic quiche recipes.

But there was no time for a vacation! There was the new show, *Eat Drink and Be*, to plan and a budget for a limited run of episodes from the end of April through September already sitting in the coffers. Alan was eager to experiment with showing first-run episodes throughout the summer, and he remained enchanted by his idea of trying out other programs between live episodes of *Eat Drink and Be*—packaging it as a CookingChannel smorgasbord of "destination television" with traditional taped shows, like the surfer chef, being sandwiched in between the brave new world that was apparently going to be the live *Eat Drink and Be*.

On top of it all, they weren't so far away from almost disappearing—the fear remained fresh—that Porter made it quite clear he didn't feel in any way compelled to take up her Carmen issues with Alan.

Which was annoying because Gus couldn't seem to make her boss come around to her view: Alan had anticipated that she'd be upset and invited her to a delicious lunch at Craft, in which he patiently—paternalistically—listened to all the reasons why she didn't like Carmen and absolutely, without a doubt, no way no how, would Gus work with her.

"I know," he said after she'd gone on for several minutes, pouring more pinot noir into her glass. "That's part of what makes it fun for the viewers—it's rather spicy with the tension between the two of you."

Gus was taken aback. "Are you using me, Alan?"

Alan leaned forward over his plate and looked at Gus with curiosity.

"No more than you're using me, Gus," he said, putting his knife and fork onto his plate and signaling to the waiter. "I don't pretend to be anything but what I am: a guy who's worked his ass off to build a place in television. I'm no cook. But I like to eat. I like tasty food. And so do a lot of other folks. I saw a market and a way to sell a product. And now I see the potential for another good product."

"*The Gus and Carmen Show?*"

"Something like that."

"So it's all about money, then?"

Alan frowned and took a long pull from his red wine. He wiped his mouth with his napkin and pushed his chair a few inches away from the table, leaning back.

"Gus, we've known each other a long time. And if you fell and broke your leg, I'd be the first person to bring you a casserole. I like you, Gus. I do consider you a friend." He cleared his throat. "But it seems you've convinced yourself that you've been doing me a favor all these years. I guess, as the fellow who signs your exceedingly large paycheck, that I have rather a different view."

An awkward silence developed.

"So . . ." said Gus.

"So," repeated Alan. "You and Carmen will be great together, and on behalf of everyone at the CookingChannel, I want you to know that we couldn't be more thrilled about your new program. Shall we?" He dropped the napkin in his hand and stood up to leave.

If it had been another day, a different conversation, the two of them would have shared a cab back to the studio, where Gus had an informal plan to meet with Porter and Oliver. But it would be too uncomfortable to sit together in the backseat now, making chitchat about the sunny April weather.

"Oh, I have an errand to run," she said stiffly, trying to come up with some task in her mind so she wouldn't be lying. Gus never lied. All we have, she'd always told her daughters when they were young, is our integrity. And good manners.

And so she thanked Alan for taking her to lunch, even as she choked on every word.

Hannah Levine sat at her desk, pouring half a pack of Sweetarts into her mouth. Crunch crunch crunch. As snacks went, it would do. Though it might need a chocolate chaser. The kitchen, spit and polished by a different Merry Maid each Tuesday—Hannah called each woman "Merry," as though it were her name—was merely the storage spot for bags of M&M's, packets of Big League chewing gum, canisters filled to the top with candy corn.

"You eat too much junk," Gus said on the nights she popped by with a Gruyère and watercress sandwich or a bit of steamed lemon pepper sole and green beans. Before there had been Gus, with her coffee-and-muffin mornings and her evening surprises, there had been only candy and delivery pizza, the nagging fear that the delivery boy would say those dreaded words: Don't you look familiar? Or: Hey, aren't you that girl who...

"I need a little sweetness in my life," Hannah would reply. Nowadays she ordered her candy stash off the Internet, and her pizza came frozen and delivered to the door in a box with cereal, milk, bread, maybe a little cheddar. It was still too much to go to the store, every turn into a new aisle another opportunity to be recognized. This much she had learned: hiding out was much easier when one stayed hidden. And Hannah made it a point never to leave home. She walked a well-worn path to Gus's house every morning but she hadn't been out in her own garage, let alone driven her red Miata, in ages. But that's what one did in the Hannah Protection Program, of which she was the president and only member.

"No one even remembers," Gus had chided gently one time, trying to get Hannah to come to a cookbook launch party in Manhattan.

"No one ever forgets a scandal," Hannah insisted. It was difficult for someone who hadn't been publicly embarrassed to understand the sting. That she could still feel it after all this time. Hannah could enjoy good day after good day if she followed her own rules: she stayed put, she never drew attention to herself, she never wrote about sports, she always used her initials on her articles—H. J. Levine—and never her full name. Because she'd once thought as Gus did, had hoped that no one remembered. And then found herself the subject of a "What Ever Happened To..." story on cable. This is what she had given up for privacy: dating (though she hadn't ever had much time for that in her previous life anyway), shopping (clothes had always been sent to her so she'd never had quite the "malling" experience as a teen), and making friends (Gus was the persistent exception). In return she could breathe.

Even so, she put in an appearance at Gus's holiday and birthday parties, so sure of Gus's power to protect her, so sure no one would dare to mention that she looked familiar. It would have been in poor taste to comment on her past troubles, of course. And Gus brought out the very best manners in all her guests.

Hannah's devotion to her only friend was strong enough that she had risked everything—her peace, her quiet, her safe seclusion—to help save Gus's show. What had she been thinking?

With trepidation she trolled online at her desk, every link a catch in her throat as she read the list of page titles on Google. A lot on Gus. Good, good. Nothing whatsoever about Hannah Joy Levine. Even better. She leaned back in her cushioned gray desk chair, careful not to tip over as she'd done more than once. And the floor was hard, still the original red oak, though worn in places and covered with a series of mismatched rugs. The room was designed to be an eating area though Hannah had never invested in table and chairs. Just a long L-shaped desk she purchased from IKEA more than a decade ago and two televisions mounted to the wall. All the better to watch the news, my dear, she told Gus the first time she let her inside. Hannah didn't want to forsake the world. She simply wanted to watch it behind glass.

The carriage house had been Hannah's first—and only—major purchase, other than a red sports car, which sat, its battery disconnected, covered under a sheet in the garage. A memento from another time. The compact home had been an investment, a cute little cottage that caught her eye as she drove to practice, her rackets stowed on the seat beside her. She'd bought it eighteen years ago, when she was still a teenager, never imagining that she would show up on the doorstep a short time later, with a suitcase and not much else. In all those years, Gus was the only neighbor who knew her. She didn't mind. She liked it that way.

Thinking about the past always made her anxious and therefore hungry. Hannah opened her bottom desk drawer, reached in without even looking. She had her candy stash memorized. Her eyes never veered from the CookingChannel website message boards.

"Who's hotter: Carmen Vega or Gus Simpson?" read the title of one thread. Hannah smiled. In one fluid motion she flipped open her cell phone and pushed Gus's number, while simultaneously ripping open a bag of peanut M&M's. Her penchant for sweets had never fully impacted her figure: she'd always had a good metabolism, thank God, even at thirty-six years of age. That, and she'd put a treadmill in the guest room instead of a bed. Wasn't like anyone was going to be visiting her, anyway.

"Hey, lady, it appears you've set the foodie world aflame," Hannah said to Gus's hello. "You've apparently reached sex symbol status." With surgical precision, she separated the blue candies from the other colors as she talked. It was a habit left over from long ago, when silly quirks, affected for their own sake, were indulged and entertained. The truth was that all the colors tasted the same to her now.

"Thank God it's you—I'm so mad I could poke out Alan Holt's eye," said Gus. "Did you eat lunch?"

"Yes."

"I'm sure you did. You're going to end up with a sugar problem—diabetes or whatnot. I'm not going to let this go on." Hannah remained silent. It was true that Gus had once—just once—tried to clear out the goodies in the house. The result was the only fight the women had ever had and it left Hannah hysterical, crying on the kitchen floor. It was just that Gus couldn't help herself: she always had to fix, fix, fix things until she thought they were just right.

Mercifully, Gus launched right into sharing the details of her lunch with Alan, from the folds of the napkins to the talk of Carmen's outfits for the show.

"And I'm supposed to be in a meeting in two hours with Miss Spain," she concluded. "I had to get away so I've made up an errand. I've gathered up a little gypsy salami, some smoked provolone, and a jar of black Puglian olives to drop off at the girls' apartment."

"Bad idea." Hannah slipped a candy into her mouth, only to suck and taste the coating. She'd never chew in Gus's ear.

"No, it's great. Who wouldn't want to come home to a loaded

refrigerator?" Gus's breathing was a little louder now, the combination of fast walking, a loaded bag of yummy delights, and wearing a heavy winter jacket under the warming spring weather.

"Gus, no good ever came of a parent letting herself into her daughters' home without asking."

"It's not like that," said Gus. "Besides, Sabrina wouldn't mind."

"Aimee certainly will," insisted Hannah.

"Oh, I'm at the building," Gus said, her voice triumphant. "I might even have time to whip up some brownies while I'm upstairs. Won't that be lovely?" Hannah knew her friend well enough to know she wasn't really asking a question.

The morning had been blissful: clear and sunny. Well, at least it looked that way out the window. Sabrina hadn't made it out of bed, save for one discreet trip to the bathroom. Her love was still new enough that she liked to pretend she didn't need to use such things as toilets and deodorant. She'd brushed away her bad breath and shaved, but didn't shower lest her boyfriend catch on that her silky smooth bikini line was something other than natural. She'd snuck back into bed without disturbing him, treating him to a breakfast that had been a series of perfect nibbles: fingers and lips and eyelids and earlobes. Who wouldn't love playing hooky for this? They'd had some juice afterward, returned for a long nap that spilled into the afternoon. Sabrina lay on her right side and watched her boyfriend's chest rise and fall with his shallow breathing. She put some strands of her deep black hair against his light blond fur, marveling at the difference. He was beautiful. They were beautiful.

The beginnings of a relationship were what she liked most, when every moment felt tinged with bright possibility, before all the expectation and obligation crept in. She placed her hand lightly on Billy's white skin, staring at the princess-cut diamond glittering on her ring finger. He'd asked her last night. Soon enough they would find themselves looking at homes and buying sofas and discussing how a dinner fork should feel in a man's hand. Sabrina had done all of that before. She'd had three previous engagement rings, all returned to the givers, of course. Two of them had been quite alike, in fact, round solitaire diamonds that twinkled and winked in the sunlight. They were more like gift certificates, rings to be exchanged when she and her fiancé of the moment went jewelry shopping together, to pick out something she would like better. The other had been lapis lazuli in sterling silver. That was her very first ring, from Stephen Campbell, her very first serious boyfriend. They were barely twenty-one, had known each other since high school. He'd tried to insist she keep it. Gus made an even bigger fuss that the ring be returned.

She wished she had it now. Not that she wanted to be with Stephen. She didn't. She just wished she had some piece of her heart from all those years ago, something she could hold in her hand and say, Yes, this mattered to me. Some way to remember what she'd wanted then.

Troy Park had never given her a ring. She'd expected it. Wanted it. He'd been different, that one. He'd demanded something the others had not. Sabrina looked up at Billy, at the shadow along his jawline, at his pink lips. Did she love this mouth? This man?

"Am I happy?" she whispered. He didn't stir. They never did.

"Am I happy?" she said again. It was the same question that came from her lips whenever she awakened in a cold sweat late at night, the room dark and quiet, her heart racing, her brain uncertain where she was. Alone with her thoughts, she didn't have to power up and turn on the cheeriness that everyone seemed to require. She wondered, in those still hours, what her father would have thought about how she'd turned out. Which one of her boyfriends he'd have liked better.

"I'm a serial monogamist," she'd told Aimee when notifying her that Troy was no longer in the picture and she was now involved with Billy. That's how she'd phrased it: in the picture. As though exclusion in her life was as simple as replacing the snapshot of the smiling boyfriend in the pewter frame on her dresser.

"You're an idiot," her sister had replied, shaking her head. She looked as though she wanted to say more but she didn't. For once.

Sabrina was relieved, didn't want to hem and haw over how she'd met William Angle. They were introduced by a guy she'd known at design school who worked as a graphic designer in Billy's office. Billy was a rising exec at a media company owned by a global conglomerate, with lots of connections to fun parties and prospective clients. That had been what interested Sabrina initially, and meeting him for a drink had been all about networking. It was a pleasant way to spend an evening: he had this wonderfully calm way of talking, which slowed everything down, and he seemed remarkably self-assured. But he surprised her, too, when he told her he volunteered as a Big Brother and had to leave early because he was taking his Little Brother golfing at Chelsea Piers the next morning.

He seemed so unlike all the other men she'd met that Sabrina was fascinated. She was always attracted to what was new. Nothing happened, mind you. She wasn't that kind of girl. She simply flirted and emailed until she was certain there was something there—Sabrina never made a move until she knew who she was moving on to—and then she packed up Troy's things in a paper bag.

"I don't know," she'd told her mother when asked what had gone wrong.

"I don't know," she'd answered when Aimee asked her if she loved Troy.

"I don't know," she'd said when each of her boyfriends, in turn, asked her what she wanted. Now she glanced about her bedroom: the walls were painted a cool blue-gray, as though looking at the sky through a veil of fog. Her double bed, an explosion of throw pillows the night before, was scarcely big enough for two. Theirs had been an impromptu stopover on their way to Billy's apartment—just for Sabrina to pick up a few more clothes—before they carried on.

Instead, they got deliciously carried away. They'd never stayed the night at her place before.

"Let's not leave this bed," she'd whispered, before skillfully convincing Billy to call in sick. "Let's pretend we're stranded on a raft no bigger than this bed and no one can find us." It was one of her favorite games. And as long as she was up to playing what he wanted, Billy had no need to be rescued.

Sabrina had just drifted off again when she heard rustling sounds in the kitchen. Noises from an empty New York City kitchen were never a good thing. She nudged Billy awake.

"We've got a mouse," she hissed.

"And you've got a mousehole," he growled, reaching for her.

"Come off it, Billy, I'm serious."

He paused. "I don't hear anything," he said in his normal voice.

But Sabrina was already up, throwing on a T-shirt and passing him his boxers. "Let's go out there."

"Don't you live with your sister?"

"It's the middle of the afternoon—she's at work."

"Okay, okay," he said, stretching lazily before sliding his underwear over his thighs. As a joke, he grabbed an umbrella from the top of her dresser and held it over his head, looking back at Sabrina as he opened the door with a flourish and took an exaggerated step, Elmer Fudd style, toward the kitchen.

"I'm hunting wabbits," he singsonged, waiting for Sabrina to laugh.

"Omigod!" his girlfriend screamed, her face flushing. Billy whipped his head forward, every ounce alert. He was completely serious now. And there, in the kitchen, still wearing her winter coat and holding a jar of black olives in one hand, stood television's most famous host: Gus Simpson.

"Mom! What the hell are you doing here?" Sabrina felt naked even though her T-shirt covered her somewhat.

"Go back in that room and put on a shirt!" Gus was practically shouting as she pointed to Billy.

"No." Billy placed his arm around Sabrina's shoulders but she shook him off. "You're trespassing."

"You—you're the trespasser!" Gus *was* shouting now. "I can come to my daughter's home anytime I like."

"No," he repeated. And simply stood there in his boxers.

Gus changed tactics. "Get yourself dressed right now," she said to Sabrina. "You and I need to have a talk."

"Mrs. Simpson—Gus—this is uncomfortable for all of us," Billy said, pleased by his own maturity. It wasn't how he had planned to break the news to his future mother-in-law, but Billy was a big believer in facing things head-on. You just had to roll with it. Now he grinned at Sabrina even as he felt the heat from Gus's glare. "But I really think you should calm down. Your daughter and I are getting married."

"Oh, sweet Jesus," said Gus, putting the jar of olives on the counter with such force that it slid right off and smashed on the linoleum. She watched the liquid seep out onto the floor.

"I'd say congratulations, but, God help me, I can't go through this again."

Although filming of *Eat Drink and Be* was to take place at Gus's home, meetings were still held at the New York studio. It was more convenient . . . for everyone else. About two seasons ago, Gus believed she was on the verge of being able to request all meetings be brought to her, in her home. She already had the knives, the pots, the pans, the salad spinner co-branded with the CookingChannel. It hardly seemed fair that the ratings dip left her in a battle for all that she'd created. To be frank, there simply couldn't have been a Carmen Vega without a Gus Simpson. And she was going to make sure that tarty beauty queen didn't forget it.

Gus's feet ached inside her black leather boots as she entered the CookingChannel headquarters: too much walking in too-high heels. It amazed her how anger could fuel the stride, leaving her blistered and more frustrated than when she started out. She hoped Sabrina's Billy choked on that little picnic! The entire day was a disaster, from Alan to Sabrina and her monstrous boyfriend, and she still had to meet again with Porter. Being late wasn't something Gus did. To be fair, Gus had always made a point of being punctual. But her life now was a far cry from when she'd just been Gus Simpson, private citizen, and sometimes it chafed. There were a lot of rules and regs to being Gus Simpson, celeb TV host. And chief among them was smiling on cue.

"Carmen—what a surprise," said Gus, even-tempered and pleasant, as she walked through Porter's open door. "Am I late?"

"Never," said Porter, watching her carefully. "Carmen was early. She was just saying how excited she is to work with you."

"I've been studying your shows like a blueprint," Carmen said, smiling broadly. "I could learn so much from you, *sabes*?"

"Indeed," said Gus. "I'm so glad *All About Eve* was playing on the classic movie channel last night. I feel so much more prepared. Porter?"

"Okay, ladies, let's go sit at the table over here. There's something I want both of you to see: a selection of videos that came in after the show. We're going to upload several to the CookingChannel website—the response has been amazing." Porter turned his laptop so both women could see the screen, taking care to place the computer equally between Carmen and Gus. He clicked "Play" to start a streaming video of a group of twentysomething men and women.

"Gus Simpson, welcome to my own March Madness party. I used to think it was impossible to be you," said an Asian woman in a Syracuse T-shirt. "But now I'm inspired! It's okay to mess up—and please, who is that cute bald guy?"

"You can have Oliver!" shouted another young woman in the

background, "I want the other one!" A chubby guy behind her playfully hit her over the head with an oven mitt before leaning into the shot to hold up an "I love Carmen" banner.

"Go, Gus!" the crowd shouted in unison as the video ended.

Porter moved the laptop out of the way and handed out copies of some notes he'd made.

"We've got tons like this—even a group who made your first dish in real time with all of you and it's hilarious," said Porter. "What's amazing is how much viewers are responding to the real-time, real-world, real-people aspect of the inaugural show of *Eat Drink and Be*."

"I'm delighted," cooed Carmen. "I love real people."

"How charming," said Gus drily. "I'm fond of them myself. So how"—Gus subtly motioned in Carmen's direction—"is this thing really going to work?"

"Ah, I have a plan for that!" Porter was up and pacing the floor. "We're going to bring them all back—Troy, Hannah, Aimee, Sabrina—and we're going to do it all again. A bit more organized, of course."

"Sabrina is apparently engaged. Again." Porter had known Gus and her girls for a long time. He knew well that Sabrina loved to fall in love.

"Engaged *again*?" asked Carmen. Gus pretended not to hear her.

"Knowing Sabrina, this guy's a hunk," said Porter. "We could bring him on, too."

"Actually, no, we can't," Gus replied coolly. Porter stopped moving long enough to glance at Gus's face.

"Okay, scratch that," he said. "Hey, where's Oliver? I wouldn't expect our culinary producer to be late to our first group meeting."

"Ooooh, yes," said Carmen. "I just asked him to do me a weensy little favor. I didn't think anyone would mind."

Gus opened her mouth and then closed it again. Porter got the message: she did mind. But she wasn't going to give in to the temptation to say so.

# 8

Don't get stuck in the elevator: that's what Oliver's favorite professor, Dr. Randall, always said in business school. Only he'd never meant it literally.

Oliver Cooper reached out his arms to estimate if he could touch both sides of the elevator at the same time. He couldn't reach but still he came impressively close. His arms, like his legs, were long and well muscled, and his skin was lightly tanned from a recent ski weekend. At six-five—and with a smoothly shaven scalp, his answer to the dreaded thinning hairline—Oliver cut an imposing figure. Thankfully he was the sole occupant of the elevator—the doors of this square box didn't seem to be budging and he didn't relish the idea of making small talk. ("This is crazy, huh?" would be the theme.) He punched the "emergency" button several times, the loud ring reverberating in his ear. He reached for his cell phone before remembering he'd left it at home—of all days!—then slid down against the wall and squatted over the heels of his brown leather loafers.

A glance at his Swatch watch revealed it was 4:05 PM. He had been trapped for eleven minutes; he was supposed to be in Porter's office five minutes ago. And he could have been. If only he was better at saying no. There were just so many times when Oliver couldn't turn down what was requested of him; it simply wasn't done.

"Oh, Oliver, I'm so happy to see you!" That's what she'd said in the lobby, quickly sweeping her eyes down and then gazing at him full in the face with her wide brown eyes, those long dark lashes. Carmen. Always pretty, always sweet, ever so slightly feigning helplessness. "I have all of this stuff to take upstairs and no one's around to help."

"Couldn't you get a dolly? From the doorman?"

Carmen shrugged as though she couldn't be bothered to find out.

"They're not heavy for you." She touched Oliver lightly on the arm. He was carrying a Frap from the coffee shop across the street. It was a guilty indulgence—he'd been trying to cut back on his caffeine—and the cup was mostly full. "It's just too much for me, Oliver." She tilted her head in a practiced way and left the question in the air. Her red satiny blouse highlighted her warm olive skin and her red lips drew attention to her even, white teeth.

He took a long sip of his drink and tossed it in a wastebasket. Too late he realized the bin was meant for recycling. Oh, well, no wonder the earth was going to destroy itself; too many careless humans who couldn't be bothered to read the recycling arrows. Oliver considered removing the cup but thought that would seem even more distasteful. Instead, he spun around to face her.

"So what do you have for me?" he asked, trying to be chipper. Of course he'd consented. Only a complete jerk would leave a delicate thing like Carmen standing in the lobby of the CookingChannel offices surrounded by heavy boxes.

Carmen mouthed her thanks but didn't look a bit surprised. Her lack of genuine gratitude annoyed him, just a bit. She knew he'd do it even if he didn't want to—knew he'd say yes even when he pretended to himself that he was mulling it over. It was almost socially impossible for a man to refuse a woman's request for help. That was one of the little inconsistencies of professional life that drove him rather nuts, to be honest: the assumption that it was okay for a woman to ask a man to do physical labor. Never the other way around, mind you.

"You're welcome, Carmen," he pretend-shouted. Oliver rolled up the sleeves of his French blue Oxford shirt. He knew he'd agreed to carry up Carmen's belongings because she was attractive and funny and, as much as he was annoyed, because it also appealed to him to be seen as strong. And because he owed her much more than a bit of manual labor. She knew food had saved him, had nourished his spirit when he looked deep within himself and saw what was missing. She shared a similar respect for the power of flavor. And because she knew about the problems he'd had with his wrists working as a restaurant sous chef, she'd whispered his name to Alan Holt as someone who would be a good candidate for culinary producer.

Oliver had known Carmen for years now—had bonded with her when he showed her the genuine *jamón serrano* he'd smuggled in after a trip to Barcelona, had even briefly dated her until they mutually decided to stick to being pals—and, as friends went, he knew the former Miss Spain wasn't a bad one to have.

But there were still things to put up with: the baby doll act, the wheedling, the expectation. Carmen was accustomed to getting her own way. It might have always been that way for her, growing up as her mother's favorite child in Seville, attracting the attention of photographers as she rose through the beauty pageant scene, winning the hearts of the paparazzi when she sent sandwiches out to them while they waited for a glimpse of Carmen and her Hollywood singer. That type of attention can alter a person, there was no doubt about it. The same way that suddenly earning a huge pile of money had changed him. Oliver tapped his fingers on Carmen's boxes: he wouldn't have carried someone's stuff back when he was on The Street.

"Just keep your head down and do your work," his father said to him the day he left for college.

"You're going to make something out of yourself," said his older brother Marcus, who had returned from school to work with his father.

"Be sure not to forget about us when you're all big and fancy," said his oldest brother, Peter, who was a bookkeeper for a local company.

Oliver hadn't expected to forget where he came from. He hadn't expected his career successes to have such an effect. He'd assumed he was stronger than that.

His mother had always said he had a good head on his shoulders. And he did. They'd called him Ollie back in those days, growing up in a farm town in Indiana. He was only the third member of his family to go to college, Marcus and Peter getting there before him. But he had been the first to get a full scholarship. The first to move out of state. The first to get an MBA. The first to get to New York and earn promotion after promotion. To make money. That's what he'd done. He made money.

Certainly the initial years working on Wall Street had been solid, more than healthy, and the update in his wardrobe, the widening of his palate (he had fond memories of his first bite of tripe, of the eating tour of Italy, of the cycling trip in Napa), the choices for his vacations all reflected his well-padded bank account. He remembered well the awkwardness of realizing that he was earning more in his first full-time job than his father, a mechanic who repaired tractors and cars. The Cooper family farm had been sold to a conglomerate a while back.

The expensive gifts he bought to bring a little luxury into their lives—the Cadillac his father always said he wanted, a trip to Aruba for the entire family—only highlighted his new position. It was hard to play the little boy when he had an overstuffed wallet and a Bulova watch; it made the pretense within the family difficult to continue.

His plan, the day he arrived in Manhattan with his tired-looking suitcases and his bike, was to make a tidy sum and then move on to doing something that fed his soul. It's not like he'd always wanted to be an investment banker or anything.

His intention was never to stay long in the city.

"These are my capital accumulation years," he told Peter when he hit twenty-eight. "I'm going to make the most of them. I'm not going to get distracted."

And he didn't. He worked long, long hours. Oliver was good at what he did. Still, at quitting time, he found that he avoided his Tribeca apartment. Oliver wanted to be around people even as he wished to remain disentangled, separate. Instead, he focused all his considerable extracurricular energies on trying out the latest restaurants, sampling the tastes and hidden delights of new cooks. Eating alone never intimidated him: he didn't even bring a book with which to shield himself, but simply allowed himself to be entertained by the food itself.

From the tiniest neighborhood bistro to the pinnacle of Le Bernardin, Oliver Cooper's most intense love affair was with food. (And, as a consequence, he also maintained a slavish devotion to his personal trainer.)

His life was just what he'd ordered up: work that paid well and food that tasted good. He'd had the occasional girlfriend, pretty and pleasant, and his family—whom he saw rarely but cared about deeply—was in good health. It was all good. It was better than he expected.

But the novelty—the appreciation—had lessened. And thus began Oliver's gradual transition from earnest, hardworking, wide-eyed Midwestern boy to world-weary, multimillionaire Master of the Universe. Oliver could still make chitchat with the cashier at the bodega, could still open the door for an elderly person without making a huge fuss. Those moments helped affirm that he was a good guy, still the same Ollie Cooper who had played kick the can on warm summer nights and rode his bike to school. Back when his hair was thick and full, when baldness seemed like something that only happened to other men. Back when he divided people up between the ones who were kind and the ones who were not.

But he lost his manners little by little. Cutting off cars as he changed lanes on the Sunday night drive from his country house, his arm—and middle finger—raised in the universal salute. Needling waiters about taking milliseconds too long to bring water, although he eschewed free tap water altogether when sparkling was in fashion. Oliver stopped saying "goodbye" when he finished up a phone call, merely clicked off when he was done saying what *he* had to say. He neglected to ask "How are you?" when he met one of those pretty girlfriends for dinner, instead talked fluidly and at length about how stressed he was. Busy busy busy. The code word for important.

He laughed with his parents the Christmas he told them that he had made more in one year than his father had made in a lifetime. He figured they'd be proud. And they were, no doubt. But also embarrassed. He chose to believe he didn't understand why.

And so it went for years. Ambitious Oliver morphed into an older, far less interesting man. Only he was the only one who didn't know it.

The food in his life was the one thing that remained consistently exciting—from the most expensive black truffle to the freshest apple pie at the bakery around the corner, the scent of cinnamon wafting through the pastry lattice. But everything else was rote. Blasé. Oliver spent long days in his large office, earned generous paychecks, cleverly turned his pennies into dimes, and so on. He had purchased a ticket on an endless rat-race merry-go-round, never even thought about getting off.

It took a while to notice that his buddies from back home had fallen out of touch, simply sending cards at Christmas. (Or, to be precise, their wives sent the cards, signed *Joe and Cindy* or *Gord and Ricki*, and he'd have to think long and hard to remember if he'd met the wife, if he'd asked his assistant to send a wedding gift. Later, he would realize he hadn't even been invited.) His brothers rarely called, when his nieces and nephews would get in touch to thank him for the belated but extravagant birthday gifts. He dropped a hefty load of guilt and dollars at FAO Schwarz every year.

"You think we're all hicks," said his brother Marcus in a rare phone conversation. "You've convinced yourself that living in Manhattan makes you better."

"Doesn't it, though?" Oliver had meant it as a joke.

"Man, what happened to you?"

"What do you mean?"

"When did you become such a pompous ass?"

"I beg your pardon?"

"Let me tell you who you are: Mom's seventy-fifth birthday and you're nowhere to be found. You're the kind of guy who sends his mother the biggest bouquet on her birthday but can't find the time to visit her more than once a year."

"I was busy."

"She cried, Oliver." Marcus was clearly furious. "All night she thought you were going to make a grand gesture and walk through the door."

"I said I couldn't make it."

"What were you doing?"

"Working."

"You always said you'd get in, get out, and get on with things." Marcus sighed. "I'll tell it to you straight: you act like you're the king of the hill but you're a sorry loser, if you ask me."

"Screw you."

"When was the last time you were nice for no reason? When was the last time you felt happy?"

"Last night, my friend, as I downed a 'ninety-five pinot with pork belly in maple glaze." Oliver's voice was triumphant. "So there you go."

His brother was quiet for a long time.

"I'm glad you have your food. I really am. Because the way I see it, you've got nothing else."

And like the perfect spice that awakens the tongue and burns the back of the throat—Oliver was jolted by his brother's words.

That was the start of it, a dull awareness humming in the back of his mind. He wanted... something else. He wanted to be more than just that guy, the one who seemed as though he had it all and yet had nothing. He'd grown up to become someone Marcus and Peter didn't particularly like. Someone he didn't particularly like, either.

He already knew he was happiest when he was around food. Certainly the eating brought him great pleasure, but so did his forays into one of the many gourmet stores in Manhattan, selecting peaches and eggplant and thick tuna steaks. But the realization was more than that. Oliver began to see that he had never expected his work to fulfill him. The entire getting in/getting out scenario was a fine one, a solid plan, but only if he remained aware enough *to* get out. If only he didn't become trapped by inertia and beholden to the zeros in his bank account.

He took a knife basics class, just in the evenings. Then a series of Sunday brunch lessons. Intro to pastry. Holiday essentials. And then he flew home and cooked his mother and brothers a resplendent turkey dinner, with sausage stuffing, maple-glazed sweet potatoes, and a chutney made with peaches, pears, pineapple, and a dash of curry.

"I'm quitting my job," he announced over apple *tarte Tatin*. "I've enrolled in cooking school full-time."

"That seems... unusual," replied his father cautiously. "Are you feeling quite right?"

"Does this mean you'll work less, dear?" asked his mother, waving at his father to shush.

"Not necessarily," Oliver replied. "But I think it means I'll be happier."

"Oh, good," sighed his mother.

"Less of a jerk?" asked Marcus.

"We can only hope," Oliver said, handing out coffees to go with the dessert.

It had been only four years since he enrolled in cooking school, but it had changed his schedule, his attitude, and his wardrobe, he thought, glancing now at the brown loafers he never would have worn in his other life. He'd deep-sixed most of his suits and currently favored a casual look. The last time he'd been in an elevator with boxes was when he had his office carted down to the lobby, his finance buddies unable to hide their pitying looks as he walked down the hall. They thought he'd cracked under the pressure. Oliver knew he'd given away too much of himself already. And so he welcomed, even as he was shocked by, the rigor at the Institute of Culinary Education.

That's where he met Carmen. He was a semester ahead of her—and several years older—when they ended up working side by side in a dessert class. He'd helped her out when she had a coconut cream disaster, her whisk scraping the metal of the bowl and turning her nice, yellowy cream into a gray-green goo. Together, they poured her mess down the sink, and then he poured half of his mixture into her bowl. It was against the rules, of course, and yet it seemed the right thing to do. Oliver had wanted to be one of the kind ones again.

And now, four years later, he'd miraculously found himself working for the CookingChannel, starting an entirely new career at the age of thirty-nine. He checked the bright plastic watch on his arm. In his heart, Oliver had parted ways with his old life from the moment he tucked his expensive watch into a box—it was too risky to wear good jewelry when cooking—and started wearing a timepiece that made him smile every time he looked at it. Well, maybe not every time: he was still hugely late for the meeting.

Curious, frustrated, and bored, Oliver pulled at the tape around the biggest box of Carmen's. Why not get a peek at what was so important? He felt bad being so snoopy.

Inside, carefully cushioned in bubble wrap, were eleven pairs of shoes: flats for cooking and heels for . . . who the hell knew what?

He pulled out a pair of glittering gold stilettos, putting one on each hand. "I'm Carmen," he said in a falsetto, his Spanish accent ridiculous. "Carry up my shoes so I can walk all over you." He pantomimed walking on the box top with his shoe-hands, then doing a cancan.

"Get me out of here," he moaned, bringing his hands up to his head automatically, even though they remained tucked into Carmen's gold shoes.

Unexpectedly the doors to the elevator opened.

"Uh, Oliver?" It was Porter, standing in the hall, taking in the sight of the tall, bald, handsome culinary producer crouched down among boxes, his fingers peeking through the peep-toe in a pair of gold shoes. "You all okay in there?"

# 9

Porter was less amused 128 minutes later as he crumpled up his seventh piece of paper in a row.

"It's just that I think we need to wow the audience with our next show," Carmen was saying, repeating her point. "I'd like to see something with squid ink. The menu has to amaze and tantalize."

"That's great for a restaurateur, Carmen, but food television is never about fuss," said Gus. "It's about making the spectacular seem easy."

"I've done a show before—this isn't my first time," Carmen replied.

"I've no doubt you've been around the block," Gus said. "But a ten-minute Internet show? It's not what we're doing here." Gus was not pleased at the back-and-forth over the menus for the upcoming episodes of *Eat Drink and Be*. Her shows without a cohost had always been easy to plan. And she wasn't impressed with the idea of presenting fussy dishes: as a mom, she had more respect for her busy peers.

Also discouraging was that Alan was forcing them to do a mini-season test run: Gus was essentially auditioning for the job she'd held for the last twelve years. It was infuriating. "*FlavorBoom* was extremely popular," Carmen said, her voice icy.

"With frat boys," said Gus. "What the hell did you do in ten minutes? Dress up mayonnaise. Make chips and dip. Toss a salad." Gus was getting cranky but she tried valiantly to keep herself in check. The last thing she wanted to seem was shrewish. She cleared her throat and tried her most professional voice. "My point, Carmen, is that the average viewer on the CookingChannel is looking to be entertained and inspired, not overwhelmed. We try to use foods that are easy to find, and that have some sort of familiarity to the viewer."

"Novelty keeps people interested," said Carmen. "And by the way, I don't do fancy mayonnaise."

"I like mayo—well, really aioli, but same idea." Oliver hadn't spoken for most of the meeting, uncomfortable about being so late, annoyed with Carmen, intimidated by Gus, worried about Porter's impression of him. "We could make a fish with aioli."

Gus and Carmen each shot him a nasty glance. Oh, brother. He slunk down in his chair a smidge.

"Ah, he speaks," Porter said, appraising Oliver. "Look, it's clear Carmen and Gus have different ideas—and I want the three of you to go shopping together, and then come back and cook. Without cameras, without pressure. See what you can put together in the studio kitchen, learn each other's styles a little bit."

"But we can't even agree on the basics of a menu," began Carmen. "My concepts aren't being respected by some of the women in the room."

"Trust me, Carmen," he said simply, "you've got innovation and spice. Gus has sophistication and a proven track record. I've had a lot of hit shows and together—whether the two of you like it or not—I'm going to make sure that *Eat Drink and Be* is my best one yet."

"When are we starting with the new show?" asked Oliver.

"Immediately," said Porter. "Here is what I really want to do: have a contest. Some lucky viewer will win an hour, on air, with the team of *Eat Drink and Be.*"

"What?" Gus had a sense that everything was spinning out of her control and, frankly, she didn't like it.

"We'll get entries, essays, videos, you name it. All why they should be lucky enough to cook with you two. Carmen's fans are Internet-based and our viewers would kill to spend time in your kitchen, Gus."

"You're turning my show into a game show, Porter!"

"It's my show as well, Gus." Carmen clapped her hands together. "And I think it's brilliant."

"Good," said Porter. "We've got an ad for the contest ready to go live."

Seventy miles away in northern New Jersey, Priya Patel opened her Web browser for the fourth time in fifteen minutes. In the background, as usual, was the hum of the CookingChannel; she liked the noise but she only paid attention to the repeats of *Cooking with Gusto!* at noon and five. The rest was just filler. Today Gus Simpson was making orange-apricot scones with a sweet glaze made from orange peel, a scraping of zest, and confectioners' sugar. Yum.

The only thing better than the repeats were original episodes, and Priya had made a house rule that she was not to be interrupted during a new episode in which Gus appeared. Only for broken arms, she told the family. Nothing else. Not that anyone in her house paid attention. There had been a lot of bustle in Gus's kitchen during that live episode and Gus seemed a bit strained. Putting on a good face, of course. Priya knew what that was like.

She'd been dismayed to see ads about an entirely new show—*Eat Drink and Be*—that was going to replace her beloved *Cooking with Gusto!* The tempo was nice, very soothing, whereas the live show seemed a bit chaotic.

Out of concern, Priya had written several emails in recent days, her points bulleted and concise, to explain why this live format wasn't the best way to showcase Gus Simpson's talents. Not that anyone from the CookingChannel had taken the time to reply. She hadn't expected that they would. Well, maybe she'd had a hope. It was okay to have hopes.

Instead, Priya had taken to outlining these points late at night to her husband, Raj, who sometimes pretended to be interested and at other times very obviously wanted to go to sleep. She knew she shouldn't take offense but still it was hard. Unlike Priya, who'd arrived in the United States when she was two, Raj grew up in India and only came to America when he and Priya had become engaged. They'd met, of course, beforehand; her parents were thoughtful in that regard.

Marriage had been a condition of going to graduate school. And besides, Priya had been more than ready to get out of the house. It had seemed a fair trade at the time. A reasonable request. Now, almost twenty years and three children later, Priya longed to go back in time and undo her decision: remain a virgin and live in her mother's house all her life. She could have manned the front desk of the Days Inn they operated in north Jersey, smiling at the weary travelers as they came off the thruway.

"Oh, let me look up your reservation," she would have said, looking calm in the air-conditioned office. "Let me make your stay a more comfortable one." And the patrons would have smiled at her and murmured thank-yous and appreciated the bowl of apples she had on the counter, washed and ready to eat. Priya prided herself on her attention to detail.

Not that anyone understood how hard it was just to keep it all together.

You should be happy. That's what her husband said. Look at the nice house we live in. Do you know how much that flat screen cost? You should be happy. That's what her mother-in-law said when she flew over to visit, each stay getting longer. When I was a bride I couldn't have hoped for such riches. You should be treating your husband better. You watch too much television. You're lazy, and grouchy. If my son wasn't so kind, he would have traded you in long ago.

Priya liked to imagine herself on a trading card, her face on the front and her vital statistics on the back. Height: 5'4". Weight: MYOB. Age: MYOB. Hobbies: canning fruit, making jam, and watching Gus Simpson on the CookingChannel. ("Those are not very Indian hobbies," she could see the collectors of the trading cards discussing among themselves as they weighed her against Lakshmis and Mayas and Indiras. "This makes Priya a very rare card indeed. Is she worth more or less?") Happiness level. That was Priya's favorite category on her trading card. Happiness level: MYOB.

She loved that phrase. MYOB. That's what she told her husband when he asked her what she'd been doing all day, when she'd forgotten to go to the Oak Tree Center Road in Iselin to pick up tomatoes, chilies, and fresh coriander to make a meal. To get *methi*—fenugreek—and put together tortilla-like *thepla*. Raj enjoyed that dish. Her teenage daughter did not. Neither did her sons, the youngest barely six and gearing up to go to school full-time in the fall.

He liked macaroni. From a box. Which Priya often made when they were home alone, swearing him to secrecy. That could go on her trading card, too. Bad habits: keeps secrets. And hides out in the bathroom to cry.

"You must be happy about Kiran going to first grade," said her mother, who came to visit often. "Then you'll have time to do all the things you want. Think how clean the house will be."

MYOB, thought Priya, sounding out each letter in her mind and smiling. Out loud, she agreed with her mother. It would be a fine thing, she said.

Now, with Kiran playing upstairs, his belly full of Kraft noodles, Priya opened a new window on her computer screen. The words *Win a chance to appear on Eat Drink and Be!!* flashed on the screen. See rules to apply, she read, clicking the link.

What could it hurt, she told herself, to enter Gus's little contest? Wouldn't it be fun to meet her and discuss spices? Priya knew all about Gus's life—she'd read about it in *People* magazine years ago—about how she was widowed with two young daughters and scraped together to open up a little food store.

A sandwich shop, Priya thought, would definitely not be nice. Everyone coming in and demanding different things: no tomato, more lettuce, my bread is stale, why haven't you gone to the Indian store to get fresh onion? She empathized with Gus, at how hard she must have worked, and took great pleasure in her success.

Not to mention Gus was very good at throwing parties.

Years ago, Raj had liked to invite over his friends from the temple. But he'd stopped doing so when Priya told him, repeatedly, how much money she was spending on food. I don't mind, is what he said, I am happy for everyone to come here and have a good time. But Priya felt it was like being in a sandwich shop, and had subtly tried to dissuade him from the idea.

"You like to cook," said her mother, during one of her regular stopovers. "So I don't see what your problem is. I think you just watch too much television."

On television, the parties were fun. Gus was so welcoming. She knew what it was like to be a short-order cook, to scrub floors even though you had several degrees, to give and give and give. Gus knew what it was like to be a wife and mother and yet she hosted her show with a smile.

"Take a seat," Gus had said in an episode of *Cooking with Gusto!* long ago. "Let me fix you a little something."

"Yes, please," Priya, all alone in her big house, had spoken to the TV screen. "I'd like that very much."

# 10

"The thing is, part of me feels as though I should try to like Carmen," said Gus as she knelt in front of a planter, using a narrow hand trowel to stab a hole in the dirt. Once the danger of frost had passed she could plant her herb garden: creeping thyme, dill, sweet basil, hyssop, French tarragon, and bronze fennel. All wonderful flavors and scents to add to her dishes.

"Part of me feels as though I should be more generous," she clarified. "It's what people expect of me. It's what Alan and Porter want."

"I know," said Hannah. "That's what's easier for them. Expectations will crush you." She sat curled up in a patio chair she'd pulled over a few feet from the outdoor table, examining a box of seedlings she held in her lap.

"It's just that I absolutely and completely feel this sense of outrage whenever I see her. She preens and she's fussy and wants to spend all this time showing off her cooking chops—" Gus leaned back on her heels, searching for words. "She sucks all the attention out of a room."

"Divas always do," said Hannah. She was dressed in what Gus referred to as her "outside pajamas"—a pair of sweatpants and a blue hooded top. "But you can't have her knowing that you're a softie underneath all those crisply ironed shirts of yours."

"Porter said something very stupid," Gus said, gesturing with her garden tool. "He said I have trouble letting things go."

"Mmm—hmmm."

"You think I do?"

Hannah half-shrugged, half-nodded, then brushed back some hair that had fallen loose from her ponytail, smudging a little dirt on her face.

"Right there," Gus said, pretending to wipe her own face. "A little bit of mess."

"So maybe a little issue letting things go?" laughed Hannah. "I'll agree with that."

"Maybe," admitted Gus. "And the thing is that I feel guilty about not liking Carmen. I came of age in the seventies, women's lib and sisterhood, all that. I went to a women's college."

"You're a true believer," said Hannah. "But maybe that's a little naive, no?"

"I know Carmen is angling for my job," said Gus. "And then I have this other feeling: shouldn't I want to help her?"

"Being female doesn't mean someone automatically wants to be part of a sisterhood. Maybe you all were so busy getting over the housewife thing that you overlooked that part."

"But I believe in mentoring," Gus said earnestly.

"Good," said Hannah. "Find some little girl who wants your help. Though don't mistake helping someone to mean being 'the good girl' when she tries to walk all over you."

"She's barely older than Aimee," Gus said quietly.

"Bad girls shall inherit the earth," said Hannah. "It's always too late after the fact."

"It's different from what you went through."

"Yes, but if I'd been more vocal, or stronger, or simply savvier, I wouldn't have found myself on the outside looking in," Hannah replied. "Or, more correctly, on the outside hiding out. You can't afford to feel guilty about a rival, especially one who hasn't shown any reason she should be trusted. I've written about this type of coworker before," she added, knowing Gus was aware she'd never actually worked outside her carriage house dining room.

"It's just that maybe I should be more understanding, have more faith in the CookingChannel," said Gus.

"Oh, Gus," implored Hannah. "This woman was thrust on the air with you and now you're sharing your show. *Your* show. You have worked at this for years, built a fan base, and now you're practically handing it all to Carmen Vega. That's not fair. Get angry!"

Gus hesitated. "No," she said, a little doubtfully. "I don't like to feel angry."

"Yes! Use your frustration to create focus. Turn your anger outward, not inward." Hannah stood up. "Listen to me: I know what it's like to be mad at yourself. And it's not going to help one bit. You have to play smart."

"And that means . . ."

"Be professional. Be on top of your game," she said. "But when it's your turn to serve, hit hard. Damn hard."

It was slightly overcast when the trio of Oliver, Carmen, and Gus met at the farmer's market in Union Square a few days later, marching silently into the throngs of gourmet yuppies looking for heirloom tomatoes and NYU students in search of a few inexpensive bites of, well, anything. Stalls were set up over a long expanse of concrete, next to a park—really just a collection of nice trees and park benches—between Broadway and Park Avenue South. Every so often the rumble of a train pulling into the subway station below could be heard, and a steady stream of people flowed up and out of the staircases underground.

Gus took a deep breath, taking in the wondrous scent of fresh herbs, ran her eyes over the stalls of red and yellow tulips and the tables mounded with ramps, asparagus, sorrel, chives, and mushrooms. Farther along she could make out the crisp spring lettuces, the romaine and spinach and what was known as a merlot, with its wonderful ruffled red edges and bright green ribs. Gus longed to crunch on a few baby carrots, dreamed of giving them a quick blanch and a dab of butter and parsley. Yum!

She wanted a chance to wander through the crowd, imagining how she'd put together an early spring vegetable soup, and savor a cup of tea as she people-watched the comings and goings of the green market.

Oliver had come prepared, carrying natural canvas bags in which they could tote away their prized goodies, and he handed them out to Gus and Carmen.

"Same for everybody," he said cheerily.

Gus noted, almost unconsciously, the double takes as the Saturday morning shoppers stared at her group. It was something she'd gotten used to a long time ago, the public persona that was Gus Simpson. There were moments when her other life seemed like a dream she'd once had and this world, this career, was all she'd ever known. Not everyone knew who she was—she wasn't a movie star, for God's sake—but enough passersby paid attention to her that it made others look and frown, trying to figure out why her face was so familiar. Was she someone they went to high school with? No, wait, she looked just like . . .

"Gus Simpson!" she heard a woman squeal behind her. "Isn't she gorgeous?" Gus inwardly brightened at the comment and looked hard at Carmen, willing her to hear. Then a horrid thought crossed her mind: what if they were remarking about Carmen's good looks?

"So, here we are," Carmen said, interrupting Gus's thoughts. "It's tremendously cold for late April."

Lacking patience or desire to listen to Carmen, Gus did what she did best: she made decisions.

"Let's split up, go shopping separately, and meet on a park bench in twenty minutes to compare purchases," she suggested. Carmen's cell phone rang but Gus pretended not to notice. She kept talking. "Porter didn't mean for us to be joined at the hip."

"Should we synchronize our watches?" asked Oliver, smiling broadly. He had lines around his mouth when he did so, friendly ones. He was a good smiler, Gus thought. Carmen wandered a few steps away from the group to talk on her phone.

"You're not mocking me, are you?" asked Gus.

"No," Oliver said simply. He stood there, calm and still smiling. "But I could stick with you and carry your stuff."

Was he commenting on her age? (In her head she heard Hannah's voice: "You're the only person who's obsessed with how old you are!") Or maybe he was the last true gentleman in New York City? Hard to tell.

It had been a long time since Gus had gone on a field trip, and she felt unprepared and overdressed in a blue cashmere cardigan and a nice pair of heather gray gabardine trousers, her gray trench coat slung over an arm. Oliver, on the other hand, was wearing a ball cap over his bald head and a pair of jeans, a green Henley underneath a leather jacket. Carmen had on a long turquoise tunic dress over leggings, her hair loosely pulled back from her face and clipped with a barrette, her makeup artfully applied to appear natural. Looking effortlessly casual. She was good, Gus had to admit—it was practically impossible to see where the foundation blended into her neck.

"I'd love to learn your favorite vegetables," persisted Oliver. "I bet you like asparagus. You know: Gus. Aspara*gus*."

"My daughters used to make that joke when they were small."

"You've got kids," commented Oliver. "Your house must be busy."

Gus threw him a quizzical look. "They're long out of the house, I'm afraid."

"In college then?"

"No, no, out of school. Working and all that." Who could stop thinking about her age with this bozo around?

"Were you a teen mom then?" asked Oliver, before holding up his hand. "I'm sorry; I have a tendency to just speak whatever thought comes into my head."

"I was not a teen mom," Gus said, wordlessly daring him to ask her age.

"You know, you're not really like a Gus."

"What does that mean?" asked Gus, clearly peeved.

"It's just that it's a very informal name and you're a very formal sort of person," he replied. "You're different that way."

Just then Carmen sauntered over to the two of them.

"Hey, something's come up," she said, tucking her cell phone back into her purse. "I've got to go."

"You can't just leave," said Gus, her disapproval apparent. "This is a mandatory activity. Porter said so."

"It's quite all right, Gus," said Carmen. "It's been cleared with the big guy."

Her words took a moment to register.

"That was Alan." Gus wasn't asking a question. "Alan just called you."

"I forgot that I'd promised to do this brunch thing with him. You know." Carmen folded up the canvas bag Oliver had passed out and put it in his hand. "Ask Oliver—he knows how forgetful I am. I'm like a—how do you say it?—absentminded professor."

"I don't think that's appropriate," Gus insisted. "We've all made a point to come here today, and it doesn't seem professional that you're marching off."

Gus had a strong belief in rules, in following through and doing what was expected. It was the only way she'd managed to get through life.

"Look, it's not personal," shrugged Carmen. "I have to go. I'll meet up with you at the studio later." And she walked away while Gus sputtered. It was like being stood up, only worse: being abandoned in the middle of the date.

"You've still got me," Oliver said, as though reading her mind. "C'mon, let's go shopping."

"She's an absolute pain," Gus said, still staring as though she could see Carmen walking away.

"How about some spring peas?" Oliver asked in a not-so-subtle attempt to change the subject.

"I hate peas."

"A good chef isn't allowed to hate a vegetable," he said, persistently ignoring her dark looks.

"I'm not a chef, Oliver," said Gus. "I'm a TV host. I can hate anything I want to. I just can't do so in public."

"Oh, I like a challenge," he said. "I could get some spring peas and whip up a little dish later that you'll love."

"I won't try a bite of it," Gus shot back. But she wasn't frowning now. She took a deep breath, trying to cleanse all the Carmen dust out of her lungs. Nearby, a young mother was wrangling two girls in pink-and-orange sweaters; one of the girls, the younger, was clearly upset. She felt a sense of déjà vu.

"I don't actually like everything," Oliver said conspiratorially, starting to walk toward the stalls and willing Gus to keep in step. "I object to foie gras for ethical reasons. Even if it tastes delicious."

Gus, he could tell, wasn't paying any attention to him, her eyes glued to the crowds of people.

"I once had elephant kebobs," he said.

She continued to watch the little girls, her heart going out to the mother trying to keep them entertained and occupied. There was no father in sight. He might have been at home. Or maybe he was simply gone.

Gus knew how that felt.

"And a soufflé of pureed tiger toes," said Oliver, running through a list of inappropriate foods in his mind. He hadn't eaten any such thing, of course. "I like penguin dumplings in sesame sauce."

Slowly the culinary producer's words found their way to Gus's ears. She turned to him.

"I've always found penguin a little chewy myself," she said, a tiny whisper of a smile on her pink lips. "That's why it's so good for braising."

"Do you know what is really a crazy food?" he asked. Gus shook her head.

"Kumquats. I once saw a television commercial in which a pregnant woman asks a grocery store manager for kumquats," he said. "And the manager raises his eyebrow and says, 'Kumquats?' as though it actually means something illicit." He laughed at the memory.

"I was about seven or eight and for years afterward I was convinced kumquats were only for ladies," he admitted. "I didn't try one until cooking school."

"You thought you could get pregnant from eating kumquats?"

"Pretty much," conceded Oliver. "I was a goofy kid."

Gus gave Oliver an appraising look, trying to see a goofy kid within the tall, good-looking man in the jeans and leather jacket. He had warm brown eyes, she decided.

The two of them wandered around the farmer's market until, as if by some plan, they stared at a selection of leeks and onions mounded high on a table.

"We could do a spaghetti sauce with ramps," suggested Oliver. "Something earthy and simple."

"A leek tart, a little vichyssoise," Gus said, feeling more in the spirit. After all, they still had to cook something up that afternoon as part of Porter's "getting to know you" plan.

"I tend to like traditional things," she added, walking over to pick up a head of Bibb lettuce, weighing it in her hands.

"Oliver," she asked sharply, remembering the beauty queen's comment from earlier. "Why did Carmen say you'd know how forgetful she is?"

"We went to culinary school together," he said flatly, seemingly fascinated with the lettuces as he avoided looking at Gus. No dummy, he knew a personal association would not be appreciated by his new boss. "But it's not like we're best friends or anything."

"I wouldn't have guessed you to be the same age," she said.

"We're not. I'm much younger," he said, then winked to show he was kidding. "I'm a second careerist."

"Well, so is she, technically. Beauty queen and all that."

Oliver nodded. "I used to be on Wall Street. You know, an investment guy."

"Didn't like it?"

"I was good at it," he admitted. "But it wasn't for me." The last thing he wanted to discuss was his background.

"So what's your favorite food trend?" he asked.

"Oh, don't tell me you're one of those! I hate food trends," replied Gus, albeit pleasantly. "Sunchokes, pomegranate, Meyer lemons, figs, foams—every year something new sweeps the foodies and it's eaten passionately and then practically abandoned. It's irresponsible to the palate."

"I love Meyer lemons," insisted Oliver.

"So do I," asserted Gus. "But I refuse to be a slave to food fashion."

"What's your motto, then?"

"Fresh. It's all about fresh," said Gus, her eyes beginning to sparkle. She brought an artichoke up to eye level. "What could we do with this?"

"Hearts with fresh pasta, cream sauce, and a dash of nutmeg," he said. "Or herbed in a tart with shavings of fontina."

"Sounds delish. So here's the real question: do you love food, Oliver, or do you love cooking?"

The tall man in the ball cap focused intensely on the slim woman in the soft blue sweater. He thought for a long time.

"That's a serious question, Gus Simpson," he said, drawing out his words.

"Indeed it is, Mr. Oliver Cooper."

"I love food," he said. "I do love cooking but my heart belongs to the food."

"Well, if that's the case, then you and I shall be good friends," said Gus. "Though a certain someone else, I suspect, is devoted more to displaying her technique."

"I would not deny that Carmen is a person who enjoys the spotlight," conceded Oliver. "But I don't think she's merely a cooking show-off."

"We shall agree to disagree, then," Gus said amiably. "But I won't hold your friendship with Carmen against you. Entirely." She smiled. "Let's talk about hothouse tomatoes: necessity or crime against flavor?"

"Both."

"Right answer, I think," Gus said, loading up her canvas bag and then, feeling the weight, distributing some of her goods to Oliver. "I could carry this but I do want you to feel useful."

"Of course," he said. "I'd like to be of use to you, Gus."

It was one thing to say you were available anytime, Carmen thought, and quite another to actually mean it. Alan, she was quickly learning, was very demanding.

Be careful what you wish for because you just might get it: that was the American saying, and it was so true. She'd called Oliver late last night to complain.

"You've got to protect me from Gus," she had pleaded. "The woman hates me."

Carmen had no problem with people wanting to look good but there was something so formal and aloof about Gus: she overdressed just to go shopping. It was as though she kept herself that little bit apart. That little bit different.

Being on television was not going as expected, that was for sure. Who wants to share a show? That had been Alan's idea, and while he seemed quite pleased with himself, Carmen was trapped: she couldn't dare refuse.

Why, she wondered, did everything have to be so unfair? She'd put her time in on the modeling circuit, sashaying about in bikinis. It had been difficult, when she was younger, before displaying her body became just a regular part of work. It was a long climb to go from Carmen, daughter of Diego and Mercedes of Seville, to Carmen Vega, Miss Spain 1999. She knew how to turn on the charm—and the walk—when she had to. She knew how to act. She'd been well trained.

But her relationship with food was all about being Carmen of Seville. It was her truth, her statement to the world. And she didn't care if she had to use her beauty queen smarts to get people to take a bite—because once they had a taste of her flavors, of the garlic and olive oil and pinches of smoked paprika, *pimentón*, they would know. Carmen Vega wasn't just another pretty face. She was an artist.

# 11

Saturday afternoon stretched out before them, bright and sunny: if Gus had been home it would have been a perfect day to putter in her garden and tend to the delphinium. After all, there was no set time to be at the studio, and Gus was hardly certain that Carmen was going to show. Although she wouldn't have minded calling it a day and taking the commuter train back to Westchester, Gus felt responsible as Oliver waited patiently, loaded down with veggies in the canvas bags.

"What's next?" he asked pleasantly.

"You're easygoing," said Gus. "Aren't you a bit annoyed at our state of limbo?"

"Oh, I had a life makeover a few years ago," he said. "Worked out a lot of my annoyance issues. I'm a much nicer guy now, actually."

"I'm sure you were always nice."

"No, not really." He was still smiling so Gus wasn't sure if he was joking or not. "Back then I would have decided all the days' moves long ago."

"But now you sit back and let someone else take charge," Gus said in a matter-of-fact tone.

He laughed. "Wrong again," he said. "Now I know when I need to make a decision and when it's time to let someone else have a turn. That's a different thing altogether."

"So . . . ?"

"So I'm at your service."

"I guess we could go to the studio and play." Gus gestured to the produce. "Why don't I call my daughters and convince them to come and eat lunch?"

Oliver nodded. "At the very least we can try to teach them a few skills before the next episode."

"I know!" Gus nodded vigorously. "Honestly, I don't think I've had a more disorganized episode since my first day on TV. Those kids can't tell a spoon from a spatula."

"That's part of the fun, I think," said Oliver. "The mad scramble of a group who can't cook their way out of a paper bag. Present company excepted, of course."

"Right back at you," said Gus. "It is rather disturbing, isn't it, that I've managed to raise two girls who are not particularly adept in the kitchen?"

"I think the taller of the two, the one with the light brown hair, has more of a knack."

"Do you? That's Aimee. She pays attention even when you think she's not looking."

"She seems interesting."

Gus turned to the man at her side and looked at him thoughtfully. He had a nice build, and friendly crinkles around his tickler eyes. And a thought began to form in her mind quite naturally.

"Aimee is interesting," she told him, making a mental note to find out if Porter knew Oliver's age. "She works for the UN as an economist."

"I'm sure she and I could have fun talking numbers," he said. "But you and I will have a better time cooking, that's for sure."

"Right," Gus said, listening with half an ear. She dialed Aimee from her cell phone and invited her up to the studio.

"She'll meet us there because she's already uptown," Gus told Oliver as they clambered into a taxi, tucking the bags of vegetables in between them.

After chopping three potatoes to Oliver's ten spuds, Aimee decided she needed a break or she might cut her fingers off by accident. She didn't typically spend her Saturday afternoons cooking: in fact, it was her routine to do her washing in the basement laundry of her building, interspersing trips up and down in the elevator with watching all the episodes of *Wheel of Fortune* she'd TiVoed from the week before. Game shows were Aimee's secret obsession and most guilty pleasure: she couldn't decide if she'd rather imagine herself winning or would simply be content to watch program after program of smiling, successful contestants. Sitting amid her comforter and watching the television, her laundry basket on the end of the bed and the liquid detergent tucked back into its spot in the linen cupboard, Aimee gave herself over to the enjoyment of watching: she experienced a deep satisfaction after every big win, a twist in her stomach when a participant landed on a "Bankrupt" on the colorful wheel and lost all potential money. The best moments, though, were when the contestants began to tear up after being awarded some large jackpot, their relief and desperation etched in every line of their face.

"Oh, they really needed the money," she would say aloud to no one at all, her room empty except for her. "This is going to make a big difference for them."

Sometimes she would tear up just as the participants were doing, crying along with them and feeling a warm happiness enveloping her. She'd hit "pause" and imagine all the wonderful things they could do with their prizes: the trips they would take, the table they would finally buy for an empty dining room, the teenage son or daughter who could finally go to college. Aimee saw all their dreams and cried for them. But that was most often only when someone won $100,000.

And then, at the end of watching hours of shows, as if to bring herself back to the real world and all its discomforts, she would warn the players through the screen: "Don't forget you'll be taxed on your winnings!"

Late at night, when she was trying to sleep, she often wondered why no one had started a game show magazine, with article after article giving updates on the winners of *Millionaire* and *Deal or No Deal* and *Wheel*. It was true she enjoyed the smarty-pants nature of *Jeopardy* but, when it came right down to it, what had a hold on her heart were the regular people just holding their breath for an opportunity that day-to-day life could not deliver.

The game show obsession had started years ago, back in the summer after her father died, when she and Sabrina had their mornings free after swim lessons and nothing to do. Gus had kept them home most of the time while she dealt with papers, sitting with the door closed in the tiny room that had been their father's office. There were a lot of papers, apparently.

She and Sabrina, still in elementary school then, had become diehard devotees of *The Price Is Right*, memorizing the price of Rice-A-Roni and Lysol disinfectant and planning a cross-country road trip when they turned eighteen and could finally become contestants on the show. They'd see Bob Barker and the Plinko board, and if they played it just right, they'd bid well enough to win both showcases. Sabrina wanted to win a car, a truck, and a Winnebago, but all Aimee wished to win was a new living room set. Something with bright flowers that would cheer up Gus and make her want to come out of the office.

Aimee put down her knife and looked up to locate her mother. Gus had been spending much of the afternoon pretend-searching for items in the pantry, and Aimee, well acquainted with her mother's penchant for matchmaking, was suspicious about what was really going on. She walked out of the kitchen studio a few steps and went to find Gus.

"Long time since you've been in the studio, Mom?" she asked. "You don't seem to want to hang out with the rest of us."

"Aimee, you startled me," said Gus, who was looking at a can of tomatoes with studious concentration.

"Need tomatoes?"

"No, why?"

Aimee gestured toward her mother's hand. Gus looked down.

"Oh, I was just . . . reading the ingredient list," she said. "It can be illuminating."

"I'm sure, Mom," said Aimee. "It contains tomatoes."

"Are you having a nice time with Oliver?" asked Gus. "He's very handsome. Funny, too."

"So go date him, then," said Aimee.

"There's no need to be ridiculous," said Gus. Her daughter well knew she had not gone out with anyone after Christopher died. It was always too soon, too busy, too scary. Too easy to avoid altogether. Even when she felt alone at times, Gus believed that remaining single was better for her girls. For herself.

"What's the deal, Mom? Hoping for a double wedding?"

"If you mean with that Billy, then no." Gus replaced the tomatoes on the shelf. "I did leave you a few messages last week that you didn't return. I want to talk about this Billy thing."

"News flash, Mom," Aimee said. "Sabrina's the one who is engaged. Not me."

She'd spent an hour or so with Billy one evening as he waited—

and waited and waited—while Sabrina changed outfits repeatedly. He'd seemed unaffected by her sister's shenanigans entirely, had read the paper, chitchatted about the midterm elections, and even offered to make a run for coffee, all the while praising every outfit Sabrina paraded around. It's not as though he became Aimee's best friend or anything, but he hadn't seemed like such a bad guy at all.

"For one, I know that. For two, don't speak to me in that tone," said Gus. "You don't have to be so prickly all the time." She leaned close to Aimee and whispered, "Help me get Sabrina back with Troy."

"It's her life, Mom. You don't have to run it. Why do you have to just, just . . . " Aimee mimed wringing someone's neck with her hands.

"I'm just trying to help. Aimee, your sister runs through fiancés like a thirsty man drinks water."

"So let her figure it out."

"I can't think of anything worse," said Gus. "Do you know what my fear is? That Sabrina is going to call me from the road, having left behind a husband and a couple of babies, because she's gone off to find herself."

"That's not going to happen, Mom. It's not like she married any of these guys."

"One day she's going to drop the 'cold feet' act and then what?"

"Then I get my own apartment."

"You're just being ridiculous. We've got to band together and take this seriously."

"She's only twenty-five years old!" said Aimee. "She's got several more fiancés to dump before she really gets serious."

"You know what she's like. Sabrina has always needed someone, and I think Troy is it. You're different. You can stand on your own. Like me."

Aimee rolled her eyes. "The toughest girl in the world," she said. "Look, I didn't come up here to talk about my sister or hide out in the pantry. I thought I was at least going to get some soup."

"This is important, Aimee—I need your help."

"What do you want me to do, Mom?" Aimee watched Gus closely.

"Sabrina won't answer my messages."

"Ah, I thought you'd been in touch with me a tad more than usual," Aimee said under her breath. Gus gave no sign of hearing her words.

"Wasn't Troy kind?" she asked.

"Yeah, but he isn't some sort of savior. Nobody's perfect."

"Exactly," said Gus. "He's real. And I believe Troy truly cares about her."

"Maybe, but you just like him better than those other stuffed shirts she's brought home."

"Neither of you girls have any idea what it's like when things go sour. You've never had to pay for your mistakes."

"So let us do something wrong," said Aimee. "You get so intense when we don't do what *you* want us to do."

"You don't know what it's like to struggle." Gus was getting angry: her cheeks were turning red. "I have done everything for the two of you."

"Maybe don't do so much, then," Aimee said quietly. "We may not have had your struggle, but we've had our own."

"Hey, Simpsons," Oliver said, poking his head into the pantry. "Soup's on."

"It can't be done already?"

"It's coming together, but I was getting lonely out there. Come out and assist."

Gus glanced at him sharply.

"Er, I mean come out and let me assist you," said Oliver, grinning.

Gus began to move in the direction of the stove.

"Oliver?" Aimee asked, pulling lightly on his sleeve. "You heard us arguing, didn't you?"

"A culinary producer never tells," he said. "Besides, Carmen just called my cell and she's not going to make it up here today. I figure your mother has used up her last bit of patience—and I was hoping to save some for our next live show."

too many cooks

# 12

Eight days later, the team was fully assembled in Gus's kitchen: Oliver in a purple cook's jacket, Carmen in a cranberry-colored wrap dress, Sabrina in a sage green skirt-and-sweater combo, Aimee in a crisp white blouse and charcoal slacks, Troy in a dark blue shirt and a very large button that said "Sabrina used to be my girlfriend" in red letters. Not bad, thought Porter, for a team who resisted direction on what to wear.

The group sat among the cameras—much to the annoyance of the camera crew—as they waited for Gus, who was upstairs with Hannah, ostensibly getting ready. Porter was going over his schedule for the upcoming hour, not in the least worried that Gus hadn't come down. She'd never let him down in all their years of working together, and he doubted she was about to start now.

One floor above the kitchen, perched on the cushioned window seat in her master bedroom, Gus waited with Hannah. Gus was careful not to crush her emerald green silk shirt and wide-legged dark pants, or ruffle her hair, expertly blown out in her signature swingy bob. Hannah, wearing a gray velour tracksuit, had flopped on the bed. She didn't want to join the others.

"You'd be better at hiding if you didn't dress like an athlete," Gus pointed out. "Try wearing a skirt or something."

"Perhaps a short white skirt, right?" Hannah said, before grabbing a pillow and making to smother herself. "I'd be better if I didn't go on television at all."

"I know you love halibut." Gus was using her soothing tone. "Hannah, it's going to be easy today: halibut in zucchini jackets, a green bean and potato casserole, and a white sangria."

Gus loved to talk about food. Late at night, if she couldn't sleep, she would read cookbooks out loud to herself until she relaxed.

"Sangria? Isn't that Spanish?" Hannah's voice was muffled from underneath the pillow. "Like Carmen?"

"Contrary to reports, I actually love Spanish food," said Gus. "I just have issues with Carmen in particular. But that doesn't mean I can't compromise now and then. We're using anchovies imported from Santoña and spicy paprika today."

"Anchovies? I hate anchovies."

"People always say that." Gus stepped over to remove the pillow from Hannah's face. "But then they don't even know that's what they're tasting. It's all about trying before deciding against something."

"Are we still talking about food?"

"If you don't want to be on the show, it's okay by me," said Gus. "But I'd prefer to have you there."

"I don't know what to do, that's the problem," Hannah said. "You cannot imagine how much I want to go home and put on my pajamas. But I hate to give in to it."

Gus wore a strange expression on her face.

"What?"

"It's just that . . . nothing," said Gus.

"I hate to quit things," continued Hannah. "Do you know what my father always said? 'Once a quitter, always a quitter.' "

"Hannah, you stay home all day long. All night long. All the time. And your father? Don't get me started."

Hannah leaned up on one elbow. "Oh, hiding is not the same as quitting," she explained. "I thought you understood that."

"Well, it's an unusual style of living!"

"Popular with cloistered nuns, hermits, and disgraced sports stars everywhere."

"You can't let the past dictate your future."

"It's called self-preservation." Hannah's face was serious. "Do you think someone will recognize me?"

Gus considered fibbing, but only briefly.

"Yes," she said. "I knew who you were the day I met you," she continued. "You haven't changed all that much in fifteen years, you know. Your head took up whole billboards in Times Square once upon a time."

"The soup!" cried Hannah. "High-energy vegetable soup. Those ads bought the carriage house."

"Did you ever eat that stuff? I've always wondered."

"All the time. I thought it would have been unethical to promote something without trying it." She felt the usual twist in her stomach whenever the topic of her disgrace came up.

"Oh, Hannah," said Gus. "That makes everything else that happened even more ridiculous."

"I know," she said. "But I did it for my dad, I guess."

"It's funny, what we do for our parents."

"Or what our parents ask us to do for them," said Hannah. She had rolled over on the bed and grabbed a pillow, pressing it into her abdomen. Sometimes, when the bad feelings came, she tried to squish them down. Occasionally it worked.

"I'm frightened."

"Of course you are."

"I don't want to ruin your show, Gus," she said. "What would happen when someone calls the CookingChannel and says, 'Is that her?'"

"Then we tell them that you're my very best friend and a wonderful person," insisted Gus. "We all make mistakes."

"You don't."

"Oh, Hannah. You, of all people, know how often I do. I just emphasize the things I do well."

Gus regarded the thin woman in the gray tracksuit sitting on her bed, her forehead wrinkled and beaded in a light sweat.

"Oh, move on over," she said, scooting onto the bed and lying next to Hannah, not caring if her bob got flattened.

"Thanks for not hugging me," Hannah said, a bit sniffly. "I hate being hugged."

"Don't worry about the show," said Gus. "I'll put on a Teflon vest so I won't feel Carmen trying to stick her knives into my back."

"Kevlar, not Teflon. For bullets. I know, I had to wear one for a while."

"Some fans take tennis very seriously."

"Yeah." Hannah's eyes were watering. She felt like such a freak sometimes, paralyzed by her fear of others' judgments. "People are reluctant to forgive when you shatter their illusions," she said. "I know you know, Gus, having so much expected of you. The truth is that it sucks."

"Professional success doesn't always make life easier," admitted Gus. "It can bring unexpected complications."

"It's the personal stuff that matters," said Hannah. "But that seems too easy to be true."

Gus well knew that the doubts and insecurities lingered, no matter how many shows she hosted or how many cookbooks she wrote.

And no amount of zeros in her bank account could bring Christopher back.

"I'm going to sneak in a squeeze anyway," she said, leaning in briefly to hug Hannah. "That one was for me, not you."

"They'll be going crazy downstairs, wondering why you're up here," Hannah said, blowing her nose. "Porter will be looking at his watch and tapping his clipboard."

"I'll be there. I'm always there."

"A persona can be a powerful trap. It can take you over."

"I know who I am."

"It's not about knowing. It's about remembering to be."

"So what's the verdict?" asked Gus.

Hannah pulled the elastic off her ponytail, then gathered up her red hair and replaced the tie. She always played with her hair when she was nervous, a leftover habit from when she was younger.

"You are truly and absolutely my only friend, Gus Simpson," she said. "The rest of the world has abandoned me but not forgiven."

"The only person who has to forgive you is you," said Gus.

"And maybe the German girl who fell down the stairs at Wimbledon!"

"Right. I forgot that bit of nasty business."

"My whole life is a disaster." Hannah took a deep breath, then another. "I'd go on that show of yours if you needed me to. But you don't. I really suffered with anxiety after that basketball episode. Please don't ask me."

"I'd never make anyone do anything," said Gus. "Sabrina and Aimee are proof of that."

Gus lay on her bed next to Hannah, her mind drifting back to the past week. To the meetings with Porter, Carmen, and Oliver to finalize the menu for the show that was going to begin in a half hour. To Sabrina's late-night phone call demanding that she ask Troy to leave the program. She wasn't asking, Gus had noticed, that she not appear herself. No, indeed. And she thought of Aimee, as well; their one conversation since the disastrous afternoon in the studio had been terse and perfunctory. In short order, it seemed, her carefully constructed world was unraveling, in fits and starts, thanks to the new show.

Not every decision, Gus knew, turns out to be the right one. It had merely seemed fun to have the basketball menu, to have everyone come and meet the stars. And now, thanks to bad weather, the sudden appearance of Carmen, and a split-second choice, she had managed to rope all her loved ones into a world that was not of their making. Not everyone actually wanted to be on television; they only thought they did.

The easiest thing, really, would have been to cut them all some slack. A lot of slack. To tell Hannah that she didn't need to come downstairs, to ask Troy to leave the show so Sabrina felt more comfortable. But that wasn't what they needed, Gus believed. It was time to shake her little darlings out of their comfort zone.

"Come downstairs, at least to watch," she told Hannah, who followed meekly along. Just as she was about to enter the kitchen, Oliver came up to her quickly in the hall.

"Gus, I need a minute," he said, a sense of urgency in his voice.

"Gus!" Porter yelled from the next room. "Get over here."

She put up a finger to Oliver. "Hold that thought," she told him. "We'd better get in front of the camera. You can tell me in the break."

Porter was motioning oddly at her, his right hand holding his cell phone near his face and his left plugging his ear to shut out the background noise. He must have noticed her hair was a little scrunched, she thought. She gave it a quick shake and shrugged. It was best to be upbeat.

"Don't worry about it," she half-shouted. "We're all good, Porter."

"Places, everyone!" called out a member of Porter's camera crew. "We're live in one minute."

She floated into position behind the center island, noting that everyone had been assembled into stations as planned: it was much more organized than last time. Troy was at the sink, washing beans; Sabrina was set up nearby on a corner of the granite counter, a bowl of new potatoes waiting to be diced, a rubber glove covering her left hand (and, more important, her ring). Gus raised an eyebrow when she caught her younger daughter's eye, then glanced briefly at Aimee to see her slowly and methodically slicing up lemons and oranges for the sangria.

Hannah, feeling guilty for wanting to back out, sat glumly off-camera, wanting to leave but too loyal to Gus to abandon her without moral support. She waved. Carmen, apparently assuming the gesture was intended for her, waved back.

Oliver, looking stressed, took up a place at the Aga stove. He'd been working frantically setting up the kitchen, putting together a *mise en place* of salt, pepper, spices, and olive oil, then arranging the produce, the knives, the bowls. It was his job to make sure the kitchen had every item necessary to create the day's menu.

Gus and Carmen stood side by side at the main island, doing last-minute touch-ups of their lipstick. Porter dashed over quickly with a folded piece of paper and extended it toward Gus.

"Full service," Carmen said, grabbing it out of his hand and blotting her lips. "Thank you very much, Porter, I'll be sure to tell Alan."

The countdown began and they stowed their items in a hidden shelf in the island. And with the red light, they were live.

"Hi, everyone," said Gus. "I'm so glad you could join us today for another live episode of *Eat Drink and Be*. Our goal is to show you how to celebrate life with food and drink. I'm here with my cohost, Carmen Vega, and our wonderful group of friends and family, and today we're going to make a wonderful, easy menu with some Spanish influences." She made a sweeping gesture with her arm. "In honor of Carmen, of course."

"Why, thank you, Gus," Carmen said, moving ever so slightly closer to Gus so that her hair, piled loosely on top of her head, blocked a bit of Gus from the camera. Gus moved several inches to her right, away from Carmen, and then walked toward the camera as she spoke.

"So let me fix you a little something," she said, reaching down to a shelf within the island. "We have a beautiful halibut, very fresh, that we've already unwrapped and had Oliver start some prep work."

Gus pulled up a platter that was a mass of long tentacles. She continued smiling while she sought out the red light, confirming the cameras were still on.

"Well, my goodness," Gus said. She looked serenely into the camera. "Imagine assuming you've bought a pound of fish and you come home to open the brown paper and you find it's octopus!" She laughed as though unconcerned. "It's happened to us all from time to time, I'm sure."

Turning to Carmen, she said calmly, "Do you have any thoughts on how we should cook our octopus today, Carmen?"

"Well, thanks for asking, Gus," said Carmen. "How about we make a warm octopus salad? In Spanish cuisine, our goal is to elevate the flavors of the seafood and to be able to taste each part of a dish. Bring out the flavors simply."

"Fantastic," Gus said, sensing Sabrina turning toward them.

"I'm not touching that," said Sabrina.

"I've always wanted to eat octopus," said Troy.

"Let's hope we have all the ingredients we need," said Gus, who could see Porter motioning to her that it was time to cut to break. Thank God, she thought.

"We're going to do a quick look in the fridge to find a few things and then we'll be right back to make Carmen's salad," Gus said, still speaking to the camera. "It's going to be an exciting hour."

And they were out.

Porter took a huge gulp of air and let it out slowly. "You did great, Gus," he called out.

"This isn't *Iron Chef*," she replied. "I don't appreciate being surprised with ingredients."

"It's no big deal," said Carmen.

"Oh, don't think I haven't noticed that you weren't the least bit surprised by the appearance of Mr. Octopus," said Gus. Without turning around, she addressed Oliver, who was behind her at the Aga. "And I imagine you prepped this?"

"Just a slap of water," said Oliver. "It was delivered right before the show."

Gus did not reply, tapping her teeth together as she considered various forms of murder.

"Well, we're back in two minutes, folks," Porter said. "And remember, I want to make sure we get in several mentions of the contest: one lucky viewer is going to become a participant on *Eat Drink and Be*. Talk about how exciting that'll be."

"Oh, that's a treat," yelled Sabrina. "Maybe we can invite her ex-boyfriend on the show, too."

"Just suck it up and quit whining," snapped Aimee. "Why do you always have to be such a baby?"

Porter waited a second, assuming Gus would jump in and referee. She said nothing.

He came close. "You okay?" he asked, his voice low. "I tried to pass a note."

Her face was grim. "Don't you know by now that I'm always okay, Porter?" she said darkly. "I've had far worse surprises in my life than a platter of seafood."

They moved to a corner of the room, as far away from the crew as possible.

"You're doing great," he said, his producer's mantra of keeping the talent calm running through his head. "Did you do something new to your hair?"

"Don't change the subject," she said. "What's the story?"

"Carmen brought the octopus in and said Alan wanted it to be a surprise."

"This is ludicrous," she said. "Does that seem like Alan to you?"

"I dunno." Porter sighed. "He's been riding everyone hard over ratings. I think he's a bit desperate."

"Why wouldn't he have called you himself?"

"I missed a call from him this afternoon and he wasn't there when I dialed back," said Porter. "But everyone knows he and Carmen are together. It's the worst-kept secret at the CookingChannel."

"Well, we've never worked like this before!"

"And we've never been a live series before, either," he said. "All the rules are changing."

Checking his watch, he tapped her on the hand and led her back to the center island. "It's time."

With a flourish, Gus stretched out her arms and spoke to the cast and crew: "Fake it like you're having fun, and for God's sake, smile!"

Over the course of the next hour on air, Oliver boiled the octopus and then Carmen showed how to clean it. It was a laborious procedure and involved a lot of skilled knife work and the removal of the eye.

"Oh my God, that's disgusting," cried Sabrina, watching over Carmen's shoulder and then covering and uncovering her eyes with her hands. "It looks like something out of *Finding Nemo*!"

Even Aimee, ever the stoic, seemed a bit horrified.

"What sort of a cooking show is this when we're all afraid to touch the food?" she whispered to Troy, not completely aware that the microphone picked up every word. "You know, I only like protein that comes wrapped in cellophane, all cut up into anonymous rectangles. I never thought we'd be butchering animals."

"Why do I get stuck with the beans?" muttered Troy. "Let me take a cleaver to that thing. I could stand to work out some frustrations."

Meanwhile, Gus strolled blithely from station to station, describing what each person was doing and talking directly to the viewer as if to an old friend. She also, by not doing any of the chopping, boiling, slicing, or dicing on her own, managed to convey the impression that she was running the show and that everyone else, Carmen included, was there to assist *her*.

Sampling the food turned into a bit of a struggle, with Aimee and Sabrina pointedly sipping sangria while refusing to try a bit of the octopus. Troy, on the other hand, scooped up a forkful and put it in his mouth enthusiastically.

"It's chewy," he began, then swallowed quickly as Carmen glared. "Chewtastic," he clarified.

Gus smiled at him fondly.

"You know, tonight's menu was a wee bit complicated—not your standard weeknight dinner," she said to the camera as Porter gave the signal to wrap things up. "But that's okay. Sometimes it's fun to try something new, when you have a leisurely Sunday like we had. Next time, though, we're going to take things a little easier and do some brunch favorites. Who doesn't love a Sunday brunch? So see you next time, and until then, remember to *Eat Drink and Be*. Right, Carmen?"

And Carmen, tired and more than a little glowing with perspiration, gave a wan smile for the camera. The show was over, for one week at least. Gus hadn't tasted one thing.

"I don't recall being consulted about the next menu," Carmen said, dabbing at her forehead, as the crew began to pack up cords and wires.

"You weren't," said Gus drily.

# 13

The question of who washed the dishes and scoured the pots after any of Gus's cooking shows had never previously been considered by Sabrina, nor by Aimee. Surely there was some sort of crew member whose job it was to take care of such things? And the moments after their first time on television, for the basketball show, were such a heady mix of relief and elation that they'd scarcely paid attention to the clean-up process.

"Since you're all sitting around endlessly dissecting the pros and cons of tonight's show," Gus said now, "I expect you to make yourself useful. After all, this is my home."

"I don't think that was part of the deal," said Sabrina.

"Oh? Have you read the fine print?"

Sabrina paused, uncertain whether she had signed on to get dishpan hands or not. There had been some paperwork but nothing she had actually bothered to read.

"But it isn't fair. Carmen's already left, and so has Hannah," she pointed out.

"I doubt that there's a 'Carmen's gone so I can't uphold my responsibilities' clause," replied Gus. "I'm sure Oliver will be happy to direct all of you."

And with that, Gus headed out of the kitchen, ready to leave Oliver, Aimee, Troy, and Sabrina mucking about in the kitchen. Her goal was to go up to her room and take a long, hot bath, the kind where the water is so steamy that every part of the body tingles upon stepping in. But first she wanted a few private words with her producer.

"Let's have a brandy in the Henry Higgins," Gus said to Porter, as she led the way to her wood-paneled study. It was an intimidating room and very masculine; the kind of place she imagined Christopher would have enjoyed, a place to work late after family dinners or to have serious heart-to-hearts when one of the girls was dating a bad boy. Not that he'd ever had that opportunity.

The walls of the room were lined with books of all shapes and sizes. On one shelf were copies of her own cookbooks, and it was directly in front of them that she sat herself down in a creased but cushiony leather chair.

Porter's job for the last twelve years had been to make Gus Simpson look good. Always. And tonight, with the surprise of the octopus, she had been placed in a most uncomfortable position.

"Alan returned my message." Porter spoke before Gus said anything. "He left a message saying he thought tonight was very intriguing and he'll have more to say when the numbers come in."

"And it's all about the ratings."

"Of course it's all about the ratings—that's what created your empire, my dear," Porter said, taking a seat in a leather chair opposite her. She recalled Hannah's encouragement to tap into her frustrations. How many times had she bent herself into a pretzel trying to get everything done? How often had she come through for Alan, for the CookingChannel? Get angry! she heard the Hannah in her head say. Be upset!

"What's going on, old friend?" Gus said softly. "If Alan wants me off the air, he could just fire me. *Adios*. A professional divorce."

"Gus, believe me when I tell you I'm confused myself," Porter said, leaning forward. "If you go, I'll go with you. But we're not out yet."

"That was just so out of control," Gus said, covering her face with her hands. "What if I'd had a meltdown? On-air hysterics?"

"He gambled you wouldn't walk off the air."

"No, I'd never do something like that." She couldn't shake the looming worry that welled up inside her, at once familiar and yet still surprising. "It all just makes me wonder who to trust."

Too often, she realized with frustration, you never know what someone is going to do until they do it. At fifty, she was still learning.

"Actually, as much as I hate to say so, it was damn fun television," said Porter. "Your energy was great."

Gus leaned her head back into the chair, closed her eyes. "God only gives us what we can handle, right?"

"Exactly," said Porter.

Her brown eyes flashed open. "That's what someone said to me at Christopher's funeral," she said crisply. "'God only gives us what we can handle.' It's a shitty line that people tell you so you don't fall apart and make things messy. For *them*."

Porter shook his head. "You're a tough cookie, good on your feet. Some people fall apart in a crisis."

She regarded him curiously.

"Oh, Porter, not you." Gus sighed. "I never thought you'd try to pass off a lame pep talk as compassion."

She got out of the chair.

"Don't think that because I've weathered many storms it's easy for me to sail on through," she said. "We all have our breaking point."

"No one is going to break you, Gus," said Porter. "I'll make sure there are no more surprise stunts. But at the end of the day, we all have to answer to Alan.

"It's a tough game in TV these days," he continued. "We've got to play it smart. I've got Ellie to think about."

Gus understood. Family first. For all their tough talk, neither of them wanted to be out of a job. Hadn't she always done everything she could to keep Sabrina and Aimee's world together?

"We'll be okay," he said.

"Of course." She nodded, her natural reaction to put someone at ease, before she was barely aware of it. But inside she was frightened.

"You know we can take care of the dishes, right?" Porter asked, trying to lighten the mood.

"Of course," she said, motioning in the direction of the kitchen. "But *they* don't."

The messy spatulas, forks, spoons, and knives were piled by the sink; the pots had yet to be collected together. Aimee stood at the center island, looking woefully at the congealing octopus salad, holding her shortish brown hair in her hands.

Oliver came up behind her. "Hey, that's how I went bald," he said, poking her hands quickly.

"Do we save the leftovers or what?"

"You could give it to the cats," said Oliver, winking.

"They're vegan," replied Aimee. But she smiled back. "At the very least we can finish off this sangria."

Oliver poured out four glassfuls from a pitcher, taking care to place pieces of sliced orange and lemon in each one.

"All right, let's get going," Troy said, rubbing his hands together. "I want to clean this up and get back into the city." He leaned over to Sabrina. "We can ride the train together."

"Umm, no, we can't," she said testily. "It's ridiculous the way you're following me around." She accepted a glass from Oliver.

"I'm not following you—we're on a TV show together."

"Get real, Troy! If my mother wasn't such a busybody, we wouldn't be seeing each other anymore," Sabrina said, her blue eyes flashing with anger. She whipped off the rubber gloves she'd been wearing to conceal her diamond. "And by the way, I'm engaged."

Aimee looked at Oliver and rolled her eyes, then mouthed, "And by the way..." The two shared a bit of mirthless laughter, feeling awkward and sorry for Troy.

"What did you say?" he asked.

"I was quite clear, Troy. I'm getting married."

Troy stared hard at the slender, pretty, black-haired girl standing in front of him.

"We've barely broken up," he said. "I know math isn't your thing but this seems to add up to 'too quick' and 'damn stupid,' if you ask me."

Aimee reached out to bring her arms between the two of them and made the time-out signal with her hands.

"Innocent bystanders here," she said. "Can't the two of you go off and talk somewhere else? There's only about a zillion rooms at Mom's."

"I'm not going anywhere with Troy." Sabrina folded her arms and waited.

"Oh, wait a second," Aimee said, looking at her palm and pretending to contact an imaginary report. "Yes, you are. Because you've just been evicted from the kitchen. And not to go all bad mommy on the two of you, but if you can't be in the same room, then just be merciful and go somewhere else. Together, separately, I don't care."

"You're very rude, you know that?" said Troy.

"Just direct," replied Aimee. "There's a difference. And I have dishes to do."

Sabrina marched out of the room toward the hall, with Troy on her heels. "Don't think we're not going to talk about this," he said.

Aimee turned on her mother's under-counter CD player for a

little music, hoping to drown out the sound of Troy and Sabrina's raised voices.

"Ah, ambience," said Oliver. "Just what I like when I scour pots."

"Oliver, what's your deal?"

"I beg your pardon?"

"I Googled you," Aimee said, opening drawers to find some rubber gloves. "And I asked a couple guys from school about you. Apparently you're a bit of a legend downtown. A money man."

Oliver scrubbed at a bit of grit stuck on a lid. He waved off Aimee's offer of gloves.

"We all have talents," he said. "Mine is cooking great food. But I'm also lucky. I made a nice chunk of change for a lot of people, including several who needed more money like they needed another hole in the head."

"I thought men like you believed there could never be enough moola."

"Men like I used to be, maybe," he said. "But don't tell me you're one of those rich kids who pretends to hate wealth? That doesn't become you."

"Oh, I don't hate money," said Aimee. "I'd just like to see more of it spread around the world."

"What's your specialty?"

"The economics of agricultural development."

"How'd you come up with that?"

"My parents both spent time in Africa working with local sugar farmers when they were in the Peace Corps," she said. "I used to love to watch old slides from when they were in Burkina Faso."

"I didn't know that about Gus."

"Yuppers, back in the day she was practically a revolutionary. Off to bring peace and salvation to all the world."

"And now she teaches couch potatoes to fold napkins and to survive Carmen Vega's octopus salad," said Oliver. "You disapprove."

Grabbing a blue-and-white-striped dish towel, Aimee took the pot from Oliver. She surveyed the kitchen: it was coming along. Every so often, the sound of Sabrina's voice floated into the room, high-pitched and even a little squeaky. Quietly she dried a dish.

"Nope," she said after a time. "My mom likes what she does. And there's no shame in a job well done. My father used to say that." She paused. "He would tell knock-knock jokes at dinner."

"Gus doesn't seem like a jokester," ventured Oliver.

Aimee opened her mouth, prepared to stand up for her mom. It was her instinctual reaction.

"She's very elegant," he continued. "She has a certain presence."

Aimee relaxed her defenses.

"Yeah, that's my mom. It's like she has this aura around her."

"Or armor."

"She wasn't always like that. She was huggier back in the day."

"Huggy? Gus?" Oliver's tone was light.

"The house was messy when we were kids," said Aimee. She felt an unusual exhilaration as she spoke, as though revealing a secret. "Mom was a terrible housekeeper."

"But now it's so neat here." Oliver continued to wash. "I wouldn't dream of leaving this place less than spic-and-span."

"She has a cleaning person, of course, but she's neater now. *Very* organized." Aimee nodded. "I like that about her—the lack of tidiness used to drive me bonkers. Dad, too."

There was something tremendously pleasant, she realized, about being able to talk so easily about her father. She rarely did that with her sister or her mother. Sometimes, with one or two of her close friends, Aimee shared her haphazard collection of memories from the time before Christopher died, when it wasn't so crucial that she be good and helpful and quiet. It hadn't been a seamless transition, but now she could almost suffocate on her own reliability. Most often, though, she just kept her thoughts to herself. She kept a lot of things to herself. It was easier for everyone.

Yet somehow she enjoyed chatting with Oliver. She told him

about the little bungalow they'd all lived in before Gus had purchased the manor house, how she and Sabrina put tape down the middle of the floor in their shared bedroom. How they worked after school in The Luncheonette, and how, after all these years, she was still sharing an apartment with Sabrina.

"She couldn't make her own rent, there's no way," said Aimee. "I've been on my own since college but I suspect Mom continues to pay Sabrina's credit cards."

Oliver laughed. "I pay my parents' credit cards," he said.

"It's not the same and you know it."

"So you wish your mom would give you money?"

"Oh, no, that's not what I want."

"What do you want, then?"

Aimee could see her reflection in the window, standing next to Oliver; it was dark outside and her face was reflected in the glass.

"You're sneaky," she said. "I'm usually not much of a talker."

"Listening is something I'm working on."

"Like therapy?"

"Like personal goals I set for myself," said Oliver. "Spiritual nutrition."

"That's big," said Aimee. "Or crazy."

"Being malnourished isn't always about a lack of food," he said.

Aimee blushed, feeling a sudden sense of unease about sharing so much.

"So you just walked away from it all?" she said, turning the conversation back to Oliver.

"I didn't walk away *from* it," he said. "I walked away *with* it. More money than any man reasonably needs. I just left the stress and the more-is-more mentality behind."

"You don't need to work on this show, then."

"Oh, that's where you're wrong," he said. "I need to work on this show more than anything."

# 14

For the second time that evening, the library was occupied, its heavy wood doors closed. This time, however, Sabrina had positioned herself in the cushioned chair behind the large cherry desk. Her hope had been to seem intimidating, or at the very least self-assured, though instead she appeared to be even more of a little girl playing big.

Troy took up a place across from her, occasionally pacing but more often yelling.

"My mother is sleeping upstairs," said Sabrina. "Can't you pipe down? You're coming onto this TV show when you should be out of my life!"

"Being on *Eat Drink and Be* isn't about you," shouted Troy. "No, wait. I'm not going to pretend here. Yes, I like to see you, Sabrina. But

I need to boost my company's revenues—a lot—and I'm just trying to promote my business."

"How?"

"I've worked out a deal with Porter to start wearing T-shirts promoting FarmFresh," he explained. "My new wardrobe starts in the next show. Deal with it."

"Oh." She shrugged. "Shouldn't you be paying for that?"

"Gus is an investor, remember?" He spoke sharply. The company was doing mostly all right, but an influx of cash would ease his mind. Going out on his own had created more pressure than anticipated: turns out that living a dream can create as many new problems as it solves old ones.

"Of course," said Sabrina. She affected exasperation, even trying to fake a bored yawn. Inside, however, her heart was racing. It was exciting to see him so riled up: the anger had brought a flush to his cheeks and reminded her of what he was like when they'd slept together.

And Troy was definitely good in bed.

Strong and intense and seemingly indefatigable, he approached the study of her body as seriously as he took running his business. Troy was a man driven by passions. All her other boyfriends, even Billy, hadn't actually demanded much from her. In bed or out of it.

"What do you want?" That's what Troy had asked her once, late at night, an invitation to play. She'd been asked that question before, a soft murmur in between kisses, but it never actually required an answer. "What do you want?" he'd asked, and then waited for her to articulate her desires. "Talk to me," he'd whispered. It was horrifying, frightening. It was one of the reasons she'd had to leave him.

Now, Sabrina stared at the finger pointing at her. The same finger that had caressed her only months ago. Funny how things changed.

"How long have you been seeing this guy?"

"Awhile," said Sabrina. "I didn't mean to hurt you."

Troy waved both hands at her in disgust.

"I didn't mean." He wondered if stupider words had ever been spoken. What *did* she mean, then? That if there had been more time, she'd have sent a handwritten note on personal stationery to break the news, gently and euphemistically? That he could have folded up the letter and put it in a drawer, sad but with a veneer of happiness at Sabrina's good fortune? Ha! No, there was no question that Sabrina wouldn't have said a word: he would have found out she was getting married by reading an announcement in the *New York Times*. Before Sabrina, he'd never even known about the wedding announcements, never even read the Style section. But she had read them carefully and often aloud, sharing the details of the marrying couple, their colleges and parents' occupations, perhaps the funny story of how they met. At one time, he'd found her obsession with weddings to be cute. Part of her Sabrina charm. Like her smiliness and willingness to laugh.

He knew he'd gotten in deep when he found himself muttering while in the shower or using the weight machine at the gym, composing an imaginary announcement to run the day of their wedding. He had planned to write it out and give it to her when he proposed. As if on autopilot, he went over the words in his mind right now:

*Sabrina Simpson, an up-and-coming interior designer and the youngest daughter of CookingChannel host Gus Simpson and the late Christopher Simpson, was wed today to Troy Park. Mr. Park, who graduated summa cum laude from the University of Oregon, is a daring entrepreneur and the CEO of FarmFresh, the first national supplier of fresh fruits to vending machines in schools, hospitals, and airports. His parents, Jin and Soo Park, both born in Korea, are the hardworking owners of a fruit orchard in Hood River, Oregon. Mr. Park also has one sister, Alice.*

*The couple met when Miss Simpson was hired to decorate the midtown office of FarmFresh.*

*"I had vision," says Mr. Park. "But she had the style."*

"Troy?"

"Do you know what I'd like?" he asked, outraged by her behavior, annoyed at having been jostled out of his thoughts. "An explanation."

"What?"

"I want you to explain, as concisely as possible since I have an important meeting tomorrow, just what the hell happened." He came around the desk and leaned back against it, his head arched in such a way that she could see the muscles in his neck. Troy had liked having his neck kissed, she recalled.

She'd liked kissing his neck.

"I had to move on," Sabrina said.

"What did I do?" Troy was pained.

Sabrina had made up a reason when she broke up with her first boyfriend: she told him his feet smelled. Later, she felt guilty about fibbing and vowed to use easy lines with other guys: It's not you, it's me. I wish things were different. It's hard to explain.

Problem was, all the lines were the truth.

Troy was unique among all the men she'd dated. He tried having smoothies for breakfast, just because he liked eating what she was eating. He suggested they have sleepovers without sex and stay up all night watching comedies and eating popcorn. (Though of course they always ended up having sex anyway.) He began reading Dear Abby when she told him she'd bookmarked the advice column on her computer.

"I just want to know what you're thinking," he'd said. "Isn't it okay for a guy to want to learn what interests his girl?"

She'd tried to fight against the dread she felt, to overcome the familiar sense of being chased down and cornered.

She knew exactly the moment when she realized she had to leave Troy, though. A Saturday afternoon, sitting on the sofa in the apartment she shared with Aimee, pretending she couldn't hear her sister applauding in her bedroom as she watched a week's worth of game shows. She kept her sister's secrets just as Aimee kept hers.

Sabrina and Troy had been flopped on the couch, her legs in his lap, exhausted from an afternoon's bike ride in the park. Just hanging out. That's when he'd suggested it. The counselor. The therapist. They could go alone and together, he said. Joint and solo.

"Let's really do some soul-searching," he said, and Sabrina had laughed, assuming he was kidding.

"I thought psychoanalysis was only for true New Yorkers," she teased. "You're just a Korean boy from Oregon."

He looked at her intently, took both her hands, and spoke to her with more kindness than anyone before or since:

"Let me know you," he'd said.

What had been most alarming was the lie it made out of her most cherished private belief about herself. That all she wanted was to be understood. To have someone "get" her and love her anyway.

But she didn't. She didn't want to be forced into that kind of trust. What if he couldn't follow through? What if he couldn't love her anyway? And in her heart she could hear a drum beat: Trust will lead to hurt. Trust will lead to hurt.

There was only one solution: he had to go. They all had to go, of course. But giving up Troy was the toughest.

Now, if her mother hadn't brought Troy onto the television show, he'd be like all the rest of her ex-lovers. Trading the once-a-year belated holiday email filled with the three-paragraph rundown of all that was new and fascinating. But Gus had interfered, as she always did, and here was Troy, pacing in the library on a cool Sunday evening in May.

"Just tell me what you see in him," he said. She liked how he was thoughtful, methodical, *interested*. He was upset, definitely, but he wasn't whining.

"I don't know," said Sabrina. It was hard to lie to Troy; she felt as though he could see through her. "He's a good guy."

"I'm a good guy." He was matter-of-fact.

"You just want to possess me!" Sabrina could hear how shrill her voice sounded.

Troy gave her an appreciative once-over.

"No," he said, his voice mellow. "I just want to love you."

He came around the desk, put a hand on either arm of the chair, and leaned in to her.

"I love you, Sabrina Simpson," he said.

"Why?" She began sobbing, guilt and regret and fear rushing out of her. "Why?" He was far too close; he smelled just like the Troy she knew, an intoxicating blend of grapefruit shampoo and spicy cologne. Sabrina breathed deeply, then again. She liked his Troy smell.

"Hey," he said softly. "Hey."

His face was very close.

Almost without being aware of moving, Sabrina tilted toward Troy.

"You don't have to cry," he said, his lips so close to touching her own. "We can work it out."

Her chest felt tight, as though he was pulling the breath right out of her. She moved nearer to get it back from him and as she did so, he caught her mouth in his. His arms moved up to grip the back of her chair, forming a box around her head.

Sabrina opened her mouth wider as Troy nudged her with his tongue, remembering how he tasted and wanting more. She reached up, encircling his neck, and pushed up from the floor with her feet slightly as Troy pulled her body into his, steering her back into the desk, pressing against her as they kissed. His body felt good: strong and taut in all the right places. She felt safe and powerful and beautiful and good. Very good.

Sabrina eased her way on the top of the desk and tugged at Troy's shirt, bringing his body closer and beginning to undress him at the same time.

"I knew," he said. "I knew."

His body was warm against her and she liked the sensation of being covered. She liked the motion of his hand running up her thigh, over her stomach. She wanted him, just as she'd wanted him before.

And then he stopped.

"Wait," Troy said. Sabrina, as if watching in slow motion, felt dizzy as she saw him reach over to her left hand and wrench the glittering diamond off her finger. Saw him throw it across the room, where it hit one of the leather club chairs and bounced onto the floor. She watched it fall and then he was kissing her again, urgently, his hands everywhere, her skirt very high now, almost to her hips.

"Come on," he said, indicating her clothes.

She began to twist out of what she was wearing and, in doing so, looked down at her hand, at the indentation where her engagement ring from Billy had been just moments earlier. In her mind's eye, she could see herself having sex with Troy, could imagine just how much she'd enjoy it. Her body ached for him.

Sabrina hesitated.

"Tell me what you want," he said, holding her palm to his cheek.

"I don't know," she whispered, before removing her hand. "But I'm engaged to Billy."

Troy's eyes went cold. A vein jerked at his jaw.

"For once I want to do the right thing," Sabrina said, crying again. Her body felt cooler now and, looking down at herself on the desk she could see how disheveled she was, her skirt hiked up and her sweater mostly off. Her bra hung loosely around her shoulders.

"Kinda late to be starting that now, don't you think?" he said, hurriedly tucking his shirt back into his pants.

He strode quickly to the door, then whirled around and moved toward her in two quick steps. Reflexively, she shrunk back, even though she'd never been hit, by him or anyone. Troy gazed at her with a mixture of confusion and pity. Then, shaking his head, he turned her body around so that he could reach behind her and fasten her bra. With care, he eased her arms into the sleeves of her top as she sobbed, then lifted her off the desk and onto her feet, checking her skirt as he did so.

Taking a Kleenex out of a box on a nearby bookshelf, Troy pressed a pile of tissues into Sabrina's hand. Wordlessly, he kissed her on the top of her head and exited the room.

# 15

Sabrina had been on Gus's mind ever since the last show. She thought about her daughter when she padded through the house at night in her bare feet, making sure the doors and windows were all locked, wondering if Sabrina was at her new fiancé's or what. Gus talked aloud to her as she sifted flour, asking her questions with each shake of the sifter, even though Sabrina wasn't in the room and the only listeners were the four-pawed snoozers, Salt and Pepper.

"I've no idea what to do about Sabrina," she told Hannah during a quiet sunny morning in her kitchen. "I've barely spoken to her since Octopus Night. Aimee is running interference."

"How?"

"Calling to talk to me and then letting it slip that Sabrina's working late on a big project, that kind of thing," explained Gus. "It's what she used to do when I went out on a book tour and called home, when Sabrina was misbehaving."

They munched on oversized blueberry-lemon muffins sprinkled with white sugar crystals and dripping with creamy butter that Gus purchased specially from a New York state dairy. Hannah was already on her second and she'd only been over for a few minutes; Gus had anticipated that her sweet tooth would get her. She was looking thinner than usual, and Gus was concerned as she tapped her fingers incessantly on the arm of her chair.

"It's okay to give them some space," Hannah said, her mouth quite full. "Whatever you do, skip the surprise visit this time."

"A family shouldn't have secrets," said Gus. "That's when things go all loosey-goosey. When mistakes are made."

Hannah began coughing on a piece of muffin.

"A family," she said, trying to swallow, "is absolutely a group of people who keep secrets from each other. Who else cares that much about what you do?"

Her own family was far-flung and distant. She didn't see them anymore, though she received a few emails from a cousin every now and then. She often liked to fantasize about all the different lives she could have had, if she hadn't needed to hide out in her little white carriage house.

"Too much knowledge never helped me," she pointed out, and Gus knew it was true. In fact, Gus had been hoping that being around *Eat Drink and Be* would be a positive in the lives of everyone around her, would draw Hannah out of her shell, would bring Troy and Sabrina closer, would bring out a little fun in Aimee. A lot of pressure on one TV program, she thought now. Especially since quite the opposite seemed to be happening. The ones she loved were—and this worried her a great deal—annoyed with her.

She went to the coffeepot and brought it back to refill Hannah's mug, pouring in some heavy cream as she did so.

"Have you and Porter patched things up?" asked Hannah, reaching for the sugar bowl and putting in two heaping teaspoonfuls. With pleasure, Gus watched her crane her neck toward the counter, looking for more muffins.

"Things are as they are." Gus shrugged.

Hannah waited for her to explain, but when her friend didn't, she took her muffin plate toward a metal cooling rack laden with fluffy deliciousness. She took two and proceeded to butter both with enthusiasm.

"What about Oliver?"

"He has continued his barrage of daily apologies," said Gus. "The last one was in free verse."

"So all is forgiven?"

"I'm rather glad he felt bad. But it's not really about Oliver, you know? The issue is Carmen and her quest for kitchen domination."

"So what are you going to do?"

"I'm going to kill her with kindness," she said. "I just woke up and decided I'm going to smile her to death. I'm going to blind her with my bright white teeth until she'll run all the way back to Spain. Or, at the very least, someone else's show."

"Speaking of, how are the ratings?"

"High, actually." Gus smiled as Hannah sat down with her muffins and tucked in. She enjoyed watching Hannah eat. Well, actually, she loved to watch anyone eat her food. "So far Alan's experiment is successful. The sight of Carmen and me squabbling with each other is a hit with viewers. It seems taste has taken a nosedive."

"A cooking catfight," said Hannah.

"We're not the only ones," Gus said. "Seems Troy and Sabrina's little snipes are also gathering them a fan base. The message boards are agog about SaTroy."

"He's a cutie," said Hannah. "The long, lean, dark-haired, Asian thing. Sexy and exotic."

"You're not the only one who's noticing," said Gus. "Troy called to tell me he landed a meeting with a Nebraska school district because the superintendent watches *Eat Drink and Be*."

"They called him for a date?"

"No, they want him to get some oranges and bananas into the school district vending machines," Gus said, shaking her head. "Besides, he's only thirty-four."

"Older women and younger men is all the rage," said Hannah. "More experience in the bedroom! I should know: I just wrote an article on the topic for *More*."

Gus tried gamely to hide her surprise.

"Should you really be writing about relationships?"

Hannah made a face. "You don't actually have to know anything to write this stuff, Gus," she said. "You just find some so-called experts and quote them. No one asked for my sexual history."

"No, no, of course not," Gus said, feeling a bit silly. She tried to change the subject. "I'm afraid Sabrina is busy plotting her latest wedding without me."

"Maybe that's why she gets engaged so often," teased Hannah. "She knows how happy you are to plan."

"He's handsome," conceded Gus. "In a Ken-doll kind of way. That's how Sabrina likes her collection."

She stood up and took the cups and plates to the dishwasher, which was empty save a bowl from her late soup supper the night before. Gus fretted about Hannah not eating, but the truth is that her own stomach of late had been feeling sour. Too much stress. That's what you got for keeping secrets.

"I phoned him," she announced to Hannah, needing a confessor.

"Who?"

"Billy," said Gus. "I was like a dial-a-stalker: I hung up on his voice mail three times."

"Oh my God, Gus! You're going to end up in a TV-movie-of-the-week: My M-I-L is a nut job."

"It's like I can't help myself," Gus admitted. "What's wrong with wanting to protect that girl from herself?"

"Nothing, Gus, but there are boundaries, you know."

"I told myself I was trying to reach Sabrina each time I dialed," she said. "But the truth is that I wanted to say a few choice things to him myself. Like what is he doing proposing to a girl who's already been engaged so many times?"

"Like what is he doing when you want her to be with Troy?" asked Hannah.

"I wasn't going to say that. *That* would have been rude. I'm not trying to hurt the man—it's just that he doesn't know her."

"Are you sure about that?"

"What's true is that if Sabrina didn't have Aimee running after her every two seconds, I don't know what I'd do."

"Hey, maybe some handsome dude will win Porter's contest and come on the show. Then Sabrina will run off with him."

"That's really not very funny," said Gus. "Though with a random drawing anything could happen. I wanted there to at least be an essay portion but no one else wanted to read the papers."

One entry per day was allowed, which was certainly more than fair, thought Priya Patel as she filled out her ballot onscreen. She wondered how many other women were sitting in their homes, just like she was, wishing for a chance to meet Gus Simpson and ask her all about plum tarts and pistachio cakes. It was foolish for a forty-four-year-old housewife in New Jersey to dream about winning but she held her breath, just the same, and clicked "send."

The children were breakfasted and off to school, lunch bags in hand. The two younger ones insisted on peanut butter and jam, like their classmates, and juice in boxes, which Raj disapproved of but which Priya didn't really mind. Her teenage daughter ate in the cafeteria with her mostly white pals. She recalled her own mother's suspicions when she'd wanted to eat nothing but spaghetti during her first semester in college, concerned that it indicated some deeper rejection of all things Indian.

"I like noodles," she'd said, and while that was true, she had also been mooning over an Italian-American boy in physics class. That was the thing about her parents and their friends: they were more Indian than the Indians back home, constantly watchful for fear that moving to America would leech away their children's understanding of who they were. Raj had developed similar fears.

Though it wasn't as if Priya didn't cook for the family. She made *phulkas* for Raj's lunch and *pakoras* to go with Sunday Night Football, American-style. (Funny, that, how being such a fan of the Giants did not impact Raj culturally. He had explained as much to her and the children.) And she had a special fondness for home-style sweets, nibbling on raisiny *bundi ladoo* and wiping her hands discreetly on a napkin so as not to make the keyboard sticky. It wasn't as though she resented all the cooking, entirely, because she often quite enjoyed the sizzle of the vegetables and the scent of curry around her. What bothered her most of all was that no one stopped to admire what she'd made. They just fell upon the dishes like hungry wolves, even Raj. How nice it must be to be Gus, she thought, able to watch an old tape and admire what you've made. She'd suggested they get out the camcorder during Diwali last year to capture the platters of *cholafali*, deep-fried *ghooghra*, *khandvi* rolls sprinkled with coconut and little balls of *churma na ladoo* that had taken such care to make, but everyone had laughed as though she'd made a funny joke, and she'd pretended to go along with it.

Cooking was a curious thing, really, how there was nothing to show after it was all eaten up. This is great, someone might say as they chewed, but in the end all that was left was the memory. It wasn't as though you could save up a portion of your best curried lentil spread and put it on display, a sign taped to the bowl saying "Priya made this." Not like when she'd been designing mechanical systems at her job back before she'd had kids.

Even a recipe didn't come out exactly the same each time you made it and so wasn't perfect proof of your cooking ability. If that had been the case, then anyone able to read a cookbook could produce a Michelin-star-quality meal. No, making good food took creativity, technique, flair. And love.

Priya loved her family, loved Raj and Bina and Chitt and Kiran. Yes, she did. Oh, she knew she was supposed to feel this constant hum of happiness—she'd read the books, seen the programs—but it was just very, very hard. She felt very tired. And plump. In recent years, Priya had started running to fat, which collected around her middle and seemed impossible to dislodge.

"I like your tummy," Raj said, pinching her rolls. If there was one good thing about marrying a man your parents had selected straight from India, it was that he still thought being chubby was a good thing. He didn't nag her when she curled up with a bowl of crunchy *tum tum* and ate every speck. He was really, much of the time, quite nice. It was just Priya. She simply felt bogged down.

If I got to meet Gus, she told herself, then it would all turn around. How would it not?

When Gus had declared the next episode would feature brunch, she had not thought out the rather simple fact that the show ran on Sunday *nights*. And there'd been some concern from upstairs, Porter had indicated, that the show was adrift.

"After two episodes?" Gus had not been convinced.

"TV is changing into a completely different world," said Porter. "Sitcoms disappear after one episode if the numbers aren't there."

"I thought our numbers were good?"

"They're way better, but we haven't been re-upped yet," he said.

"Well, it would help if Alan wasn't making us all play chicken and would air us week after week," said Gus. "I'm surprised anyone keeps tuning in."

"Our demos are great, actually: lots of frat boys with an empty Sunday who want to watch Carmen, lots of twentysomethings caught up in the drama of SaTroy, plus the diehard Gus fans," he said.

"I assume those are the old ladies?"

Porter laughed. "You've got your own following with the frat boys, I can assure you. Something about HotOlderMamas-dot-com?"

"Oh, don't even tell me that," Gus said, though in truth she was quite curious and made a mental note to check it out later. Then Carmen and Oliver had shown up—riding together in the elevator this time around—and the group of four had brainstormed everything from frittatas to congee.

"I've got it," said Oliver. "Why not make the show more thematic? As in, 'You've spent all day in bed—say, with your cute girlfriend—and now you're going to treat her to a little breakfast in bed, even though it's nighttime.'"

Carmen giggled. "I like it!"

"Typically my theme isn't sex," Gus said. "Though I'm not opposed. Just not quite onboard."

"But think about this whole SaTroy thing going on," said Porter. "It's perfect, Oliver. Make pancakes, but call them 'sexy pancakes,' or whatever."

"I was really thinking more along the lines of little breakfast bites," said Gus. "You know, breakfast as appies."

"Great idea," said Porter. "But let's go with the sex. Er, romance. Soften it up and say it's all about romance."

They'd agreed to no more surprise ingredients, either, though Gus wasn't entirely reassured, and settled on a menu of pancakes with fruit compote and fresh whipped cream, Spanish omelet, and a wonderful blood-orange mimosa. It pleased her to have an episode that was going to be all about the classics, and she'd felt a renewed sense of enthusiasm. She was even resigned to Porter's contest, and agreed to announce the randomly chosen winner on the air: Priya Patel of New Jersey.

The truth was that Gus enjoyed being on the air, and tonight's show was no exception.

"Places, everyone, places," she shouted, as though directing a high school musical. Troy had arrived wearing a blue T-shirt emblazoned with "FarmFresh for schools!" on the front and back; Aimee was in black on black; Carmen was in a V-necked blouse that was just a little too low-cut, as always; and Oliver wore a navy chef's coat. (Just how many cooking outfits did this man own? she wondered.) Gus, for her part, wore a long tunic-style cardigan over a fitted tee and a pair of dark-washed jeans.

Gus never dressed down on the air but, after a visit to the website Porter had told her about, she'd been rather flattered by a plea to "see Gus's ass." It had frankly been rather a long time since anyone had made such a request. So while she was, of course, wearing a rather substantial sweater, it was still the thought that counted. She did feel hot. And it was fun.

So far the show was their most successful, helped along by the fact that Sabrina was conspicuously absent. Hannah, just like last time, was perched on an equipment box behind the crew. A popping sound grabbed Gus's attention.

"Bring out more potato chips, Oliver," Carmen shouted, as she ripped into a bag and began crunching. "Just one for me," she told the camera. "The rest are for my twist on a wonderful tradition in my country, the Spanish omelet, or what we call *tortilla de patatas*. Okay, one more." Carmen pointed at her full mouth and Gus took up her cue.

"Okay, avoid a flavored potato chip—no barbecue," she said. "Just a good, plain chip, such as kettle-cooked. You'll want to crush them down," she was saying, as a bang made her jump. She threw a world-weary look to the camera.

"Open the bag first," she said, before gesturing to Troy, who had exploded a bag of chips on the counter.

"Oops," he said, in a fake whisper. "Sorry."

"Then mix the eggs and the chips together," Carmen said, cutting in, but not in an unfriendly way as she usually did.

"Let them soak for several minutes," said Gus. "And then ask the big bald man in your kitchen to heat up some oil in a sauté pan."

"We'll start cooking during the break, and you can see how it's all coming together when we're back," said Carmen. "You won't want to miss a minute of our sexy Sunday night brunch."

"Perfect, you guys!" yelled Porter. "It's great to see you working together."

Most of the next segments were filled with only minor issues, and were far less chaotic than the previous episodes of *Eat Drink and Be*.

Aimee accidentally poured salt into the simple fruit sauce instead of sugar within the first fifteen minutes of the program, and then managed to do the same thing again immediately and ruin a second batch.

"Don't worry about it," Oliver told her. "We've all sweetened with salt from time to time."

"This tastes disgusting," she said, after dipping in her spoon.

"Normally we don't say that part on air, dear," Gus said, grinning at the camera. "See why I love to cook for my family and not *with* my family?" She walked around the island as though coming closer to the viewer. "But we're going to make the lightest, fluffiest pancakes, and if we don't have any fruit syrup today, then we'll just use good old maple syrup."

"Go for Grade A dark amber," said Oliver. "It's rich and velvety."

"And very, very good for dipping apples in," Troy said, pointing to his FarmFresh shirt.

Gus handed Carmen some eggs. "Separate those out," she told her, "because when I make pancakes, I always fluff the whites separately. Then I fold them in when the batter is mixed . . ."

"And that's how you keep them high and light," said Carmen. "Very nice, Gus."

"While we get those on the griddle, and sip our blood-orange mimosas, we're going to get ready for a special treat," said Gus. "Just because it's breakfast doesn't mean we can't have dessert." She saw Porter motioning to her. "And I mean a *sexy* dessert."

Behind the cameras, Porter put a friendly arm around Hannah. He simply wanted to share a bit of good. "This is it, kiddo," he said. "We're finally getting it right."

Hannah, who hated to be squished, hugged, or generally touched, pretended she had to tie her shoe and squirmed away.

"Everyone ready for an espresso sundae?" asked Oliver.

"I put the kettle on a while ago," said Aimee. Although Gus had her own espresso maker—and she assumed most viewers had coffeemakers—she also wanted to show them how to make the simple dessert in a matter of minutes using instant packets. The kettle was Aimee's second big responsibility of the night, and after mucking up the fruit sauce, she aimed to get it right. Her mother's plan was to serve one delicate scoop of vanilla gelato in a wineglass, then drizzle it with piping hot espresso that had been lightly sweetened. With sugar this time.

Aimee, Oliver, Carmen, and Troy crowded around the island, watching Gus scoop out the gelato as though they'd never had ice cream before. There were only four minutes left in the show, just enough time to finish and spoon up, and the entire cast could barely fit in the shot. The cameraman panned out, enough to get everyone in the scene, but the rest of the kitchen was blocked from view. Porter nodded to let him know it was fine, wrinkling his nose at a strange smell as he did so.

"I love ice cream and fruit!" Troy shouted, catching Porter's attention. It was energizing to see the typically subdued guy so riled up. He knew Troy's growing fan base would love it; his goal was to get clips of *Eat Drink and Be* posted to YouTube.

"But today we're having it with espresso," Gus reminded everyone. "So let's get our instant mix and some boiling water from the kettle—" She turned to the counter and realized the kettle hadn't been plugged in.

"Aimee, I thought you started the kettle?" Gus said, a rising panic in her throat. How would they finish out the dish? How could she make another mistake?

"I did," said Aimee, clearly annoyed.

"Shouldn't it have whistled by now?"

The other members of the group began turning around, looking for the kettle. Carmen was the first to spot it.

"Oh my God, she put it on the stove," she screamed, everyone moving at once. "And it's on fire!"

Flames and sparks were coming up from the white plastic; Aimee had put an electric kettle on the Aga stove. The cameraman, now that the group was jumping around, could finally get a full view of the kitchen. He'd wondered if he'd gone a little out of focus. Now he could tell that the room was filling with smoke.

"We're burning up!" screamed Carmen. She grabbed a box of baking soda from the cabinet and threw it on the flames, causing them to flare higher, redder. Oliver, dish towel in hand, pulled her back and ended up setting the cloth on fire.

"Drop it, drop it!" Troy pushed Oliver's hand down to make him release the towel and began jumping on it with his feet.

It had been about fifteen seconds since Gus had asked for the kettle, and now her kitchen was filled with yelling and commotion and camera people pushing their way in to get a close-up.

"We're still live," Porter yelled, hoping to be heard over the din. "We're still on the air."

And then, without a thought other than protecting her friend, Hannah—who had written an article on kitchen fires not more than two years ago—ran into the melee and reached under Gus's sink to find the fire extinguisher she'd put there herself after turning in the piece.

The kettle was beginning to melt and the flames were high enough to scorch the ceiling.

"Stand back," shouted the thin woman in a red hoodie as she sprayed the Aga with white goo. "Get out of the way."

She let off a second surge from the extinguisher for good measure, a camera in her face as she did so. Hannah gave a blow of air out her mouth, trying to calm down.

"We almost burned down," Carmen cried. "Thank you, Hannah."

Hannah had an instant of happiness—she loved to be a help—before her dawning awareness of the cameras all around the kitchen.

"I didn't recognize you until now," Troy said. "I was such a huge fan."

Her eye caught Gus's and they knew: Hannah Joy Levine, the disgraced former tennis star who'd been kicked out of the sport fifteen years ago for throwing matches, had just been rediscovered in Gus Simpson's kitchen. Damn.

# 16

In no time at all, the message boards on the CookingChannel website were overrun with viewers trying to suss out if the girl in the hoodie really was Hannah Joy Levine, one-time Wimbledon champion forever banned from tennis.

It was the first question Alan asked when he called, barely two minutes after they went off the air. Not a "Hey, you all okay?" or even a "Don't worry about the damage" for Gus. Nope. He moved right in to the big question: How come no one had told him Hannah Joy Levine worked on his camera crew?

"She's doesn't work for us, Alan."

"It'll be great to have her on the air."

"Uh, she still doesn't work for us."

"I don't get it," Alan said, his voice breaking up slightly over the phone. He was probably in his car. "Surely she hasn't been hiding out in Gus Simpson's cupboards for over a decade?"

"No, they're neighbors."

"Well, having Hannah Joy Levine on Gus's last show would have been a huge help when the ratings were in the toilet."

"I'll be sure to pass along your message of concern," Porter said, giving Gus the a-okay sign.

"Well, whatever," Alan said to Porter. "This is like finding Amelia Earhart. Al Capone's vault. Following up with the kids from *Diff'rent Strokes*. It's beautiful."

"No, no one had smoke inhalation." Porter faked a chuckle as though he was reassuring his boss.

Alan ignored Porter's running patter. "The important thing is how we're going to play it. Get that Hannah signed to something, then start running promos about our new mystery guest on *Eat Drink and Be*. Is she or isn't she you-know-who? I'm just going to sit back and count the ratings."

Hannah appeared shaken when Porter expressed Alan's personal "invitation" to be on the air and looked plaintively at Gus.

"This is turning into a freaking circus," Carmen yelled before Gus could speak, slamming pots around for effect. "No, no, no! I am not having one more person on this damn show. Alan promised me he'd put *me* on television, and instead I've got half a show and a team of idiots who don't know what they're doing!"

"Oh, I don't think so, my dear," said Gus. "I'm the one who's been stuck with the idiot. They've clearly brought you to me because you couldn't hold your own program." She lowered her voice and spoke slowly. "No one with any sense would make octopus in their very first episode of a new series."

"I don't care about middle of the road," said Carmen. "I want to be creative."

"There's creative, and then there's experimental," said Gus. "Open a restaurant and experiment all you want, but not on my show. We're lucky any viewers came back after putting on that octopus salad."

"Well, if they did watch tonight, then they picked a heck of a night," shouted Carmen. "We nearly had a fantastic episode—for once you weren't messing it up! But then your frowny little daughter ruined it with her fire starter routine."

She ran over to Aimee and grabbed her by the collar, half-dragging her toward Porter for several steps before Aimee shook Carmen's hands off her blouse and, with a well-placed kick, swiped Carmen's feet out from under her.

"I want her off the show," Carmen demanded, having landed on her butt. "Now!"

She was strong for such a slight woman, Aimee thought, trying to catch her breath. The neckline of her shirt was torn.

"Absolutely not," said Gus, knowing full well that Aimee would have been thrilled to be off the air. "You sit down," she said to Aimee, hustling her into one of the wing chairs in the bay window. She wasn't about to let the beauty queen take on her kid, thank you very much.

"If you touch my daughter again, I will boil you in oil," she said quietly, her face very close to Carmen's. "And don't worry, I'll make sure it's Spanish olive oil."

"Get the hell away from me, you *zorra*!" Carmen began to cry and scream at the same time. "Get out, get out!"

Gus began talking to no one in particular. "I had a nice show," she said, addressing the room at large. "I worked hard. I kept long hours. For twelve years. And how do I get repaid? With a Carmen Vega. A silly prima donna who can dish it out but who can't take it."

"Get out!" hissed Carmen.

"No," Gus said, pretending to be calm though her red ears gave her away. "Because not only is this my kitchen—and believe me, every viewer knows it's *my* kitchen, Carmen—we're all still actually in my house. The one I own. The one where I am going to kick your sore little butt to the curb. Unless Aimee wants to do it, of course. Dear?"

Speechless for once, Aimee sat in her chair, watching her mother with wide eyes.

"You don't have to fight," piped up Hannah. "I don't want to be on TV. Really. It was an accident."

"Oh, no it wasn't," Carmen said, still on the floor. "Gus had Aimee do that on purpose."

"You think I tried to burn down my own kitchen intentionally?" Gus shouted "You know what you are? Crazy. Unbalanced. Unhinged."

"I think we all just need to go home and get some rest," Oliver suggested pointedly, holding Carmen by the shoulders. He was at least a foot taller than she was and it didn't require much exertion on his part to keep Carmen still.

"Let go," she wailed.

"Look, let's all cool it," said Oliver. "We've just had a bit of a crazy night, that's all. By tomorrow it'll all be behind us."

But Monday found the entire PR staff of the CookingChannel working in overdrive, trying to dance around the issue of Hannah's sudden appearance on the show.

She and Gus sat in their chairs in the bay window, Salt and Pepper in laps, and watched a clean-up crew that Porter had sent over tidy up the stove and ceiling.

"It's out there," said Hannah. "Me."

Is it liberating when what you've dreaded most comes to pass? Does it make you feel as though all the agita and bad sleep was silly somehow? A wasted effort? No, Hannah thought, it doesn't. It made her feel as though she'd been punished for dropping her vigilance. She'd spent all night watching the news on her computer and on her two televisions in her dining room office, braced for the past to be dredged up again.

"Sometimes suffering is just suffering," she told Gus. "It doesn't make you stronger. It doesn't build character. It only hurts."

"I know," Gus said, and Hannah felt like hugging her friend, though she didn't, of course.

They sipped their coffee as the workmen scrubbed the white ceiling, clearing off all the dark smudges and leaving it spotless again. No trace of the ugly. All cleaned up.

Hannah wondered if her father watched the CookingChannel, if he would get back in touch with her, would send her a letter or email. Though it seemed unlikely, and not just because he didn't have her email address.

Porter pushed the PR team to reframe Aimee's blaze as part of a very special episode on fire safety.

"That's insane," Gus told Porter when he called her at home to tell her not to answer her phone if media called. "We nearly blew up my kitchen!"

"If the public buys it, then that's what we're selling," he said. "Look, we're getting calls from everywhere: one night of a burning kettle has gotten *Eat Drink and Be* noticed by everything from *Entertainment Tonight* to CNN. Not to mention it's the number one clip on YouTube."

"Yippee," said Gus. "Must be a slow news day. I'm so glad all my years as a television host have led me here. My reputation is going to be ruined."

"Oh, no, Gus, you don't get it," said Porter. "This is going to boost your cool factor in a big way."

"Do I need to be cooler?"

"We all need to be cooler. It's the new publicity. You and Carmen and all the rest are becoming famous just for being stupid."

Gus was speechless.

"Look, you've been booked on *Regis and Kelly* to talk about the importance of fire extinguishers in kitchens," explained Porter. "The two of you are going to go out there—happy to be together, I might add—and be upbeat. And whenever anyone asks if the woman who put out the fire was Hannah Joy Levine, I want both of you to just smile like the Mona Lisa."

By the end of the week, Carmen and Gus had done morning shows and late-night chatfests and been forced to write heavily sanitized "behind-the-scenes" blogs for the CookingChannel website. (*Carmen is certainly unique,* Gus wrote, as Hannah munched on licorice twists and edited over her shoulder.)

They'd even been informed, by Alan via Porter, that the two of them were expected to be judges on the current episode of Cooking-Channel's *Kitchen Kingdom*, in which two restaurateurs squared off to create competing meals with one unusual ingredient and win the crown of Royal Chef.

It was not one of Gus's favorites on the CookingChannel roster, a fact that she had previously kept discreetly to herself.

"I assume," she said to Porter, "that the secret ingredient will be octopus?" She even managed to look amused.

"I can put in a special request with the producer there," said Porter.

"No thanks," she replied. "I've been using enough of my considerable energy to ward off Carmen's evil. It'll be a while before I can enjoy octopus in the same way again."

On *Kitchen Kingdom*, the two hosts of *Eat Drink and Be* were seated side by side, glued at the hip as they had been for over a week. The two sat grimly next to each other until either one spotted a camera moving to the judges' table and banged the other on the knee. Then, in unison, they would look up and flash toothy grins, mouthing words at each other as though engaged in scintillating culinary conversation. In reality, they were literally not speaking.

Jeffrey Steingarten, the food critic from the *New York Times*, rounded out the judging panel, and he quite openly stared at their silent "talking." A pair of odd ducks, he'd called them, which embarrassed and irritated Gus. She told him she was saving her voice for when she was on-screen.

The previous week's winner of *Kitchen Kingdom*, who owned a restaurant in Chicago, was paired against a popular Spanish chef, Karlos Arguinaño.

"Don't you vote against him just because he's from Spain," hissed Carmen when it came time to write down their scores, covering the mike clipped to her dress.

"What you don't realize, Carmen, is that I'd be quite happy to eat your food if I never had to see or speak to you," said Gus. "Just because I don't like you—and I don't—doesn't mean I don't like your food."

But the public la-di-da act was draining: she was more unhappy about Carmen's presence than ever. Carmen had made it quite clear she was not going to make working together easy. Sabrina continued to be evasive. And Aimee was mortified by the nonstop emails she was receiving from old high school classmates who saw the clip online. Gus was mad and fretted that everyone she cared about was mad at her. Only Troy, who'd seen a huge increase in hits to the FarmFresh website, was remotely happy. And he was still pining for Sabrina; she could hear it in his voice when he refused to talk about it with her.

She took to crying in the shower, where it felt safer to sob, and stayed up late at night, baking chocolate cake and oatmeal bars and chewy cookies, when she couldn't fall asleep. Salt and Pepper enjoyed the late night company, and Hannah came over dutifully every morning to eat her midnight productions.

Overtired and cranky, Gus found herself wishing that some teen starlet would drive over a paparazzo's foot or that a movie star—anyone would do—would wear a loose-fitting shirt to jumpstart another baby bulge countdown. Anything so that the celebrity journalists had something else to write about instead of her and Carmen and their great, great show together. It was ridiculous. Kelly Ripa had even told them they were a super example of girl power.

"Girl power?" Gus had said. "How interesting."

"Gus isn't actually a girl anymore," Carmen had interjected, with saccharine sweetness.

Every interview had been like that with Carmen. It was exhausting.

"Why is everyone making a big deal about this fire thing?" she asked later in the week, as she dragged herself into the Cooking-Channel studios to shoot some promotional commercials. Alan had started advertising *Eat Drink and Be* heavily during other programming, and had even bought spots on other cable channels

"Because it's funny when no real damage was done," said Oliver. "And then there's the fact that Carmen's pretty and you're hot."

"Ha ha ha," Gus said, before calling out to Porter. "Why doesn't Mr. Clean over here have to do any of the interviews?"

"Don't worry, we'll exploit him when the time comes," replied Porter. "But right now the fans want you and Carmen. Well, and Hannah, but that's another situation."

"She's not going to do it, Porter," said Gus, who had already phoned Alan to try to convince him.

"Smart cookie," Carmen said through gritted teeth as she put on a well-practiced fake smile for the camera.

"We all love to watch great television," Porter was saying to Alan in his office later that day. "But we also find ourselves rubbernecking when we see a roadside accident. And *Eat Drink and Be* is turning into just that."

"Switching up the menu was an interesting tactic," Alan said, as though it hadn't been his idea. "It forced Gus to break out of her shell."

"She was excellent," said Porter. "Sharp, like in the old days. I liked that."

"When she's on, she's on. I'm rooting for her even when she doesn't know it."

"And we couldn't have scripted anything better than the kettle fire," added Porter.

"The media frenzy has been good for the network," agreed Alan.

"But I don't want this to become about stunts, intentional or not. We've got to find our rhythm. And Carmen and Gus . . ." Porter let his words trail off.

"We're heading for a seven-car pileup, am I right?"

"The team needs to learn to work together," said Porter. "Or else the last episode of our little mini-season is going to end up as a food fight. Literally."

Although the full team of *Eat Drink and Be* typically didn't see one another in a professional capacity between episodes, Porter called a special Monday night meeting of the entire crowd. Carmen, Oliver, Troy, Sabrina, and Aimee sat around a long table while Hannah, who was being wooed, in a purely work-related way, by Alan with gift baskets of Tootsie Rolls, was there via conference call as she sat next to Gus in her library.

"Great news, everyone," said Porter. He sat near the phone to address everyone at once. "Alan has invited all of you to attend an all-expense-paid weekend retreat together. It's going to be wonderful!"

None of the participants on *Eat Drink and Be* looked happy in the least.

Aimee silently raised her hand like a schoolgirl. Porter waved her off before she could speak.

"Let me be clear: attendance is mandatory," he said. "Just be happy I talked him out of taking you camping."

# hot potato

# 17

The cool blue lake glistened as the minivan carrying Oliver, Carmen, Sabrina, Aimee, and Troy made its way up the winding drive through miles of treed green woods to the impressively large resort overlooking the water. It had been a long trip up the Hudson Valley on this hot, humid May holiday weekend, delayed by all the Friday traffic getting out of the city, and mostly silent except for the buzz of the air conditioner.

Carmen, upon weighing her options between sitting in the back with the riffraff and placing herself next to the driver, chose the latter. Aimee, acting on an unspoken plea from Sabrina, positioned herself next to Troy in the back of the van. She'd been through many boyfriends and breakups and make-ups and regretful mornings-after with her little sister. It hadn't been necessary for Sabrina to explain what had really taken place on Octopus Night, and it didn't matter. She didn't have a thing against Troy, either. It's just that this was her job, Aimee told herself. Holding her sister together with paper clips.

Oliver, lounging next to Sabrina in the first row, made a few attempts at chitchat—"Hey, it's not like we're being sent to prison" was among his least successful conversation starters as he read from a brochure detailing activities from water sports to volleyball to croquet on the great lawn—but the overall mood in the car was so dour that it seemed impossible to get anyone talking.

So they fairly flew out of the van when it finally pulled up outside the lobby, Aimee and Sabrina coming together like a pair of magnets. Porter was there already, as was Gus, who had been brought in a car from her Westchester home.

"Okay, team," said Porter. "Let's get you into your rooms and get going."

The good news—if there was any good news, Gus thought, following the porter with her bags—was that everyone had their own accommodations. She'd been rather anxious that she and Carmen would be forced into one room. Or worse, each given half of a king-size bed, tussling over the covers and fighting over whether the window should be open or closed. Bringing up such a scenario was how Gus had tried to convince Hannah that she ought to come along. Hannah, thoughtfully chewing her way through a pack of original Hubba Bubba, had been unmoved.

The most annoying thing about unpacking is realizing what's been left behind. Carmen was, after years of travel, expert at rolling her clothes so they didn't wrinkle and zipping up her toiletries in plastic bags to avoid spills. And yet, she thought as she crouched down to open her suitcase on the floor, she invariably did something wrong. Forgot her toothbrush, left behind her perfume, neglected to bring the skirt that went with her suit jacket. There was always something.

She rooted around inside the case, glancing with annoyance at Porter's packing list that he'd emailed to everyone days before.

*Attention, Eat Drink and Be-ers!*
*Be sure to bring:*
*Jeans*
*Sweaters*
*Loose-fitting pants (think sweats)*
*T-shirts*
*Swimsuits!!!!*
*Don't forget sneakers!*
*p.s. Dinner has a dress code*

The weekend was destined to be a fiasco. Carmen was sure of that. She grabbed her panties and bras and carried them over to a dresser drawer, placing a towel on the bare wood before she put them down. She'd been doing that ever since she left home, still a teenager, to model. Her mother had supplied her with plenty of hand towels to line dresser drawers, uncertain about the cleanliness (or lack thereof) Carmen would encounter in the great wide world. The towel habit stuck, all through the beauty pageants and runway work and the blip on the screen that was her Hollywood debut. She'd always tried to do what her mother would have wanted. Mostly. The romance with the boy-band singer had not won the approval of her loved ones back home.

Home. It had been years since she'd spent more than a few weeks in Seville, something she supposed she hadn't realized at sixteen, packing up her *coletero* hair scrunchies, hoop earrings, and Panama Jack boots, confident of the nonstop adventures that lay before her. "So this is it," she'd said to her older sister all those years ago as she sat on her suitcase to zip it closed, feeling courageous and proud and more than a little self-satisfied. Wasn't she special? Wasn't she unique?

She was braver at sixteen than she was now, Carmen realized.

Back in the day, she'd had little concept of the unpleasantness that life could bring. Had only envisioned the triumph and perfect thrill of it all. Never knowing enough to be scared.

With one swift movement she had pulled the comforter off the bed and rolled it up into a ball, tossing it in the bottom of her closet. No matter how upscale the hotel, she never slept under a comforter, which, unlike the sheets, was unlikely to be washed daily. One of the many tricks she'd learned along the way. Like stopping the deli man before he put twenty slices of ham on a sandwich. Americans were strange that way. Just one was fine for her; she liked to taste the bread.

She curled up on top of the white sheets and regarded her half-unpacked luggage. "I want to go home," she said, though there was no one there to hear her. "I miss . . ."

She didn't bother to finish her sentence.

Carmen was more homesick now than she'd ever been in her life. She'd gotten over the ridiculously shocking price of tomatoes in the grocery store and the way the coffee shops poured giant cups; she'd adjusted to the streets seeming dark at night, thanks in part to the fact that streets in Spain had more lights. No, it was more than that. She had a greater appreciation for what she'd given up to follow her dreams, had a secret envy of her sister Marisol, who lived so close to her parents.

"*Tu vida es tan glamorosa, cariño*," her mother said when she came home for the occasional Christmas or birthday. It was easy for them to believe hers was a glamorous life, but it didn't feel all that glittery. Oh, sometimes it had been surreal, during the most dressy of events, but mostly it had been hard work and many late nights staring out the window—after a date, after a nightclub, after a long photo shoot—and wondering what everyone was doing back home in Seville.

These were the parties she had missed over the years: every *Nochevieja* for the past seven years, her niece Maria's baptism and then later her *primera comunión*, the wedding of her best friend from childhood, her aunt and uncle's *bodas de plata* celebrating twenty-five years of marriage. Not to mention the endless Saturday afternoon lunches with the entire family, savoring *calamares*, gazpacho, *pescaito frito*, flounder seviche, *solomillo al queso*, a fillet in blue cheese sauce, and *arroz con leche*.

Everyone understood how busy her schedule was; no one criticized her for not being able to come home often.

She'd made it home for her grandmother's funeral, though.

It was all rather backward.

Her sister Marisol had made fun of Carmen when she revealed, over light, flaky *tortas de aceite* and several generous glasses of *Jerez*, that she thought Marisol was the lucky one.

"You get to be with the family," Carmen said, as Marisol laughed and laughed, amused by her jet-setting little sister.

"You wouldn't give up your life for anything in the world," her sister scoffed. "There's nothing fancy here."

No one understood. Fancy doesn't fill you up. It doesn't nourish the soul. She had remained silent then because that was easier than arguing. Than to make her sister or her mother see. Because Carmen had traded everything—her family, her friends, her culture—for some so-called great career. That she'd already had to reinvent more than once, down on her luck after failing to make it in Hollywood.

Her only option was to succeed on this damn cooking show or it had all been for nothing. All the years away, all the missed birthdays, all the lonely nights. In truth, she knew that it was never going to be worth it. Even as she joked with her family about the kettle fire clip they'd watched on YouTube, and she replied to the emails from old friends. They all acted as though her life was simply grand and were invested, in their own ways, in her success. Privately, she knew she had lost far too much and made too many sacrifices, and there were moments, more often now than ever, when she wished she'd never packed her bags at sixteen and left home. But it wasn't as though she could just go back. Returning had to be on her terms or it would seem a failure. To her. To everyone. And besides, the family had learned to function well without her presence.

Hers had been an uneven bargain that cost her far more than she realized.

She called down to the lobby for Oliver's room number.

"Come on over for a drink," she told him. "I need your shoulder."

Dinner was rather pleasant, since Porter had allowed Gus, Aimee, and Sabrina to sit at their own table, and he kept counsel with Oliver, Carmen, and Troy at his own.

"I just want to go to bed," Sabrina said as everyone marched out of the dining room and turned toward the elevators.

"Hey, gang!" said a short, red-haired man standing in the lobby. Gus assumed, for half a second, that he was a fan recognizing the *Eat Drink and Be* cast, until she noticed the clipboard he held and the determined way that Porter beelined for him.

"Is this our camp counselor?" Oliver spoke in a low voice, close to her ear, so only she could hear.

"Guess so," replied Gus. "This could be the worst Memorial Day ever."

Although the redhead wore a short-sleeve Hawaiian shirt, his face appeared flushed and pink, and he puffed as though he'd just been exercising. For no reason that Gus could see, he began clapping as the group formed a semicircle around him.

"Good show," he said, nodding vigorously. "Welcome, everyone."

The "gang" stared.

"Welcome to what, exactly?" asked Aimee. You could always count on Aimee, thought Gus.

"Welcome to a very special team-building weekend." The man grinned broadly, showing a little too much gum line.

"Very special?" Troy looked wary.

"C'mon, gang, grab a seat," the man said, motioning to a collection of chairs in the lobby. "I just want to give you some idea of what's coming up tomorrow and send you off to bed."

"Who, exactly, are you?" Gus was polite but firm.

"Right, right, first things first." He held up his arms as though trying to quiet a stadium of raucous concertgoers. "I'm Gary Rose, but you can call me Gare."

"Call you *Gare*?" Aimee was unimpressed. "Why would we need to shorten a name that has only two syllables?"

"Who are you, again?" Gus, again, on point.

"Are you the contest winner?" asked Troy.

"No, that was Priya Patel of New Jersey," replied Oliver. "Gus announced it on the last show. Unless you're Priya?"

"No, still just Gare. I'm here to facilitate our coming together as a team," he said, enunciating every syllable in the word "facilitate" to add extra emphasis.

"How very special," murmured Sabrina, sharing a glance with her sister. They always got along better when they had a common enemy.

"Anyway, here's the schedule for the weekend," Gary said, "and, boy oh boy, do we have a lot of fun things planned."

"We?" asked Carmen. "Is there another like you around here?"

Gary Rose chuckled heartily, beads of sweat flying off his pink forehead. "Good one," he said, looking at his clipboard. "Carmen. Okay, gang, so Team Sports are tomorrow at seven AM."

"I don't do mornings," said Sabrina.

"Another good one," said Gary. "But it's not optional." He began handing out stacks of papers. "Don't hate me but we have a little homework tonight."

Troy looked disheartened upon receiving his pile. "What the . . . ?"

"Good question, Oliver," Gary said, a bit too loudly.

"I'm Troy, the Korean guy with the thick head of hair?" He looked amused. "Oliver over here is very white and very bald."

"Oh, right, right," said Gary. "Sorry about that. You'll all have to help me out with your names for a day or so."

"Haven't you seen our show?" asked Carmen.

"Part of the reason Alan chose Gary is that he's not a fan," Porter explained. "A fresh slate, if you will."

"And part of your homework is to answer this questionnaire all about yourself," said Gary, passing around a box of pencils. "And then answer a second one about your teammates, giving me all sorts of juicy details. So go, team!"

"This isn't about sports," said Aimee. "We're not actually a team, you know."

"I know," said Gary. "That's what I'm here to fix."

Carmen had changed into a pink nightie and curled up in her bed, but she hadn't bothered to fill out the questionnaires from that stupid Gary. She wasn't even sure if she still had his pencil. Was he expecting her to return them? She thought of calling her publicist to complain about the enforced ridiculousness but she was aware there was nothing that could be done, and besides, it was after eleven on the Friday night of the May holiday weekend. Even Carmen Vega had her limits, right?

She'd called Oliver a few times, both in his room and on his cell, though he hadn't answered. He and Troy had gone off to the video arcade after Gary released them all, and she supposed they could still be there. Playing Pac-Man and whatnot. Oliver, she knew, had his very own Galaga console in his Tribeca living room; it was his present to himself when they graduated from the ICE.

Pulling on sneakers, a pair of light cotton pants, and a cardigan sweater over her nightie, Carmen grabbed her key card and left the room.

Twenty minutes later, upon discovering the video game room was closed for the night and not seeing either Troy or Oliver anywhere (or having Oliver answer his phone, yet again), Carmen headed outside.

"Catching a little night air, ma'am?" asked the college kid manning the front desk. Carmen waved, buttoning up her sweater and bracing for a blast of cold air. However, it had been a hot day, and the air was warm.

She loitered outside the lobby for a moment before wandering down to the gardens. She was all alone, feeling more than a bit brave to be walking about on her own in unfamiliar surroundings. After several minutes she arrived at the resort's tennis courts, row after row of green concrete. There, sitting slumped on a bench with head pressed to knees, was a figure in a hooded gray sweat suit who seemed somewhat familiar. A tennis racket lay at her feet.

"So you're coming out of hiding?" Carmen asked the bundle of cotton.

"Not sure," Hannah said, raising her head to reveal her face. "I've only gotten as far as all this."

"You haven't checked in, then?"

"Nope."

Carmen sat down next to her. "How'd you get up here?"

"I drove," said Hannah. "In my 1990 red Miata, the one I bought after winning the U.S. Open. My driver's license isn't even valid."

"Well, I won't tell Gus," said Carmen. "I have no doubt she'd disapprove."

"Gus is the one who called me," said Hannah. "She phoned tonight to tell me I was fortunate to not be here. Said there's some short little man named Gary who's going to make everyone play games."

"And you just couldn't resist?" Carmen raised her eyebrows. "This weekend is going to be a huge waste of time."

"I thought maybe I'd come help Gus, I suppose. I don't really know. Making a plan isn't really my thing."

"Isn't your thing that you're a recluse or something?" Carmen tightened the laces on her sneakers. "I've tried not to follow the news. I prefer to watch my own coverage."

"Thank God."

"Being famous isn't all it's cracked up to be, right?"

"True enough," said Hannah.

"So what do you do, then, when you're not putting out fires at Gus's house?"

"I'm a writer," said Hannah. "Health stuff mostly, but sometimes I write about dating and parenting. No sports, though."

"That's sheer genius," said Carmen. "A woman in constant fear of being found out by a journalist becomes a journalist herself!"

"I admit I didn't think about it that way." Hannah tested the weight of her racket in her hands. "No one stood by me publicly, you know. But in private, some people helped me out. That's how I got my first writing assignment—a sports reporter called in a favor."

"You wrote about tennis?"

"No, about summer travel bargains. I mainly called up hotel chains and found out what specials they were running. It paid next to nothing: ten cents a word."

"But it was a job." Carmen thought about living in that California guesthouse, not knowing where to turn.

"It was," admitted Hannah. "I learned how to become a reporter just by doing it. It was a good thing, too, because I never went to college."

"I went to culinary school," said Carmen. "But not until after all the pageants and stuff. Not like Gus, with her alma mater and all that."

"Maybe we grow up faster when we're out working." Hannah shrugged.

"Wish I'd brought my racket out here with me," said Carmen. "I play a bit."

"Oh, yeah?" Hannah stared out into the court. "I haven't played for years."

"You kept the racket, though."

"I have seventeen rackets sitting in my guest room closet," Hannah said. "I couldn't throw them out. I've been afraid to touch them."

"Let's play," Carmen said. "Come on, let's go." She pulled Hannah to her feet.

"You don't have a racket," said Hannah. "We don't have any balls."

"We'll just volley. In our imaginations." Carmen walked to one side of the net, threw a pretend ball in the air with her right hand, and swung with her left.

Hannah watched her without moving.

"Well, point for me," said Carmen. "If you're not going to even try to hit back, then I'm going to win by default."

Carmen served again.

"Ace!" she shouted. "Damn, I'm good."

In a few quick steps, Hannah was on the other side of the net. "Is there a referee?"

"Of course," Carmen said. "Can't you see him in his chair? What makes me mad are the hecklers who are trying to distract me. They must be your fans."

"Hah! There aren't any of those anymore," Hannah said, connecting with Carmen's serve in her mind. Every muscle in her body seemed to be waking up from a long, dreamless sleep, every step forward a memory.

"The fans are here," Carmen said, lunging for the ball. "I missed it. Your serve."

"This is loony," Hannah said, even though she leaned back to toss the imaginary ball in the air. She swung a tennis racket for the first time in fifteen years, a moan coming out of her as she did so. "Aaaaah," she screamed, feeling pained.

"Back to you," Carmen shouted across the net. "Right-hand corner."

Hannah ran for the ball, feeling the weight of the racket, instinctively using her backhand.

"Go!" She spoke to the ball, the tennis ball that was only in her mind.

Carmen ran up to the net. "Smash," she said, practically dancing on the court.

"Far left, bounced behind your head," Hannah screamed as Carmen ran back toward the line.

"It's in," Carmen yelled. "You got the point."

Hannah stood stock-still on her side of the net, tears streaming down her face, and a deep cry coming from her very depth.

"Screw them," she yelled as Carmen trotted down the court toward her. "Screw them all!"

They sat side by side on the bench inside the tennis courts for a long time.

"I know about being tough," said Hannah. "I wasn't always a crumpled mess."

"Obviously not," said Carmen. "Two Wimbledons, a U.S. Open, and the Australian. That's pretty good."

"Not a Grand Slam, though."

"I do that, too," said Carmen. "Put myself down. This sauce isn't spicy enough, Carmen. This *croqueta* lacks pizzazz. Criticize, criticize, criticize."

"I always believed in meeting players head-on," said Hannah. "I thought your octopus prank was underhanded."

"It was a joke."

"No. There are no jokes when it comes to live television. No one wants to get *Punk'd*. They just pretend."

"All's fair in cooking."

"Is it?" Hannah wasn't convinced. "Things can quickly go too far when you start rationalizing. Take it from me."

Carmen crossed her arms. "Octopus can be very good, *sabes*? Sea urchin, eel, lots of seafood that isn't common here. My mother makes a seafood stew that is so fragrant all your taste buds water as soon as you smell it."

"That's nice," Hannah said, before admitting the truth. "I hate to try new things. I wouldn't want to eat that."

"Just because something is different from what you're used to doesn't make it bad," she said. "I didn't want to include sangria on that episode."

"But everyone thinks sangria and paella, that's Spanish. I thought it was generous of Gus to do some Spanish stuff."

"Yeah, but that's just perception of what Spanish food is," she said. "Sangria is for party night. For teenagers. And I've never had a white sangria in my life."

"What would you have made?"

"Nothing," said Carmen. "I would simply have served a good wine, maybe an Albariño."

"You have to create something while the cameras roll," said Hannah. "You can't just pour stuff."

"Well, maybe I would have made a popular *merienda* like *chocolate con churros*," she said. "It's like eating melted chocolate with a spoon."

"That sounds good to me!"

"Yeah," Carmen said, playfully punching Hannah in the arm. "I'll make it for you sometime and you'll see."

"I thought you didn't want me on the show?"

"Oh, I don't," she said. "I'd lock you in a meat freezer if I thought you were going to be a regular." Carmen smiled to show she was kidding around. "I promise I won't kill you. Just because I don't want yet another person stealing my well-earned attention doesn't mean I don't like you, Hannah."

"You're not that nice," Hannah said, approvingly. "You're a competitor."

"Nice is for cocktail parties and wedding showers." Carmen flexed her arm into a muscle. "Tough and smart is for the workday. I find American women odd."

"Why?"

"They want to rule the home with an iron fist and let everyone walk all over them in the office," she said. "That's not how to live. It's topsy-turvy."

"They think they're being kind, I'm sure."

"Letting yourself be pushed around is not the same thing as kindness," Carmen said. "And having you on the show is going to further distract from my brand."

"Your brand?"

"That's what I'm selling," she said. "The food of Carmen Vega."

"Like you want entrees in the freezer aisle?"

"No," said Carmen. "I want investors for a restaurant. I want to be named an Iron Chef. I want to be the best chef in the world."

"But that's on CookingChannel's competitor!"

"Would you have stayed with a coach who wasn't making you win?"

"My father was my coach," said Hannah. "I didn't have much choice."

"And look where that got you. Don't worry, I'm not about to blab to the papers. The last thing I need is for you to take away any more attention from me."

"My father was a gambler," Hannah said bitterly. "He was a gambler, first and foremost. He liked thrill."

"What did your mother think about all of this?" Carmen motioned for Hannah to follow. "I'm like ice, let's go inside."

"She wasn't around," said Hannah. "She died when I was still a toddler. My father remarried a viper of a woman. My stepmonster."

"Tennis was your escape."

"No, not really." They were walking briskly through the gardens now. "I had to play every day. My father wanted a champion."

"Not everyone can simply be turned into a champion," said Carmen. "I know."

"It's amazing what a hell of a lot of effort gets you," said Hannah. "But I had the talent. My father had been a strong junior player himself. But he lacked the discipline."

"And you were his proxy."

"More like his meal ticket," said Hannah. "The rumors of tax evasion came up the second time I won Wimbledon. I was only eighteen."

"Both of you were investigated?"

"My father handled all of my finances," she said, gently bouncing her racket in her hand. "I just played. Practiced and played. It took a couple of years for them to build their case."

"So did he do it?"

"Yup. He took most of my money and hid it away."

"For investing?"

"For gambling. And when it looked as though we were going to have to pay the piper, he started betting on me."

"That must have been a lot of pressure," Carmen said, a bit out of breath keeping up with Hannah's long strides.

Hannah looked at her quizzically. "You really didn't read the stories. I'm surprised."

"I am busy, you know," said Carmen. "And I prefer reading my own press." She grinned.

"Right," Hannah said, as they entered the lobby. The clerk glanced over briefly and then went back to his computer. Hannah lowered her voice.

"He bet *against* me, Carmen. My own father."

"That's terrible! So he thought you would lose?"

"He *told* me to lose," Hannah said, looking this way and that to see if anyone was around. "It was a sure thing. Get it?"

"Why did you agree?"

"I was a kid," said Hannah. "He was my father. What did it matter that I fell to seventh seed? Besides, the big problems only really came when I refused to do it anymore."

"Because then what happened?"

"Because then my father placed a bet against this German girl, Heidi Mueller. She was the number one and my main rival."

Carmen unlocked her room door and rushed inside, motioning for Hannah to sit down. She jumped onto her bed, ready to hear more.

"It was the semifinals at Wimbledon, which had always been my best tournament," she said. "I was determined to stage my comeback, start climbing back to number one. So my father decided he had to shake up Heidi."

"He threatened her?"

"Crazier," said Hannah. "He bribed someone to get an extra press pass and gave it to this lunatic who had been stalking her."

Carmen sat on the end of the bed, her mouth open. She'd had more than a few overeager fans when she was Miss Spain.

"The guy came into the dressing room and all hell broke loose," said Hannah. "Heidi freaked—she recognized the guy right away because he'd tried to break into her house a few years before—and she ran out the door and down the hall, the guy chasing her and screaming that he loves her, and ultimately she fell down some stairs and broke her arm."

"Holy crap," said Carmen. "At least she didn't get hurt worse."

"There was an internal investigation, and all signs pointed back to my father," Hannah said, quietly. "So he called a press conference to refute the allegations."

"And that's where you broke."

"I never knew about the press pass thing until after it happened," she said. "But this one reporter just wouldn't drop the topic of why I'd been playing so poorly and he wore me down. I confessed to throwing games."

"Switching up a little octopus has nothing on you," said Carmen. "Now I really don't want you on the show. You'll kill me."

"It's no joke," said Hannah. "I was banned from tennis forever. My whole life was over by the time I was twenty-one."

"And your dad went to jail?"

"For a millisecond," she said. "He cut some sort of deal—he wasn't the only one betting on games—and ended up with a light sentence. Now he and the stepmonster have another kid. A junior golfer."

"You're kidding?"

"Nope, I have a brother I've never even met," said Hannah. "Doing the wrong thing only hurts if you have feelings." She stood up and stretched, then resettled herself in the chair.

"I'm beat," she said.

"Yeah, let's get some sleep," Carmen said, throwing her a pillow from the bed. "It wasn't totally your fault, Hannah."

"We all do bad stuff," agreed Hannah. "Like you sleeping with Alan to get onto Gus's show."

"Like sleeping with Alan," Carmen repeated softly.

Hannah, drifting off to sleep in the armchair, couldn't tell if it was an admission or a question.

# 18

Gus awakened Sabrina with a phone call. Sabrina then dialed Aimee.

"Mom doesn't know what to wear," she said, before immediately hanging up and going back to sleep.

Five minutes later, Aimee was banging on her door, dressed in navy workout pants and a white cotton tee. "Get up," she said through the wood. "I'll be in Mom's room. If you're not there ASAP, I'm going to break into your room."

Aimee was hardly a morning person but she also didn't want to be the last person to arrive at Gary's little sports class. She found Gus sitting at her laptop, idly checking email and her online portfolios.

"That's strange," she told her daughter. "I can't access one account at all and the balances seem off in the other."

"Maybe it knows you're not at home," said Aimee, not really paying attention. She was busy trying to fashion a better outfit for Gus than the lumpy, oversized sweats she had on.

"Why did you bother calling Sabrina?" Aimee asked. "You had to realize she was just going to get me to come down."

"What?" Gus was intent on reading her computer screen. "Oh, I just thought she was more into clothes than you are." She looked up at Aimee. "I'm glad you're here, though."

"Try these," Aimee said, tossing her mother a pair of her own stretchy capris and a cap-sleeved top that she'd brought with her. Reluctant to leave her computer, Gus changed quickly while keeping one eye on the screen, and tried to reach her investment adviser's private line. But Sabrina, in a body-hugging velour tracksuit, showed up before Gus could make contact with something other than a voice mail directory. Quickly, Aimee herded them all into the elevator, where they ran into an irritated Porter.

"Anyone see Carmen yet?" he asked, before hurrying down the hall.

Down in the lobby, Troy stood waiting in a pair of shorts and—what else?—a FarmFresh T-shirt next to Oliver, who was also wearing a FarmFresh shirt and shorts. "The two of you could be twins from different families," said Gus. Oliver had a pair of flip-flops on his feet, which were quite nicely groomed, she noticed. She hated men with scraggly toe-nails.

"I want to go back to bed," Sabrina muttered sleepily, as Troy instinctively reached out to her and then let his arm drop, mid-reach.

"Let's sit," said Aimee, guiding her sister to some chairs.

The group waited quietly, all tired except for Gus, who loved mornings. She gazed fondly on her sleepy team until Carmen finally appeared on Porter's arm, dressed only in a red bikini and a sarong.

"Whoa," said Troy, admiring Carmen's figure but more pleased by Sabrina's sharp look in his direction.

Standing awkwardly next to Carmen was Hannah in a gray tracksuit. She smiled shyly at Gus, who moved quickly to be next to her.

"You were crazy to come here," Gus said. "But I'm glad you did."

A half hour later they were all regretting their weekend jaunt. Gary was putting them through their paces on the big lawn, making them crouch around in a circle and pretend to be seeds who would slowly "grow" to their full height and jump into the air.

"And stretch, flowers!" he said, leaping into the air with them. "Come on, Porter, you, too."

"Yes, Porter, I think that's only appropriate," murmured Gus. "Aimee, less shrub, more flower." She shook her head to show her daughter she was kidding. See? she told herself, she could have as much fun as anyone.

Carmen certainly was, fairly bouncing out of her bikini top with each flower hop.

"It is hard to look away," Troy said quietly to Oliver, who nodded.

"It's as though we're in kindergarten," said Sabrina, who, as the youngest of the group, took particular offense. "We're like little kids."

"Exactly, exactly," shouted Gary. "And remember how important it was to share?" He jumped again, though the rest of the group seemed ready to revolt.

"I think we've all grown to our maximum potential," Gus said drily.

But Gary was only getting started, watching them as they played games of Red Rover, Red Light Green Light, and Freeze Tag, in which the only way to be defrosted was to have someone who wasn't "it" crawl through one's legs. ("Oh, bloody hell," muttered Gus to herself, rapidly losing the ability to laugh at herself. "I'm being forced to relive Aimee and Sabrina's childhood.") She ran very, very fast so as not to become frozen.

"Aren't we having fun, gang?" Gary called out as they ran around the lawn, this way and that. Gus could see, out of the corner of her eye, he was making notes on how well they were playing together.

Sabrina seemed to be chasing Troy most of all, which she considered a good development.

Aimee tagged Carmen, then attempted to block Oliver as he tried to free her.

"No, you don't," Aimee told Oliver as he scooted around her, but the two of them had a playful tussle that ended up knocking over Carmen—who was not very pleased by that outcome—and they all fell to the ground in a pile.

Gus ran over to check on her daughter.

"Dammit," she said as Hannah tagged her once she got close. "Have you lost your mind?"

But Hannah was exhilarated by running around in the open air; it was such a change from her daily treadmill jogs. Everyone else may have been grumbling but for Hannah it was sheer joy. She'd forgotten how much she liked the feel of her body moving, arms and legs pumping, the pull of crisp air into her lungs. "Whooo," she cheered. "Whooo!"

Gus, although just tagged, attempted to walk off the field.

"You're frozen," bellowed Carmen, still on the ground in her bikini. "Get back there."

"Don't worry, Mom," said Aimee, as she moved on the grass through her mother's legs. "We'll get through it together. I've freed you! Run, run!"

But Gus had had quite enough. She marched over to Gary and announced she had been a good sport for as long as could reasonably be expected and that was that. She was quitting. Gus Simpson, she told him, did not play games.

"Umm-hmm," said Gary, scribbling furiously.

Hannah was on the far end of the lawn, running around even

though no one else was there, and it took more than a minute to grab her attention.

"Okay, everybody, it's circle time," Gary called, cupping a hand behind his ear as the entire group let out a collective groan. "I can tell we're going to have a fabulous weekend, you guys. Just wait till group hug!"

The group plodded forward, attempting to stave off the inevitable sharing.

"I'm freezing," said Carmen. "The grass is dewy."

"And you're just in a bikini," Gus said.

"So let's be flexible," Gary said. "Why don't we move it on inside? Oh, and if anyone tries to bail, there will be consequences. Right, Porter?"

"Uh, yeah," said Porter without conviction. "Alan is coming by later today, everyone. He'll want to know how we're doing."

"We're doing terribly," said Aimee. She was staying put only because her mother had pointedly told both her and her sister that she wanted them on *Eat Drink and Be*. "I wish I'd done more research because I have a suspicion that enforced summer camp violates common labor laws."

But Gary only chuckled. "You're a crack-up, Aimee," he said, much to her annoyance. He gave everyone a quick break to return to their rooms and gather their homework.

"Homework?" said Hannah, feeling more than a little panicked. Even when she tried something that should have been easy, like a corporate retreat, she failed. It was difficult to be outside the carriage house. Complicated.

"No worries," said Gary. "I've actually got lots of info on all of you."

Gus was almost inside when she heard his comment; in an instant, she turned on her heel and returned.

"And who, exactly, filled you in? Was it Alan? Or Porter?"

Gary shook his head. "I'm afraid that's confidential, Gus. Now hurry along or you won't have time to get a coffee before we meet in the circle."

"I don't like coffee," she replied.

Gary peeked at the clipboard that seemed permanently attached to him. "Yes, you do," he said, a bit too perkily for Gus's liking. "I'll bring you back a cup."

By 9 AM, the cast of *Eat Drink and Be* had played tag, stretched like growing seeds, and found themselves sitting on hard chairs arranged in a shape somewhat akin to a circle, awaiting Gary's return from the coffee machine. The mood was grim.

"I've never had to do anything like this in all of my years on the CookingChannel," Gus was saying. "I think we should complain."

"It's a stupid waste of time," agreed Carmen. "We should be discussing menus or something."

"Why don't we make a formal request to Porter that we'd rather be together ourselves than with this Gary guy," said Oliver. "He might be amenable. Everybody in?"

There were murmurs of agreement all around.

"I do have some other things to do this morning," mused Gus, who had used her five-minute break to try to call her bank again. She'd begun to feel rather anxious.

"We all have more important things to do, Gus," snapped Carmen. "It's not just you."

"Hey, gang, why so intense?" asked Gary, as he strolled back, coffee in hand. "All set now?"

Gus, having designated herself group spokesperson, stood up and addressed Gary.

"We've decided that we are dropping out of this program," she explained. "We appreciate your enthusiasm but we must let you know that we don't like it."

"And everyone is on board?"

"Yes, it's unanimous."

Gary beamed and clapped his hands. "Oh, this is fantastic, gang!" His face was as red as his hair, and he rocked on his heels in delight. "I don't think I've ever had a group come together so quickly."

"We're not 'together,'" clarified Gus. "We're only agreed that we don't want to work with you. No offense intended, Gary, I'm sure you're a very good facilitator for other people."

"I'm top-notch, Gus," said Gary, still smiling. "Otherwise I wouldn't have been able to make you come to an agreement so quickly. Excellent."

"You're misinterpreting this, Gary—"

"I must say, I find all of you to be utterly fascinating." He dropped his smile. "But there are no dropouts in a Gary Rose program. We're in it to win it."

Gary took a handkerchief out of his pocket and wiped his brow, then settled himself on a chair in the sort-of-a-circle.

"Sit down, Gus," he said in a no-nonsense voice. "It's time to get to work."

Gus looked around to see if she had any allies but everyone seemed to be watching Gary, waiting to see what he was about to do next.

He pretended to scan the crowd. "Carmen," he said. "What was it like being frozen for so long during tag?"

"Annoying," she said.

"Did it make you feel bad that Aimee wanted you to stay frozen?"

"I wasn't surprised," Carmen said. "She hates me. They all hate me."

"I do not," huffed Aimee. "I barely know you."

"Now that's interesting," said Gary. "Aimee feels she doesn't know Carmen, and yet Carmen feels that Aimee doesn't like her." He was interrupted by two uniformed resort staffers who came and whispered in his ear.

"Perfect," he said. "I've been waiting for my white boards to arrive."

The staffers carried in oversized easels upon which they placed a very large dry-erase white board. Gary whipped out a package of chunky markers from his canvas satchel.

"We're going to make two lists here," he said, using a green marker to draw a line down the middle of the board. "On one side we're going to write down all the things we liked about being kids. And on the other, we'll make a list of what we like about being adults."

Each second seemed to pass with excruciating slowness for Gus. The facilitator droned on, and she saw, without really hearing, the members of the group raise their hands and call out answers and even laugh every so often. She hadn't been joking when she told Gary that she didn't play games; an evening spent playing Scrabble did not strike her as a good time. At some point, back when the girls were younger, she supposed she had helped them dress their dolls and decorate their Barbie house, but that seemed to belong to some other, more carefree life. Long before her name had emblazoned a slew of stainless steel cookware.

"Gus?" It was Gary, calling her out in front of everyone. "Someone has been daydreaming, guys," he said.

She tried to appear focused and professional. Gus hated to be unprepared.

"As we've been discussing, part of playing childhood games is to remember the freedom and the exhilaration from long ago," Gary explained, apparently for the second time. "Before stresses and ambition eroded our sense of teamwork and loyalty."

"Not every child likes being part of a team." Gus remembered well how Sabrina and Aimee fought when they were younger.

Gary nodded. "Maybe they want to play a new position," he insisted. "And that's what we're doing: figuring out how we can find our places in the kitchen. When it's time to start, start at the beginning: let's share our favorite childhood memories."

Gus pursed her lips with displeasure.

"Making gazpacho with my *abuela*," said Carmen, eyeballing Gus as she spoke. Challenging her.

"Gus, what about you?"

"I don't know," she said. "It was a long time ago."

"Don't try that lazy 'I'm too old' garbage on me, Gus," said Gary. "You're hardly geriatric."

"I liked *The Andy Griffith Show*," she said finally. "I watched it with my cousin when she babysat."

"Did you have a favorite episode?"

"When Aunt Bea got her own television cooking program and Opie and Andy struggled to make their own dinner." She frowned. "But then Aunt Bea gave it all up simply because she felt she had to be home."

Aimee let out a snort.

"Did you always want to have your own cooking show?" asked Troy.

"No, I wanted to be a photographer when I was a college student," Gus said. "I wanted to be Margaret Bourke-White and travel all over. But I liked to cook. I always enjoyed exotic flavors."

"Thank you, Gus, for honoring the circle," said Gary, much to her chagrin. "What's your favorite memory from childhood, Troy—and no more TV answers. We're not going to discover that the most important thing we share is a deep attachment to *The Brady Bunch*. That much can certainly be assumed."

"I liked apple season at my parents' farm," he said. "No, wait—I liked to *eat* apples. I recall that I resented the picking part."

The facilitator consulted his clipboard. "And now you have a fruit vending company," he said, tapping with his marker. "Is everyone seeing the connections?"

"I had a Play-Doh restaurant kit," piped up Oliver, though Gus was quite confident he was pulling one over on Gary.

"There we go again!"

"Pong was my favorite arcade game," Hannah shouted, her cheeks burning. She was never a good one for fibs.

"Shazam!" shouted Gary.

"Are you expecting me to say I liked counting Monopoly money or running a lemonade stand?" Aimee was openly scornful, which embarrassed Gus. She didn't like Gary, either, but there was such a thing as discretion. Typically she didn't have to worry about her eldest in that regard.

"I'm the economist," her daughter explained to Gary. "And my sister, the mess monster who could never pick up her clothes—and still can't—has turned into an interior decorator who specializes in minimalist designs. Guess the two of us just shot your theory all to hell, huh, Gare?"

"Sabrina, do you agree?"

"I dunno." Sabrina had barely been participating, not that Gus blamed her. The entire morning had been like living in *The Twilight Zone* with Gary Rose as the host. "I guess when I was a kid I liked hanging out with my dad. He played games with us."

"What sort of games, Sabrina?" asked Gary.

"Cards and board games," she said. "He had a bowl of candy on his desk."

Aimee's face was an angry mask. "That was grandpa who had a bowl of candy, you idiot. You barely remember Dad."

Aimee addressed the group. "She was seven years old when he died," she said. "She doesn't recall anything. It all went over her head."

"I do so remember him." Sabrina could hear her voice, could hear the childishness of her phrasing. She felt diminished, as she often did when Aimee took her on, and she felt angry, which always made her cry. She hated that: the way the sheer boiling frustration set her off. It was humiliating.

"Oh, not the waterworks," Aimee said. "That melodrama is so ten years ago. You've always been overemotional, and frankly, I'm sick of it. It sucks all the oxygen out of the room. There are other people who need to breathe around here, too."

"I miss Dad," said Sabrina, betrayed by her slick cheeks. "Is that some sort of crime?"

"He died almost twenty years ago, and it's not like you see me crying. Dry." Aimee patted her face. "Still dry. No tears here. That's because what's done is done. Move on."

"If you were so good at moving on, you wouldn't be so angry all the time," Sabrina pointed out.

"You just breeze in and out, don't you?" said Aimee. "Happy little baby Sabrina. Wanting everyone to look after her."

"She don't look so happy to me," piped up Carmen.

Oh, God. The sense of mild embarrassment that Gus had had all morning was blossoming quickly into outright horror. Private things, she believed, were better kept that way. Within the family.

"That's enough, girls," interrupted Gus. "This has nothing to do with *Eat Drink and Be*, and I can assure you, no one here is interested." The rapt faces of her colleagues said otherwise but the rest of them had better manners than to speak up.

"Tough stuff with the family, Gus?" Gary asked, his face thoughtful. She stared at his pen, just daring him to make some notes.

"No, we're quite fine," she said. "A little overtired and cranky, perhaps, but *fine*."

"*I* don't feel fine," Sabrina said, staring down her sister.

"It's not your own personal tragedy," Aimee said quietly. "It didn't just happen to you."

"Aimee, let's not upset your sister," said Gus, more sharply than she'd intended.

"Quit coddling her," Aimee replied. "We've been tiptoeing around her for way too long, if you ask me."

"No one asked you," Gus said. As usual, she couldn't bear to see her most sensitive child upset and the familiar reflex to soothe kicked in. "Sabrina, dear, why don't you switch seats with your sister and come sit next to me?"

She very much wanted to get things back on track, get Gary the facilitator back to coaching them through renditions of the hokey-pokey or something equally frivolous.

"No," said Aimee. The rest of the group, even Carmen, who exulted in defying and tormenting Gus, squirmed in their seats. It wasn't like her, Aimee knew, to resist but she was just so tired of making everything better for Sabrina. We could all be as happy-go-lucky if everyone was picking up the pieces behind us. And it's not like anyone was handing out medals for it.

"Aimee!" hissed Gus. She heard a loud rip of paper from across the room and knew immediately that Hannah was opening a bag of candy. The crinkling sound told her the drug of choice today was caramels.

They were making everyone anxious.

"I'll switch," said Troy, who was sitting on Gus's other side. He was already out of his seat.

"No," said Gus, in a tone that left no room for discussion. "I want Aimee and Sabrina to switch." She could hear the collective intake of breath, the furtive unwrapping coming from Hannah's direction. Troy hovered for a moment, then sat, then stood up again. Gus studiously ignored Gary, knowing he was watching her every move.

"I am not giving up my seat to her," Aimee said. "I refuse."

"What are you doing, behaving this way?" Gus spoke in a low voice, only to Aimee, without turning her head toward her.

"I like my chair," said Aimee. "You're not even looking at me." She sounded sulky, so unlike herself.

"You're a grown woman."

"Sabrina's an adult, too."

"Aimee, really, just move for your sister. It's no big deal."

"No!" Aimee stood up and shouted. "No! Why are you always like this? What happened to *you*?"

"Can I be excused?" It was Troy, still standing, a look of alarm on his face. "I, uh, need to . . . go. Uh, to the restroom."

"I could use some air myself," said Oliver.

"Me, too," mumbled Hannah, doing more caramel chewing than talking.

"Me, three." Well, it had to be even worse than it felt when even Carmen wasn't enjoying the spectacle, thought Gus. She was mortified.

"Okay, everyone, there's a lot going on here," said Gary, making the time-out signal with his hands. "We're going to take a group break and meet up again later, at two PM in the conference room here. Grab some lunch, take a walk, have a talk. Lots of talking, people."

Oliver approached Gus, looking concerned. "Want to join me for a little stroll?"

She shook her head. "No, no, I can't. It appears to be time for a Simpson family meeting. I want to meet upstairs with my girls."

There was no conversation in the elevator: just three women riding in stony silence. Aimee and Sabrina followed their mother to her room, which had seemed so spacious earlier but now felt cramped and uncomfortable. Gus's cell phone, which she'd left in her room during the morning's festivities, gave out a chirp to let her know she had a message. She ignored it.

"Sit down," she said. "We can order up some lunch."

But Aimee was pacing the patch of carpet near the bathroom.

"Aimee, please sit," implored Gus.

"You don't have to control everything, Mom! If I want to sit, I'll sit."

"What's all this?" Gus was genuinely confused. "I always let both of you do whatever you want."

"Let? *Let*? That's the problem." Aimee ran her fingers through her brown hair and let out a groan of frustration. "We're not little kids here. Or, I'm not, anyway."

"Why are you so pissed off? I'm the one she's smothering." Sabrina sat cross-legged on the bed, her arms folded. "You've always been a miserable bitch, Aimee. You're the anti-joy."

"No, you're the one who's always running over to Mom, taking up all of her time. You suck the oxygen out of every room you're in," said Aimee. "I'm sick of it. Aren't you sick of it?" She turned her attention to Gus, who was trying to sneak a peek at her cell, which had continued to beep. What was odd was that most of the people who would call on her personal cell phone were already at the resort with her.

"I don't understand what's going on with the two of you or why it's coming up now," Gus said. "Is this about being on the show?"

"I never wanted to be on television," Aimee said. "That's you. That's all you."

"It's not easy when your mom is famous," agreed Sabrina.

"Don't be ridiculous," said Gus. "This has never been an issue before."

"Not for you," Sabrina said. "You'd never guess how many people want to know me because they want to get to you."

"But you're a lovely young girl."

"I'm not a kid, Mom," Sabrina said. "I'm twenty-five."

"Yes, of course, dear."

"Please don't condescend to me," insisted Sabrina. "Really, I'm not a child."

"You don't act like an adult." Aimee sounded triumphant.

"Is that what you do? Play the adult?" Sabrina grabbed a pillow and squeezed it into her lap. "Unlike you, I don't think that means being the black hole of happiness."

"You're not happy," said Aimee. "You just pretend."

"Well, then we're all a bunch of fakers," Sabrina said, motioning toward Gus.

"What on earth are the two of you talking about?" Gus's body was tense, her jaw clenched. "I can't believe all this childish bickering. What, in God's name, do you want?"

"I want *you*," said Aimee softly. "Call me sometime and don't ask about Sabrina."

"I do that, darling," Gus said. "You never want to talk to me."

"No, you don't," Aimee said. "It's always about something else."

"Aimee, you've always been so self-sufficient," said Gus. "Independent. I've always counted on you because of it."

"Aaaahhhh!" Aimee screamed and hollered as tears began to fall. Gus felt almost light-headed with confusion and alarm.

"You know what I want? I want Dad. I want it like it used to be. We were happy then."

"Things were better then," agreed Sabrina. "You were different."

"We were all different," said Gus. "Don't you think I want him, too?" She could sense, even before it happened, the trembling in her bottom lip, the way the fears and memories rushed to the edge, eager to spill out. Stuff it down, she told herself, stuff it down. Because she knew the truth of what she had always known: once the pain started, it might never stop. And she couldn't risk it.

She rushed over to soothe Aimee, not merely to comfort her but also to distract her from her own emotions. It's what she'd always done in the past. Taking care.

"Everyone used to be nice to us because our dad was dead." Sabrina looked worriedly in her sister's direction, as though she'd be in trouble for revealing their shared secrets. Never tell Mom, Aimee had always said, she doesn't need the stress. You be happy and I'll be good. That's what she'd told Sabrina when they whispered, late at night, their words floating over the tape running down the middle of their bedroom floor.

We can make it okay, she'd said, if you act happy and I'm good.

Gus brought Aimee over to the bed and guided her to sit next to Sabrina. She could see, of course, that physically they were grown women, but those were simply wrappers around them. She could much more clearly see the chubby thumb-suckers they once had been. The way they had waited on the stairs the night of the accident, long after the babysitter should have put them to sleep, Sabrina dozing and clinging to her sister, Aimee playing tough. It was all just tucked away inside.

"Then people treated us differently because you were on TV," continued Sabrina. "It's weird having a famous mother. I just wish we could be a normal family."

"We are normal," said Gus. "We're unique."

"We haven't been normal since Dad died," Aimee said, hiccupping a bit from her tears. "We hardly ever talk about him, do you know that?"

"That's not true, Aimee! We did all that grief counseling."

"It's not the same," she said. "We talked to some outsider whom you paid."

"We can't let you know the bad stuff," whispered Sabrina. "Gotta stay upbeat."

Gus felt physically ill. She'd been expert at scraped knees and college applications and bad boyfriends, and she'd been justifiably proud of how she supported the family after Christopher died. But seeing her beautiful daughters crying before her was too much.

"That's not true," said Gus. "My whole world revolves around you two."

"No," Sabrina said glumly. "We're just stuck in your orbit. I told you I didn't want Troy around but you didn't care."

"I do care," said Gus, "and that's why I asked him on the show. You love him, I know you do."

"You talk a lot, Mom," Sabrina said. "Yabber, yabber, yabber. Always telling everyone what to do as if you have some secret recipe for happiness. Well, I can't be happy all of the time. And it doesn't make it easy to tell you about the bad stuff."

"So what do you want to tell me?" cried out Gus, though inside, her heart was breaking. Of all the things that had hurt over the years, her daughters' criticisms cut deep. She'd spent her entire life trying not to let them down. How strange, she thought, to be known publicly for being so nurturing and yet fail to comfort her own children. She felt naked. Disappointed.

Her instinct was to end the conversation, change the subject, and do something with her hands to keep busy. Let's bake a pie, she could imagine herself saying if they were at the house. Don't we all love banana cream? And they would have gone along. Glossed over things. It's what the Simpsons did. What they all did. She could see that now.

"I thought we were doing so well," she confided, reaching out. She held each of her daughters by the hand and squeezed gently.

"Okay, girls," she said, taking a deep breath and not caring that she'd begun to cry. "Lay it on and start at the beginning. We're going to figure this out. I don't know how. But we will."

They sat there, holding one another on the bed and sniffling a bit, bursting to talk and yet not knowing where to start. Over on the desk, Gus's cell began to ring, at the same time as there was a knock at the door. A voice called Gus's name.

It was Alan.

# 19

He'd rehearsed what he was going to say for the last hour. I've got good news, he'd say, and then hit her with the bad. Or perhaps he ought to just come right out with it. Alan had hired and fired, but he'd never had to do anything quite like this. Hell, he'd never had anything like this happen to him before.

"Hello, girls," he said, stepping into the room when Aimee opened the door. "I need a few minutes with your mother, please."

They'd clearly been crying; maybe they'd heard it from someone else?

"We're doing some family stuff right now, Alan, though it's nice to see you, as always." Gus was pleasant but cool. She and Alan had been in limited contact since her lunch with him almost two months ago. And the Octopus Incident had truly altered her impression of Alan.

"It's imperative we talk immediately."

"Alan, if this is about that game of tag this morning, I can assure no one was being particularly mean to Carmen," said Gus. "Whatever she might have told you."

"Uh, okay," he said. "I haven't seen Carmen yet but no doubt I'll hear all about it. That's not what I'm here to discuss."

Gus looked from Aimee to Sabrina to Alan, who all waited expectantly; she felt a strong sense of déjà vu.

"A family shouldn't have secrets," she told Alan. "You can talk to me in front of the girls."

"Up to you," he said.

And that's when the thought hit Gus: Alan was here to fire her. Carmen was getting the show to cook up all the overcomplicated dishes she wanted to. That's how it was going to come down: Carmen was sleeping with Alan and now Alan was going to crown her Cooking-Channel's Foodie Queen. Well, it didn't matter, did it? Gus was more than set, thank you very much. She'd tucked her pennies away with care. And now she could take her daughters and go get Hannah and say a firm goodbye to Gary Rose and his silly pseudo-therapies.

"I know what you're going to say," said Gus. "So don't bother."

"You do?" Alan appeared visibly relieved. "Did you get the call?"

"So that's why my phone has been ringing?" Gus picked up her cell phone from the desk and flipped it open.

"18 missed calls" was displayed on the screen.

"Couldn't wait to tell me, could you?"

"I just phoned once, but I didn't leave a message."

"That would have been tacky," Gus said. "Don't you think?"

"Yes, I do," said Alan. "Look, I'm really sorry. I feel responsible in a way."

"In a way?" Gus was incredulous. "That's rich."

Alan laughed bitterly. "Or something," he said. "It's happened to me, too."

"Oh, please, Alan," said Gus. "I don't think it's quite the same."

"No, it isn't," he said. "I still own the channel. That's cushioned the blow."

Gus appraised Alan closely. "I could just quit, make it easy."

"What? First off, we have a contract. And second of all, what are you going to live on?" Alan looked around the room, then picked up the ice bucket and handed it to Sabrina, motioning that she should get some ice. Aimee joined her, hoping to give her mother some privacy with Alan.

"It's the shock, that's all," he said. "Let's get you a drink."

Rummaging through the minibar, he pulled out a selection of tiny bottles.

"What's your poison?"

"Don't be ridiculous," said Gus. "Those things cost a jillion dollars."

"It's on the CookingChannel," Alan said with a flourish. "C'mon, I'll make it a double."

"I thought I'd at least get a going-away party and a cake," spat out Gus. "After twelve years it's a drink from the minibar and the old heave-ho?"

"A triple," Alan said, as Sabrina came back with the ice. "Drinks all around."

"We're celebrating," Gus said to her daughter, feeling woozy even though she hadn't had a drop. "Alan is firing me but I'm quitting first."

"What?" said Aimee and Sabrina in unison.

"What the hell? Gus, have you seen the news today?"

"Hardly, Alan," Gus said, a bit primly. "I've been running around on the lawn in capri pants. By your decree."

"I only insisted on a weekend retreat, Gus," he said. "The capri pants were optional."

"I always thought I'd write a rather sentimental resignation letter," she was saying, more to herself than to anyone. "Something handwritten, about how much I've loved the CookingChannel and how it's changed my life. But that it was time to move on. Kisses and hugs and all of that."

"Did your mother hit her head out there this morning?" Alan asked Sabrina.

"It's been a rough day in general," said Aimee.

"We'd have a clip show, all the bloopers. The kettle fire, of course." Gus continued to talk. "That would have been fun."

"Focus, Gus, focus!" Alan was shouting. He put a tumbler filled with an amber liquid in her hand. "Whiskey. Now drink up."

"Why not, right, girls?" Gus tilted her head and gulped down the entire thing.

"Holy crap," said Alan. "Slow down there, cowgirl."

"You can't tell me what to do anymore," said Gus. "You are not, as they say, the boss of me. Anymore."

"Yes, I am," Alan said. He grabbed the remote control and flicked on a twenty-four-hour news channel, which had a "Breaking News" graphic flashing on the screen.

"*Looks like a lot of your favorite TV and Hollywood stars are out of a heckuva lot of cash,*" the perky newscaster in a blond helmet/hairstyle was saying. "*Turns out that popular money manager David Fazio was a con artist. Federal agents have been investigating—*" Alan pressed the mute button.

"You're not out of a job, Augusta." He soberly poured her another glass of whiskey. "You're out of a lot of money. And so am I."

"I beg your pardon?"

Aimee adjusted the TV to closed captioning, so she could read what the announcer was saying. It appeared that her mother's investment manager had stolen from an impressive list of trusting celebrities. He, and the cash, had vanished.

"Here's the deal: David Fazio has taken all our money and is sitting on a beach in Brazil with a floozy in a thong." Alan added more ice to his glass.

"What?"

"Maybe she's a brunette," Alan said drily. "Maybe it's the French Riviera. Either way, he's run off with our cash."

"Go slower," Gus said, sinking into a chair. "Though I'm quite sure you're mistaken. Last year I got a twenty percent return."

"So did a lot of people. That return wasn't from your money being invested," Alan said. "It was simply taken from the new dumb schmuck investors who wanted to work with the guy who was the money manager to the stars."

"I'm, I'm . . ." Gus found herself at a loss for words. Aimee came over and stood behind her, rubbing her shoulders.

"Your money isn't sitting in a bank somewhere, Gus, nor mine, either," he said. "It never was. He's been using it, spending it, all along."

"But the statements . . ."

"Fake," Alan said, coming around with little bottles to top up everyone's drinks.

"Alan, I've been David's client since you introduced us. And he's beaten the stock market every year. I had some trouble reaching him this morning but this news makes no sense," she said.

"Fazio played us all," he explained. "He used our funds to try and attract new clients with expensive parties and flashy dinners, then, once he had their money, too, he took it all."

"I can't believe this," she said. "How did you find out?"

"The story broke this morning. Some reporter called me for background. And let me assure you, there are far bigger names caught in this guy's trap than you and me."

Alan squatted on his heels to be at Gus's eye level. "Call your lawyer immediately," he said, ticking off an imaginary list with his fingers. "Aimee, I want you to help your mother take stock of what's where. Go through her papers. The good thing is that you've got the house, and you've still got the show."

"There's only a handful of episodes left in this ridiculous miniseason you ordained," said Gus. "Then what?"

"Then anything you want," said Alan. "You're a smart one, Gus. Use this anger to fuel the show to new heights of ratings glory."

"How?"

"Hey, I'm just the president of the channel." Alan stood up. "You're the creative around here."

"What about Carmen?"

"She adds a certain spice to the show, don't you think? I've made a lot of mistakes but she's not one of them."

"So you're serious about her, then?"

Alan shrugged. "I guess," he said. "But right now I've got to focus on the situation at hand. We both just lost a heckuva lot of zeros and I'd like to make some back."

Chutes and Ladders. That was the game Sabrina had been trying to remember for Gary. Going up one, two, three spaces and then oops, all the way back down.

The memory of Christopher playing with the girls came back to her swiftly, a sudden spark in her brain. Gus opened her eyes: she was under her covers, the curtains closed. Was it night? she wondered, until she looked at the clock and saw it was only 4 PM. There was a faint scent of whiskey, wafting from the half-empty glass on the bedside table, and she recalled Alan, and the news, and her rapid drinking without benefit of lunch. Aimee and Sabrina had tucked her in, she recalled, and it had felt nice, being looked after. It reminded her of long ago.

Her head throbbed.

Christopher had been enthusiastic about Chutes and Ladders but would always—always—manage to turn the spinner so that he could land on a chute before he got to the top and then slide, slide, slide down behind the two of them. "I don't believe in teaching my girls how to lose," he would say over her protests. "I want them to be outrageously confident."

Christopher had wanted her to be outrageously confident, too. Would he have been surprised to see her on television? She thought so early on but as she'd gotten older she'd come to suspect that maybe he wouldn't have been surprised at all. His belief in her success never wavered, and he'd seen her through all her various attempts at different careers, when she was still intent on figuring out what it all meant. Life.

He'd converted part of the basement to a darkroom so she could do her own prints, putting in a sink and everything, and stayed up all night helping put the wicks into the swirly multicolored candles she made in her kitchen and sold in a nearby boutique. She had imagined a line of housewares even then, she thought wryly, not wishing to get out of bed now.

All that, even after he'd abandoned his career ambitions in journalism to make supporting her and the girls his number one priority.

"You gotta do what you gotta do," he would say.

She appreciated it, inasmuch as she needed to eat and sleep and buy shoes for the girls, but secretly she had judged him for giving up so easily. She'd lacked compassion, she could see that now.

In the weeks after he died, she focused bitterly on all the ways in which he was difficult. How he was often late for work, and how he interrupted her when he felt she'd gone on too long.

It had been simpler somehow, to hate him for abandoning her. What she hated most of all was the knowledge, deep within her bones, that he had taken so much of her happiness away with him. That even those moments of sheer joy—when Aimee won a soccer game, when Sabrina won the lead in the school play—would be accompanied by the twist in her stomach and the inevitable guilt. She hated him for leaving her behind, and she hated herself for all the moments she had been petty and selfish with him.

She hated him for not being able to forgive her. For not being able to make her feel better. For leaving it all up to her. Gus had not been able to see her way to the future but stumbled blindly forward because there was no other direction to go.

Her dream, when she'd been studying photography at Wellesley, wasn't to open a gourmet shop that sold sandwiches and soup. But she liked running The Luncheonette well enough and the family still needed to eat and sleep and wear shoes. Ironic, really, as it gave her an entirely different insight into Christopher. He was always very good to talk to about things. He'd have had good advice about how to deal with his death.

Eventually it became hard, really, to remember any of the bad. Nothing he'd done seemed so terrible anymore.

She even forgave him for dying.

Gus became a better mother—more organized, more efficient, more capable—than she'd ever been in the years beforehand. She pledged to Christopher that she would keep their daughters safe and happy, no matter what.

Only now, apparently, they weren't.

And the money was all gone.

It was as though she'd landed on a giant chute and slid, unable to stop, all the way back to where she'd been twenty years ago, with two emotional daughters and financial woes and nothing but questions and uncertainty. Wash, rinse, repeat: her life on an endless spin cycle.

"Oh, God help me," Gus said aloud. "We're broke."

# spilled milk

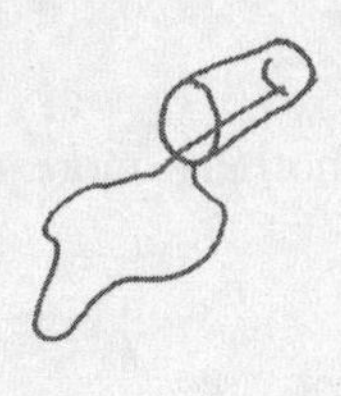

# 20

The rest of the group had loitered in the lobby for a while after Gus went upstairs with her girls, a residue of awkwardness in the air.

Hannah, who'd pulled up the hood on her sweatshirt, had whipped a pack of Fruit Stripe gum out of her pocket. She packed an entire duffel of treats, just in case she stayed for the weekend. Just in case she had to hide out in her room.

Oliver had a piece, even going so far as to try to put the temporary tattoo from the bubblegum wrapper onto his skin. Carmen declined and went off in search of carrots, she said, though Troy seemed to waver.

"No thanks," he said. "I'm kind of anti-candy. Vending competition and all that."

"Right, of course," Hannah said, thinking of the Velvet Crumbles and Aeros and Flake bars she had waiting upstairs. Her years on the tennis circuit had left her with a strong desire for international candy.

She popped two sticks of gum into her mouth.

"I'll have yours, then," she said to Troy.

"Damn," he said. "I was just about to change my mind."

Oliver showed off his tattoo of a striped zebra. "I think I like the gum with the jokes better," he said.

"Bazooka Joe," said Troy. "Don't let Gary hear us or we'll get caught sharing candy memories."

"That was intense today," said Oliver. "It was a lot to handle."

"You're worried about Gary Rose?" Hannah tried to blow a bubble.

"Not so much," said Oliver. "But I can imagine there's some serious chatter going on upstairs."

"That was hard on Sabrina," said Troy.

"And Gus," said Hannah.

"And Aimee," said Oliver. "All three of them. They've lived through some rough stuff."

He looked again at his tattoo. "How long does this thing last?" he asked Hannah.

"If you don't go near water, possibly a day," she said. "Maybe even two."

"Good enough," he said. "I want to put one on my other hand. See if anyone notices."

"Whatever you say, man," said Troy. "You're unusual."

"Nah," Oliver said. "Just a free spirit." He waved behind him as he went off to get something to eat from the lunch buffet.

"Well, that leaves just us," said Troy. "I can't promise they have more bubblegum in the dining room but we could grab a bite. I'd love some company. Sabrina's up with her mom."

"No, I can't go in there," said Hannah. "Too many people."

"But we're standing right here in the lobby," Troy said. "You aren't invisible."

"I'm harder to recognize with the hood," Hannah explained.

"Um, only in your own mind. Look, I hate to eat alone. Let me go in, get a couple of sandwiches, and then we can take them outside. Find somewhere to hide and have some chow."

Hannah agreed because she loved being outdoors again and because, with Gus busy, she had no one else to talk to. It wasn't as though she and Carmen had become bosom buddies in a night, though Carmen had given Hannah a second toothbrush that she had packed. That was nice.

Troy returned with turkey on white, chicken salad on rye, and a nice selection of fruits.

"That's not candy," said Hannah. "I'm allergic."

"I got you something good." He pointed to the cans of soda sticking out of the pockets of his shorts.

"How can you drink cola? They have those in vending machines, too, you know."

"Shhh," said Troy, leading the way to the gardens. "I love pop. It's a nasty little problem I have."

Walking behind him, Hannah smiled to herself.

"I prefer to drink organic, made with cane sugar and all that," he said. "But a man's gotta have what a man's gotta have."

"Are we still talking about soda?"

"Right, right," he said, sitting down under a tree. "Gus would have told you all about Sabrina and me."

"Nope," said Hannah. "A little. Not a lot. She's good at keeping secrets." She tugged off her sweatshirt to get a little sun on her arms. "Case in point."

"Man, do I ever remember you!" Troy said. "I was big into tennis when I was a kid. And you were all over the sports pages."

"Uh, thanks?" Hannah leaned against the trunk. "Don't think I've forgotten you're the one who outed me on live television."

"Sorry about that," said Troy. "I was just so excited. It's like finding out Martina Navratilova is my meter maid or something."

"Funny guy," said Hannah, getting herself settled so she could eat.

"You must be what now? Thirty-four?"

"You must be what? Rude?" She made a face. "I'm thirty-six. You can confirm that on Wikipedia."

"Actually, you look pretty young," he said. "All that sugar must be preserving you or something. I'm thirty-four. Do I look it?"

"No. You look forty." She took a big bite of the chicken salad.

"I do not," he said. "I play pickup basketball whenever I can. I wanted to be an NBA star."

Hannah narrowed her eyes and peered at him. "Exactly how tall are you?"

"Five-eleven," Troy said. "I coulda done it. If I'd been better."

She smiled.

"Basketball still owns my heart."

"And let's not forget Sabrina."

"Do you know she hates basketball?" he said. "Shocking but true."

"They say opposites attract," Hannah said. "Look, were you really into tennis?"

"Totally," he said, between bites of sandwich. "I went to tennis camp in the summer. It was the week after basketball camp."

"You liked it?"

"Loved it," he said. "I got a kick from getting out there and playing, just moving around. Always have."

"Me, too."

"My idol was John McEnroe. But I had a poster of you on my wall. You were like eye candy who could also kick ass."

"Okay," said Hannah. "I'll choose to be flattered. I think."

"You wouldn't have recognized me back then," said Troy. "I didn't grow until I was almost eighteen, and I had braces for years."

"Your teeth are pretty perfect," she said. "Good gums. I did a piece on the importance of healthy gums last week."

"Do you ever miss it? The sport, I mean."

"I like health reporting," she said. "But of course I miss tennis. It was my whole life."

"And it was lucrative."

"Yup," agreed Hannah. "I gave my entire life over to training to get there, too. Going pro doesn't come easy. Never had a piece of candy ever when I was training."

"And now you keep the Hershey company in business?"

"Look, I had to repay all the money I won—everything was under suspicion—and it wasn't easy. If a spoonful of sugar makes the medicine go down, so be it." She wiped her mouth with a napkin. "You do know that if you rat me out to the tabloids that Gus will make sure you never see Sabrina again, right?"

"Getting to the point," he said, nodding. "I like it. No worries. Besides, I'm pretty much beholden to Gus in general. She invested in FarmFresh when things were down to the wire. I operate on a shoestring budget."

"She's good people," said Hannah.

"You must be, too, if Gus likes you. And you did some pretty cool stuff when you were playing. I admire that."

"But how could I throw the games, right?"

"Your father asked you to do it."

"So why didn't I say no?" Hannah rubbed the bark of the tree. "That's what you want to know, I bet."

"He's your father," Troy said. "And he asked you. That's it. End of story. It's the only thing about you that isn't weird."

Hannah eyed him suspiciously.

"Okay, the stuff with the German girl, that was crazy, I'll grant you," he said, collecting his garbage. "But obeying your father? That's what a good kid does. I'd do anything for my old man."

"Yeah?"

"Sure," he said. "I still go back to Oregon every year to help with the harvest. And I'm running a frickin' company in New York City that could go under at any minute. Do you know what the failure rate is for start-up ventures? But I want to help my parents, so come harvest time, I'm chief picker in the orchard. Maybe more like chief foreman, but still. I'm there."

"Good for you," said Hannah. "Family is important."

"What about you?"

"I've got Gus. All anybody needs is one good friend. Then you can take on the world."

"One friend," he repeated. "It's hard to see how things are gonna go, isn't it? Like who would have guessed when you won your first Wimbledon that it would all end up like it did."

"You really should open a charm school," said Hannah. "Your talents are wasted selling fruit."

"Sorry again," said Troy. "I have this tendency to just blurt out. Comes from the whole adman brainstorming thing."

"Huh? I thought you were Mr. Fruity?"

"FarmFresh," he corrected. "Mr. FarmFresh."

"I know," groaned Hannah. "I've seen the T-shirts."

"I could give you one, you know."

"I'd like that. I could wear it while I run on my treadmill."

"You still work out?" Troy was surprised. "I mean, you look good and everything, it's just that you're constantly eating."

"Rock-solid metabolism," she said. "That, and I run for an hour every day."

"No way! How do you find the time?"

Hannah threw her head back and laughed, a deep, throaty sound. "Newsflash, fruitboy," she said, slowing her words for emphasis. "I . . . never . . . leave . . . the . . . house."

"Well, you're not in the house right now," Troy said, jumping up. "Let's go do something. How about canoeing?"

"How about canoe *races*?"

"You should know a man has a stronger upper body," said Troy. "And I play pickup basketball every chance I get."

"Well, you should know I do fifty push-ups when I get off that darn treadmill," Hannah said. "And I'm not talking girl push-ups, either.

"Wiry, smart, and lean," she added, waiting a beat.

"That's Hannah Joy Levine," finished Troy.

They raced down to the lake, whooping and hollering the entire way, and Hannah didn't even stop to put on her hooded sweatshirt.

The games resumed promptly in the afternoon, with Aimee and Sabrina, who had made such a scene in the morning, seeming curiously chummy to the rest of the crowd. They made a point to sit together in the circle, though Sabrina made sure to get a seat next to Troy, who leaned over and spoke to her for a few moments when she came in. He could tell that she'd been crying again.

"Where's Gus?" Carmen asked. It wasn't like her to be late, though in truth Carmen wasn't worried. She simply didn't want Gus to get any special treatment that she wasn't getting.

"Not here," Gary said. "Now quit being nosy."

Sabrina and Aimee shared a glance: had Alan said something?

"I just want to know if she's at the spa," insisted Carmen.

Gary ignored her. "Good news, everybody: we're being joined by Porter later this afternoon. So don't worry that we won't have enough people for our games."

"Can't we just write essays?" Aimee, drained from the day's events, was not in a mood to play. "I feel like I've pretty much reconnected with my childhood."

"Next thing you know we're going to be passing Life Savers on toothpicks," grumbled Sabrina.

"Hey, gang, Sabrina's suggested a game," cried Gary. "Let's make Sabrina feel valued by playing it."

"No, I didn't mean that, you—" Sabrina was frustrated. "A person can't even make a comment without you using it against them."

"Am I using it against you, Sabrina? Or am I listening to you?" Gary bobbed his head up and down as though reaching an ah-ha moment.

"I'm up for this," Troy called out. "If I play with Sabrina." He winked at Hannah.

"Go get her, tiger," she said, making a squidgy sound with her loafers. She remained half-wet from her canoe adventure but she felt more comfortable than she had in ages.

"Put me next to Oliver," purred Carmen.

"Alan's in the building," blurted Aimee. "You might want to think about that."

"He is?" Carmen asked. "How come I'm the last to know? Is he at the spa?"

"Enough, enough," said Gary. "Form up in pairs—Aimee and Sabrina, you can't be together—and we're going to practice making recipes."

"Okay," said Oliver. "But won't Carmen and I have an advantage?"

"Good point," said Gary. "You two can't be together, either. We'll go with Aimee and Oliver, Sabrina and Hannah, Carmen and Troy."

"Let's do a seviche," Carmen said. "Get up, Troy, let's go to the kitchen."

"No, no, gang," Gary said. "We're not cooking." He held up several sheets of paper. "I'm going to cut up some written recipes here, mix them up in this paper bag, and then each team has to put the recipe back together. When you're finished, yell '*Bon appétit!*'"

"Oh my God," Aimee said. "I didn't believe we could actually do anything more stupid than this morning but I think we're on track to do just that."

Oliver leaned over and whispered in her ear, causing her to laugh.

"All set there, kid?" asked Gary.

"Indeed," she said.

It was a simple exercise, really: allow yourself to fall backward into someone else's arms and assume—hope—you'll be caught. Gary explained the instructions with the excitement of a four-year-old going to a birthday party.

"This is worse than detention," Aimee hissed to Sabrina.

"You never had a detention," she replied. "That's just sitting around. This is like a version of hell."

However, after an afternoon of endless activities, including having to explain what type of vegetable each person would be and why, even the arrival of Alan and Gus and Porter couldn't perk up the atmosphere. Her daughters watched closely as Gus walked gingerly into the room and took a chair without comment. But Gary's lack of commentary resulted in highlighting Gus's sudden appearance.

Hannah changed seats with Carmen so she could sit next to her friend, and Carmen neither complained nor refused.

"It makes me nervous when Carmen isn't a bitch," said Aimee to her sister.

"C'mon, gang, let's stand up and get going," said Gary, interrupting her thoughts. "It's our last game before you're off for the night."

"I'm up for it if we're getting out of here," said Oliver. "Somebody catch me. Anybody."

"Don't you want to know who's behind you, Oliver?" Gary asked.

"Don't care," he said. "I just want to get out of here."

The group tittered as Gary held a finger to his lips. "This is no joking matter," he said. "We're going to learn how to trust each other."

"Falling into someone's arms doesn't tell you about trust," said Hannah. "It just tells you that they won't drop you when other people are watching. There's a difference."

Gary pointed to Carmen, Gus, and Porter, and motioned them closer.

"Wait your turn, Oliver," said Gary. "Okay, Carmen, close your eyes and when I tell you, I want you to let yourself fall backward into Gus and Porter's waiting, wonderful arms." He rubbed his hands with glee. "Everyone else, gather round and offer her words of encouragement."

Alan leaned forward eagerly in his chair.

"You can do it, Gus," he said.

"Don't you mean 'You can do it, *Carmen.*'" Carmen's mouth was turned down in a prettyish pout.

"Of course," Alan said. "You'll both be great."

"I'm not sure this should be required," started Aimee.

"We're good, we're good," murmured Gary. "Go for it, Carmen."

A flash of scenarios ran through Carmen's head, all of which had her landing on the floor. Hard.

"These people wouldn't unfreeze me during tag," she said. "That was only this morning. And now I should let them catch me? You're nuts, Gary. Naive."

"Porter, would you drop Carmen?" he asked.

"No, she's a great asset to *Eat Drink and Be,*" he said.

"And Gus, would you drop Carmen?"

"No, I would not," she said. "It wouldn't be appropriate."

"There you have it, Miss Vega," said Gary. "Gus and Porter have pledged to offer you a safe landing."

Carmen whirled around to face Gus.

"Are you sure?"

"I'll catch you, Carmen."

"Why should I believe you?"

For the first time in her life, Carmen did not want to be watched. Standing in the center of the crowd, with each person waiting—to see her drop, to see her fall down—was more pressure than she could ever have imagined. More than anyone else, Gus had no motive to want Carmen to succeed. Everybody—even the viewers—could sense the tension between the two of them. So how crazy would she have to be to free-fall on the vague promise that Gus wouldn't let her down? Carmen hadn't gotten to where she was in her career by letting go.

"If you replace Gus with Oliver, I'll do it," she said.

"Oh, no," Gary said. "This isn't a contract discussion. There's no negotiating here."

"So what happens if she doesn't go?" Sabrina was desperate to get out of the room. Billy had called; he was upset when she let it slip that Troy was at the resort with them. Billy rarely got angry, she had to admit, but he'd been very unhappy that she hadn't been forthcoming.

"We stay here until she does," said Gary.

"That's not fair," said Hannah. "She'll never do it. She's afraid to muss herself."

All her life, Carmen thought, she had never given in to fear. And she wasn't about to start now.

"*Madre mía*," whimpered Carmen as she covered her ears with her hands. She just didn't want to hear when she hit the ground. "Call the chiropractor, call the doctor," she yelled, as she took gulpfuls of air into her lungs and used every ounce of discipline and courage she'd ever experienced—her first teetering steps on a runway, the call to the culinary school admissions office, that overwhelming moment when she walked into Gus's manor house and thought her heart would pound out of her chest—and simply let go.

She expected a whoosh, a feeling of wind on her cheek, but instead all that was there was a glorious nothingness. A speck of time, really, when it felt as though she was wildly, fantastically out of control, knowing she'd gone too far to pull back. "Ay, *Dios mío*," she said silently to herself, and it was more of a prayer than any she'd said in years.

And then Carmen could feel Porter and Gus holding her, their bodies strong around her, as they dipped back with her slightly from the force of her fall, and then brought her upright. The relief and adrenaline whooshed through her body, making her feel tingly and . . . powerful. It was almost better than sex.

"*Genial!*" she screamed, running around the group and bopping anyone within reach in the arm. "I did it!" Carmen pumped her arms in the air as though she'd just won a James Beard award. "Me, me, me!

"Did . . . you . . . see . . . that," she shouted in Alan's direction. "I am awesome!"

Porter grabbed Gus in a one-arm hug. "Good job, lady," he said. Gus was pleased and strangely exhilarated herself, and surprised, most of all, by the warm feeling she had seeing Carmen so happy. Now that, she told herself, was unexpected.

Gary was wiping tears from his face. "You guys fulfill me so much, gang," he said. "Does anyone want a group hug?"

"No, no, no," Troy said, backing away from the puffy redheaded man.

"Okay, Troy," replied Gary. "Go next. You should fall into Sabrina and Hannah's arms. Whenever you're ready."

"She's going to drop me because I beat her in the lake," said Troy, grinning. "It's going to be up to you to save me." He locked eyes with Sabrina. "I'm counting on you."

Sabrina nodded and tucked her long black hair behind her ears. Hannah bent her knees and hopped on the balls of her feet, as though waiting for a serve.

"Go for it, mister," said Hannah, as Troy crossed his arms in front of him like an Egyptian mummy. He pressed his eyelids together and leaned back, keeping his legs taut to fight the urge to step back to stop his descent. His stomach was in his throat as he began to fall but he held fast, confident.

He had great faith in Sabrina. He always had.

It was happening before she was ready: Sabrina's arms wanted to leap away—she could feel them jerking internally. Whammo! Troy would fall cleanly to the floor. Would he cry? She didn't know. But the urge not to catch him was overwhelming. No one asked me if I wanted this, she thought. I never said you should trust me. Her body was in another direction before she was even aware of it moving, stepping sideways toward Hannah and knocking her off-balance.

"No!" Troy heard Hannah's voice in his ear in the same instant as a searing pain cracked his shoulders and head. "Holy shit," hollered Gary, running over to Troy. "I've never had this happen before."

Gus was already by his side, cradling his head in her lap and worrying over him.

"You okay, fella?" Porter asked, his face looming overhead, fuzzy.

Troy waved weakly, then moaned and rolled over onto his side.

"I think it's time we called it a day," said Porter.

Gary did not resist. And Gus, though fretting over Troy and highly alarmed by Sabrina's behavior, was rather grateful the game was over. She'd never have been able to fall backward with her eyes closed. She'd learned her lesson from the day's events.

Gus was never going to trust anyone again.

Barely three hours later, Sabrina knocked on the door to Troy's room. The light was still on, she rationalized, so a visit wouldn't wake him up. She could hear his footsteps as he came closer, could see the peephole get dark as he looked through it.

"Come to poison me or something?" He spoke through the door.

"Let me in," said Sabrina. "I want to apologize."

Troy poked his head into the hallway. "I think I have a concussion," he said. "I have to stay awake for the next several hours."

"Are you alone?"

"No," he said.

"No, really," Sabrina said, trying to crane her neck and look inside. "Can I come in?"

"No," he said.

"I just want to talk," she wheedled. "I think I'm confused."

"No kidding," Troy said, before closing the door. He hesitated a moment and then, holding his breath, he turned the lock.

# 21

Sabrina wandered the hallways for a while, shuffling up and down the carpeted corridors until she flopped down on a bench near the elevator bank. She smiled thinly at the happy couples who came and went, loving on each other.

It was rather gross, actually, when you weren't the one doing the kissing. Seeing them slobber all over each other.

Talking with Troy would have made her feel better. He'd surprised her by not letting her in. And he'd lied, too. Lied about not being alone.

Just goes to show you. You think you know a person only to find out you don't. Not really.

Returning to her room was not an option: no doubt Billy had been calling her there. Her cell phone was back there, too, though she'd turned it off hours ago. It was unlikely that her fiancé appreciated being sent directly to voice mail. He was always saying the most important thing in a relationship was mutual respect—and no doubt he was feeling that he wasn't getting it. Best to avoid him altogether, then.

Sabrina had never done well with demands.

But it wasn't as though she would have gone back to her room anyway. There was no one else there.

Sleeping had always been difficult. Ever since she could remember. Drifting off was easy but after a few hours, she'd be awake again and all alone. Sabrina hated the middle of the night.

There was only one place to go. The same place she always went. Because there was comfort in old habits. She ambled down the corridor, playing the old "I'm fine" game with herself. The rules were simple: she merely had to repeat those same words over and over. In less than a minute, she had come to the room where she should have known, really, that she'd end up.

"I'm fine," she said aloud.

Her sister, wearing a T-shirt and pajama bottoms, flung open the door as if on cue. She said nothing, merely walked back into the room and sat down at her desk. Papers were spread all around her laptop and it was clear that she had been working. Aimee continued to focus on her computer without a word to Sabrina.

"I'm fine," repeated Sabrina, kicking off her shoes and crawling onto Aimee's bed. "Troy didn't want to talk to me."

Aimee shrugged.

"I don't know why I did it," she said. "Are you working on Mom's stuff?"

"Uh-huh."

"Is it bad?"

"Not good."

"So I guess I shouldn't ask her about my wedding, then," said

Sabrina. "Though maybe the planning would take her mind off things."

Aimee didn't answer. After a few moments of silence, Sabrina flicked on the TV. The eleven o'clock news was on, and, sure enough, the third segment covered the money manager who'd been stealing from all his big-name clients.

"We should call Mom, maybe," said Sabrina.

"She wanted to take a bath and go to sleep," said Aimee. "I spoke to her a few hours ago."

"Right, okay."

"It's time you were put on a budget," said Aimee. "Tighten your belt a little bit."

"Okay." Sabrina was used to Aimee's criticisms.

"No, really."

"Wanna do face masks? I've got the stuff in my room."

"Nope."

"Okay, I'll just go get it." Sabrina dashed out but turned the dead bolt so the door didn't close behind her. "So you don't have to get up again," she explained.

Aimee watched her exit. In about twenty minutes, she knew, her face would be green with cucumber mush. Or Sabrina would read aloud from a quiz she'd found in a magazine, trying to determine what guy was Aimee's right type. It was what they did when there was too much to say.

Sabrina used her back to shove open the door. "I brought hair goo," she said. "We can make ourselves glossy and gorgeous."

"I don't do gloss," said Aimee. She knew her lines. They'd had years of practice, years of Sabrina scurrying over the tape that ran down the middle of their shared bedroom when it was late. Go back to sleep, Aimee had grumped then, even as she slid over to make room. You can't stay here all night. But of course she let her: Sabrina was the baby. And then she had dragged her back to her bed in the morning, before Gus opened the door to wake them up. Morning, Mommy, she'd said. We're fine. We're all fine.

Aimee didn't look up from the screen as Sabrina started rummaging through her sister's suitcase. "Do you have an extra sweatshirt?" she asked, even as she had it in her hands. "I brought my pj's."

Sabrina was infuriating, of course. She was needy and spoiled and had an unwavering ability to be self-involved. It surprised Aimee, sometimes, just how much she could hate her, the anger that welled up inside when Gus was fawning over yet another of her sister's indiscretions. And then, with equal intensity, she'd worry about the way Sabrina bounced around, always reacting to her emotions, never thinking anything through. She just went along with anyone who was nice to her.

Aimee had watched her like a hawk when they were young, following Gus on her errands at the mall or the grocery store. Sabrina, she suspected then, might just become distracted and walk off, getting herself lost or stolen by some stranger. Disappearing and leaving them heartbroken and all alone. And then what?

"Do I really suck all the oxygen out of the room?" Sabrina asked, opening jars, and Aimee felt a wash of guilt run through her.

"I never said that," she mumbled, submitting to the slathering of the cold green lotion on her face, grateful for a reason not to speak.

"Yes, you did," said Sabrina. "You might be right. Who wants to be around that?"

She continued talking—about Billy, about Troy, about the discussion with their mom—as she administered to Aimee, whose hair was slicked back under a shower cap, absorbing the proteins and nutrients that were supposed to make her brown hair shine.

"Do you think it's possible to love one man and still want another?" Sabrina asked.

"I guess," said Aimee. "But you've got to stop comparing guys. They're not always interchangeable, you know."

"A lot of it is the same in the beginning," said Sabrina. "Sharing the excitement of getting to know each other. New sex."

"TMI," Aimee said. "What I don't get is why they all put up with you."

"Billy says he likes me because I'm creative and I take risks," Sabrina said proudly. "He's actually very encouraging."

"Well, I'm not very optimistic about what you're doing to my hair," said Aimee.

Sabrina pretended not to hear. She enjoyed pampering her older sister in ways that Aimee would never make time for on her own. In middle school, she'd once bedazzled Aimee's book bag with gold and orange sequins. The gesture had not been appreciated.

"Do you think I'm lovable?" she asked, and Aimee couldn't say a word, her face genuinely tight from the hardened cream.

She'd never have given her sister a straight answer anyway. That would have been too much. Instead, she would have admonished Sabrina for fishing for compliments. She knew it. Being kind felt too much like weakness sometimes. And Aimee had worked hard to be brave.

She headed to the bathroom to rinse off, returning to find Sabrina tucked into the bed. She'd stolen the extra pillows, leaving Aimee with just one on her side.

"Typical," she said, clicking off the light. The computer screen still glowed over on the desk.

"You're glad I'm here, right?" asked Sabrina.

"No," said Aimee. "And no snoring. I hate when you do that."

# 22

When Sunday morning arrived, it seemed to Gus as though a lifetime had gone by since playing tag even though it had only been twenty-four hours. She'd barely slept all night, worried about her daughters, her finances, her future.

"You're fine, you're fine," she told herself, a familiar refrain she used to repeat to herself when she cleaned the house after a long day at The Luncheonette. The puffy face she saw in the mirror proved otherwise.

She dressed quickly, or at least she tried to, but somehow she ended up being the last person down to the lobby. Everyone was milling about until Gary Rose came bustling up, his clipboard swinging. Close on his heels was a plumpish, dark-skinned woman, her hair pinned in an updo.

"I see you found us a yoga expert," Troy said to Gary. He had a huge lump on his head but was fine otherwise.

"Who is the yoga teacher?" asked the woman.

"Not you?"

"No, no, I am Priya Patel," she said, beaming broadly. "I am Gus Simpson's biggest fan."

"The contest winner," prompted Porter. "You know, the new participant on *Eat Drink and Be*. In our effort to make things smoother on set, Alan and I decided it would be best that you all meet Priya before we shoot again. We don't want any personality conflicts on air."

Carmen snickered.

Porter cleared his throat. "Priya, welcome. Everybody..."

"Hello, Priya," said the group in unison. They'd been well trained after a day with Gary.

"So you must be good at karate," she said to Troy, who looked at her strangely. "Well, you assumed I am good at yoga; I am assuming you are good at karate."

"That's stupid," he said.

"Quite precisely yes," said Priya.

"Point taken," said Troy. "So we can be bad at yoga together. I've never done it before."

"Oh, no, I'm very good at yoga, in fact," Priya said. "They offer it at my gym. It's free with the membership."

"But I thought you just said that—"

"Just making a point. One must never assume."

"I have a feeling," Gus said, walking over to join Priya and Troy, "that you'll quite enjoy your hour on the show with us, Priya. I think you'll fit in just fine."

After they had all properly twisted and turned their way through various poses, Gary had an instructor take the "gang" on a group hike through a beautiful section of forest.

"You should know where your buddy is at all times," he explained. "We don't want anyone wandering off now."

Priya was quite excited to see Gus waving at her. Would the two of them become buddies? She could think of nothing more splendid. "And then we went walking together," she could imagine herself saying to Raj later that night. "She loved my recipe for banana mousse pie, said it sounded delicious." And he would be impressed and agree, finally, that it was a very good thing for her to be on television. You were right, he would say, to apply to that contest even when I told you not to.

She waved back vigorously.

"Did you meet Hannah at yoga?" Gus asked Priya as she neared. "Why don't the two of you do the hike together?"

The redheaded woman in the ponytail and hooded sweatshirt smiled shyly.

"Hi," she said softly. "Do you know who I am?"

"Of course!" Priya watched with disappointment as Gus was paired off with the tall, bald man. Now what would she tell Raj? "You're the one who put out the fire," she said to the redhead. "I watched that segment several times."

The last thing she wanted was for anyone to think she hadn't been paying attention.

"I used to play tennis," pressed Hannah.

"Well, that's very nice," Priya said, trying to keep an eye on Gus as the entire group moved farther away from the resort's buildings. She was relieved when the bald man handed Gus a red ball cap and she put it on. It looked very cute with her bob, Priya thought, and made her much easier to spot. "Exercise is good for you."

"I used to play professionally," Hannah said, feeling ever more confident that this woman not only had no idea who she was but simply didn't care.

"Do you know that we will typically have over five different careers in our lifetime?" replied Priya. "That's from a study I read on the Internet."

"How many have you had?"

"Two," said Priya. "I used to be an engineer before I had kids."

"You're a stay-at-home mom?"

"Yes. It's very important work, very necessary and therefore fulfilling." Her voice was flat and she sounded as if she was reading a speech off an index card.

"Well, you certainly seem . . . happy," Hannah said weakly.

"How did you get on the show?" Priya asked abruptly.

"I live next door to Gus."

"Really?" Priya stopped walking. "That must be wonderful, living next to Gus. Do you go to her world-famous parties?"

"I don't know if they're *world* famous, but I've been to a few. I don't really get out that much, though."

Up ahead, Oliver was pointing out a red bird in a tree to Gus and she could hear Gus's laughter float all the way down the line of hikers, over Carmen and Aimee and Sabrina and Porter and Troy and Gary. That's what she needed, a little bit of Gus's joie de vivre that she could bottle up and bring back to Jersey, to sprinkle around when she was sad. She had never expected that being at home would be so much harder than working in an office. There were no promotions, no raises, no vacations. Just a group of people who wanted, wanted, wanted from her. No one had ever asked Priya if she wanted to be the heart of the home. It was simply her birthright. Her own mother had told her so.

Gus knew how to make a happy home: anyone could see that just by watching her on television. Priya had been surprised by how much she liked watching her because, up until the day she saw Gus on TV, she had strenuously avoided all those channels with perky hosts baking muffins and planning parties. But Gus was the real deal.

It was Raj's fault, really. He had left the television on because he thought it would help, the day after he'd found her lying on the floor of the walk-in closet, crying her eyes out. I don't know what's wrong, she told him, and he had sat down with her, right there in the closet, and held her hand. Don't worry, he said, the malaise will go. We'll just think good thoughts and the bad feelings will simply melt away. We can all afford a bit of patience, she had heard Raj tell her mother on the telephone, let's have a little wait-and-see.

But the feelings didn't go away. They hardened into an invisible lump that only Priya could feel, absorbing all the joy she knew she was supposed to be experiencing. Why couldn't she delight in all she had? Other women felt that way. Would look at her big tidy home and her healthy children and tell her to just get over herself. She'd said the same words to her mirror image a million times over. The disconnect between the truth in her heart and the way her mind told her she should be feeling left her exhausted and defeated.

"You're so lucky," she sighed. "To be able to have a friend like Gus."

"If we run, we could catch up to her," Hannah suggested, wanting mainly to savor this last chance to jump around in the open air. She felt conflicted, part of her brain craving the familiar routine back at the carriage house and the other part starting to feel angry that she'd frittered away so much time in hiding. "Let's move," she shouted, jogging on the spot.

"Oh, yes," Priya said, very glad she'd worn sneakers after all. She'd been nervous about getting dressed that morning, Raj nattering at her as she changed out of a navy suit and even considered wearing a sari. Certainly the email from Porter Watson had specified casual clothing but seeing as she was only coming up to the resort for the day—and it was to be her introduction to Gus—she had spent a long time choosing an outfit that seemed quite right. She's not really your friend, Raj had said, and she won't care what you wear, which Priya thought was more unkind than was necessary. Of course not, she'd told him, Gus hasn't even met me yet.

In the end, she opted for khakis and a long cardigan, just like the sweater Gus had worn on the last episode of *Eat Drink and Be*. She had recognized immediately when the show aired that Gus was trying out a bit of a different style, and Priya wanted very much to support her in her fashion choices.

"Let's move," she repeated, though Hannah was already far, far ahead.

Carmen watched Hannah dash on by, her ponytail bobbing as she weaved her way around the members of the group, followed a few beats later by the contest winner, her khakis straining a bit over her well-padded derriere.

"This isn't a race," she called out after them. She and Aimee had, without discussing anything, agreed to exert themselves as little as possible. They weren't about to jog an inch.

"I'm sure Hannah's running over to talk to my mom," said Aimee. "As usual."

"I don't know about you, but I can't wait until this weekend is over," Carmen said. Alan had left shortly after dinner, and she and Oliver had stayed up late in the bar, enjoying a good bottle of cabernet, talking about old times. She'd suggested a second bottle but he declined and went up to his room. Alone.

"You're burning a hole in the back of Oliver's head," said Aimee. "It wasn't my choice to be your partner, you know."

"Don't have a problem with you," Carmen said testily. She tilted her head toward Aimee. "What are you doing watching Oliver so closely anyway? Do you like him?"

"Yeah," said Aimee. "He's a good guy. I think he might work well with someone I know."

"Aha!" Carmen elbowed her in the ribs, rather aggressively, in an attempt at chumminess. "You mean yourself," she said. "Are you . . . interested? He and I go back a ways."

"No," said Aimee. "Not my type, really."

"He's good-looking. Likes to cook. Quite adventurous in the bedroom."

Aimee threw her a look of surprise. "Too much information here, thanks," she said.

"So who are you looking for, then?"

"Anyone who isn't a fan of my mother or in love with my sister," Aimee said. "And, seeing as that rules out a heckuva lot of people in New York, I'm pretty much single. And quite happy about it."

"Umm, yes," said Carmen. "'Happy' is in the dictionary next to your picture. With a big X over it."

"I am actually a very nice person when someone takes the time to get to know me," huffed Aimee. "I just have a lot of responsibilities."

"The UN stuff."

"Among other things. But that's how I know Spain produces thirty-six percent of the world's olive oil. I work in trade and development," Aimee explained.

"Very good," Carmen said. "You may just be the smart one out of this bunch of *idiotas*."

"I speak Spanish, too."

"*¿Ahora sí entiendes lo que digo?*"

"Yeah, I hear what you mutter in the kitchen," said Aimee. "Like when you called my mother a—"

Carmen held up a hand to stop her from speaking.

"It's unexpected," admitted Aimee. "You swear like a sailor."

"Well, what do you expect," Carmen said. "I spent years in beauty pageant dressing rooms."

Marching along at the front of the group, just behind the hike instructor, was Gus, Oliver's extra ball cap on her head. He'd noticed her squinting against the sun—she'd forgotten her sunglasses—

and promptly presented her with the hat. She always appreciated preparation.

"Slow down," Oliver said now. "Sunday is a day of rest."

But Gus couldn't stop moving, had to keep going to outrun all the fears and anxieties that had crept into her bones the previous night. Onward, she told herself, don't look back. It's how she'd dealt with it all before and it had worked, hadn't it?

She felt angry with Alan for setting her up with that damned investment adviser, had been too shocked to tell him so, though later she felt somewhat mollified knowing he was in the same sort of pickle. Aimee had delivered her a snapshot of what she'd found so far; all was not lost. It was just so much less than what she'd had a few days ago. No doubt it was all about numbers to her former money manager, but for Gus, being conned felt deeply personal.

Still, there was the manor house and some miscellaneous investments she'd made on her own over the years, more as an experiment than anything else, a savings account, and the chunk of insurance money she'd put aside for the girls' weddings and had continually rolled over in a certificate of deposit for the last eighteen years. A fluke, really, since she'd often considered cashing out the CD and turning it over to her financial adviser.

"It'll be okay, Mom," Aimee had said. "And if it isn't, you can come live in my room in the city." They'd laughed at that, a shared joke. Sabrina had felt left out then, she could see it in her face.

"Let me help, too," Sabrina had said but Gus demurred, pointing out Aimee's skill with numbers. Later, though, she'd wondered about that, knowing she'd have been less comfortable with her younger daughter knowing what was what. "There's no need for you to worry," she'd said. It had just seemed necessary, somehow, that Sabrina remain innocent and in need of babying.

"Saw the papers today," Oliver said, keeping pace with her. He pointed to a red bird hopping on a tree branch. "And I've asked that little fella to peck out that guy's eyes." He whistled and the bird flew away.

"Message transmitted. My buddy's off to the Cayman Islands to find and torture him," he said matter-of-factly. She laughed, though in truth she wouldn't have minded if something had befallen the crook who stole her money.

"It's all quite embarrassing, really," said Gus. "I'm not as smart as I thought I was."

"Nah," said Oliver. "Never feel bad for being swindled. Scam artists are pros."

"You handled other people's money. Were you ever tempted?"

"No. It wasn't mine to take. You must have serious delusions to want something that isn't yours."

"Well, I've lost all my leverage with Alan," confided Gus, a nice achy feeling creeping into her legs. She hoped she'd be able to sleep that night, that the day's exercise would knock her out. "Now I can't throw up my hands and threaten to abandon the show."

"No one believed that anyway," he said, offering her a sip from his water bottle. She declined. "You have too much pride in your work."

"Pride goeth before the fall." Her skin was starting to feel warm.

"You're still standing," he said.

"With no one to catch me if I collapse."

"Doesn't have to be that way."

"I'm sure I don't know what you mean," said Gus.

"Sure you do. I am asking you out. On a date."

Gus frowned. "I am your boss, you know."

"Okay, then I'll quit," he said. "Although I checked out the CookingChannel policy—there's no restriction."

"No one sent me the memo," she said.

"I have a lot of virtues," he continued. "Like being patient. When I want something, I have all the time in the world."

"Well, I don't. There's too much going on in my life right now. And besides, it simply wouldn't be appropriate. The end."

"Don't fall into that routine with me," said Oliver. "I see you behind the scenes, and frankly, I like the real Gus better. She's just as cute but far less proper." He leaned his head in close, which immediately sent every nerve in her body on alert. She took several quick steps to get ahead of Oliver; he kept pace. Don't talk, she told herself. Not a word.

"So you want real Gus, do you?" The fresh air and lack of sleep was going to her head, loosening her tongue before her brain cells transmitted the message to shut up. "What would you even know about real Gus? This isn't actually the life I'd planned to be leading, you know?"

Shut up, Augusta! Simply stroll silently the rest of the way. Just zip those lips.

"I didn't plan to become a widow in my thirties," she blurted. Oh my God, she was still talking.

"I didn't plan to become a TV star," she continued. "I didn't plan to become Carmen Vega's meal ticket. I didn't plan to go on Gare's little resort adventure. And I didn't plan to have someone else hatch my nest egg. So there!"

Ah, yes, giving the silent treatment. Clearly she was very good at it, she thought sarcastically.

"There's the life we dream," Oliver said, "the life we deserve, and the life we get. I'll take what I got over what I deserve any day."

"And now you're the sous chef philosopher," said Gus. "How clever. I don't want to encourage you any more or pretty soon you will want your own show. I've enough competition, thank you very much."

"I just want to savor what's on my plate," he said simply. "Maybe explore a relationship for a bit of seasoning."

"Not much flavor here, I'm afraid. My cupboard is pretty bare at the moment."

"Okay, okay," said Oliver. "Message transmitted. For now. But look, I really can offer you some solid advice about the money stuff.

Put you in touch with some people. Just don't let this guy take away anything more than what he's already stolen. Don't lose faith, Gus."

"Because I'll be fine, of course."

"You will."

"I hate that, you know, when people say that," she said. "It doesn't actually make me feel any better. But don't worry, I'm the champion of turning that frown upside down. That's what I do." Her tone was laced with sarcasm.

"I'm not trying to diminish anything you've faced," he said. "But you deal with everything with such grace. Another person would be crying and moaning about the theft, and instead you're out here doing yoga and hiking and putting me in my place. You're something to watch."

"Like yesterday's blowup with Aimee and Sabrina," she said. "That was so well handled, I almost popped a vein in my head."

She paused. "I apologize if I'm testy. It's just been a very bad weekend."

"You're great," said Oliver. "Every family has its issues. My own brother didn't call me after nine-eleven."

"That's terrible!"

"He checked in with my mother. And that was good enough for him. Peter had kind of written me off back then. But we've reconnected."

"You knew a lot of people downtown." It wasn't a question.

"Yeah, of course," he said. "It's part of being on Wall Street."

"Is this why you got into cooking?" she asked. "Most folks in your position might have invested in a restaurant rather than trying to work in a kitchen."

"I was already into food," he said. "But maybe a bit, yeah."

"I have this funny thought sometimes," admitted Gus. "That the people who die young get to escape the pain while the rest of us are left picking up the pieces."

"I'm sorry about your husband," said Oliver. "But that's not what defines you. Yesterday was awkward in the session but I think you've truly raised two nice girls."

"Far from perfect, I'm afraid."

"Aren't we all?"

"Excuse me, Gus?" It was Priya, huffing a bit as she jog-walked to get closer to them. She had the look that Gus knew all too well: the wide eyes and wistful expression, as though she believed Gus was going to impart some secret about life that only she knew. She'd met fans like that before, of course, but it wasn't just strangers who looked at her that way. Gus had seen that look on Aimee and Sabrina, sitting on the stairs waiting for her to bring their father home, and on Hannah the summer she kept dropping by with pies, and even on Troy, when she'd gone to visit him after Sabrina had stomped all over his heart. "Will you save me?" said the face. "Can you make it all better?"

What was funny was how easily she had slipped into the role when Christopher had always watched after *her*. Gus had been the coddled one and she hadn't even known it. But there was no warm-up, no practice session, just the sudden transition and Christopher there in the hospital bed and every decision was hers and hers alone. It got so that she almost welcomed the challenges and the crises, big and small, in the lives of those around her. She was very good at knuckling down and just getting on with it, Gus had learned, something her younger self would never have believed. She was very good at taking care. The bitter pill was that it took Christopher dying to finally figure things out. And she'd been spending years making it up to him.

She'd fretted that there hadn't been enough I-love-you's between them. Even though there had been plenty. She just wanted one more. One more "I love you," one more night together, even just one more minute. She would have accepted that, too, and gratefully. Gus made little changes—she stopped scattering her shoes across the closet floor and began using the rack Christopher had purchased—and she made big ones, sticking with a profession even as the novelty wore off. In a vague way, she'd had a notion that she could date again at some point, but she'd had no idea when that time might arrive.

"You'll know when you're ready," was something her mother used to say to her in the early years after Christopher died. But what if she didn't? What if she never did? She missed being with Christopher, ached for his hands on her, and was frankly freaked out by the thought of really feeling another man's touch. Even as the fantasy excited her.

Instead, she'd tried hard to fulfill all her longing for connection by nurturing everyone else. It had worked, for a while, but after eighteen years of being alone it wasn't satisfying in the same way. Still, she knew others continued to count on her.

"I'm so glad you're here, Priya," Gus said, rubbing the woman's arm very gently, and being rewarded with a flash of white teeth. "You have a lovely smile," she said, waving goodbye to Oliver and leaning in closer to hear every word Priya wanted to share.

They'd tramped around for more than two hours before they finally made it back to the lobby.

"Thank God you're back," said the resort manager. "We've got a dire emergency. Our chef's fallen ill and we have two hundred salespeople here for an executive conference. They've paid for a special tasting menu but he didn't write anything down."

"What happened?" Gus was genuinely concerned.

"He broke his leg falling off a trampoline," the manager said.

"Well, surely he can offer instructions from a chair," she said.

"No, he's been taken away in an ambulance. I know this is terribly inappropriate, seeing as you're a guest here, but I was hoping, Ms. Simpson, that you could do something for us?"

"Are your sous chefs still here?"

"Of course," said the manager. "They're familiar with the regular menu for the rest of the diners. But the conference attendees... I'll be blunt. They've paid extra for something special."

She conferred with Oliver. "We'll have to see what's in the kitchen but I suppose we could help out."

She motioned Gary to join them. "What are your plans this afternoon?" she asked the facilitator.

"Three-legged races," he replied.

"Yes, Oliver and I will cook for you," Gus said quickly. More games were definitely not on her agenda. "Hannah, run back and see if you can rustle up Carmen. She and Aimee are dawdling on the trail. The rest of you, I wish a pleasant afternoon with Gary."

Four hours later, Gus, Carmen, and Oliver shared a celebratory bottle to toast the best meal they had ever cooked on the fly: plates of a paella-inspired risotto with clams, salt-crusted trout with fennel, thinly sliced Wagyu beef with thyme butter, and a trio of cream puffs flavored with ginger, green tea, and chocolate-chili, among other dishes. Exhausted, they left Oliver behind, to meet up with Troy and finish their arcade game tournament, and headed over to the elevator, too tired even to find anything to bicker about.

It had been illuminating to watch Carmen really dig in and cook without commercial interruption, without cameras. Her pout was gone, replaced by a look of studious concentration, and she had chopped and minced and blended spices to create amazing bursts of flavor. The *sofrito* she had made, saucing together onion, tomato, and garlic in olive oil, had elevated the roasted chicken into a fragrant and unforgettable dish.

The men and women working the line in the kitchen had been shocked, initially, to see Carmen, Oliver, and Gus make their entrance, but in quick order everyone had gotten down to business. As a team. There were paying customers to be fed, after all.

It was, quite frankly, the first time she'd ever worked *with* Carmen and not just next to her. The rivalry remained, certainly, as they tasted and sampled and continually suggested to each other how to improve their dishes. But, for once, the food took precedence over personality. After all, there was no one watching: no Alan, no Porter, no millions of eyeballs on the other side of the camera.

The elevator came up from the lower-level ballroom and opened. Gus and Carmen stepped on in silence, exhausted from a day of yoga, hiking, and running around the kitchen. A thirtysomething man was already inside, slightly unsteady on his feet, his arm around an attractive blond woman who seemed somewhat off-kilter herself.

"Are you here for the sales conference?" The woman slurred her words, clearly tipsy.

"No, though I'm sure it's quite lovely," Gus said, moving to one side. Carmen looked at the floor, wishing for her bed.

"Hey, aren't you the broads from that cooking show?" The man elbowed the woman at his side as though she could have missed what he said. "Hey, hey, that's that Gus Simpson and Carmen Vega."

"Oh my God," the woman said, peering closer as Carmen shrunk back from the scrutiny.

"It *is* her," the woman said to her boyfriend/husband/colleague/whatever he was. "Gus has been around forever but that Carmen is completely obnoxious," said the man. "With that Spanish accent. Like we don't know she comes from Des Moines or something."

"I'm from *Sevilla*," Carmen said hotly, even as the couple continued yakking, oblivious to anything but themselves.

"And those fake boobs," said the woman. "All 'hi, how are you.'"

"Those are the only things I like," said the man.

The woman snorted. "Pig," she said, though she didn't seem the least bit unhappy. "I bet she can't even cook."

Gus cleared her throat. "You do realize, don't you, that we are standing about half a foot away from you?"

"It's all a scam anyway," the man said to his companion, ignoring Gus entirely, as though he was merely at home talking in front of the TV.

"Hello, real people over here," she said. "Yoo-hoo."

"I can't stand how they mix up the ingredients and then pull the finished pan out of the oven two seconds later," said the woman. "Like we don't know they cooked it ahead of time."

"Exactly!" said the man. "Anyone could be on a cooking show. I could do that and I can't even cook!"

His companion turned and addressed Carmen and Gus directly. "You two amateurs should get a real cooking job, like the chef at the resort here. Our dinner was fantastic."

"Let me guess," Gus said coolly. "You had the marinated crab with green apple and yuzu."

"Yeah," said the man. "How did you know?"

"Because Carmen and I just prepared that elaborate feast you and your friend here consumed," Gus said, her voice rising. "We diced and spiced every last mouthful."

"And Gus made the baked figs with port and cinnamon," Carmen said. "Did you eat that, too?"

"Yes," said the woman, shrinking back a little. "It was nice."

"It was goddamn delicious and I think you ought to say so," said Carmen, jabbing her finger in the woman's face. Gus quickly put a hand on Carmen's shoulder and pulled her back, just as the elevator door opened.

"Celebrities are such jerks," the man said, as he scurried out the door. "All we did was try and talk to them."

"And her boobs aren't fake!" Gus shouted to the retreating duo as the elevator doors began to close. She turned to Carmen. "Are they?"

# 23

It was well after midnight when a sheet of paper came sliding underneath Gus's door.

*Get a move on!* was written by hand in large green bubble letters.

Another game? Gary Rose was insufferable, the way he demanded everyone do what he wanted all the time, shoving notes into people's rooms.

She thought about staying put but she really didn't want to be the only one not there.

Gus skipped putting a robe over her emerald nightgown, tramping briskly to meet up with the group. Why hadn't he put this activity on the schedule? Gus marched through the gardens near the main building and found the tennis courts, walked past them until she had made her way down to the lake.

"I forgot to wear shoes," she said to Hannah, who was juggling tennis balls on the sand. Hannah shrugged, intent on her game.

"Mommy!" Aimee sounded urgent but her voice was faint. There she was, waving, all the way over on the other side of the lake. "I've lost Sabrina," she called.

Without hesitation, Gus dragged an abandoned canoe out in the water—it was cold!—her bare feet splashing and her nightgown getting wet, trying to pull her down. It took great effort but she managed to get herself in, rowing frantically, though the lake was choppy.

The water bubbled near her canoe, making her nervous, but then Oliver popped his head up through the waves.

"Hi, Gus," he said. "Would you like to go swimming with me?"

"But I haven't got a bathing suit," she said.

"That's okay." Oliver reached out a hand to pull her in. "I don't mind..."

Oof! All ten pounds of Pepper the cat landed squarely on Gus's chest, jarring her awake. She had been dreaming.

"You're better than an alarm clock, you know that?" she told her cat. Pepper meowed back, not so subtly encouraging her to get up and plate his breakfast.

"And a bowl of milk, you say?" Gus said, petting behind his ears. She threw on a robe and started to head downstairs in her bare feet, then turned back to her closet for a pair of slippers. Salt, snoozing on the stair landing, stretched lazily and followed them into the kitchen.

Her neck, shoulders, and butt positively burned with ache: she'd put herself through the paces with yoga, the hike, and the frantic dinner in the kitchen Sunday night. But none of that caused as much tension as the twenty minutes she spent as a passenger in Hannah's red Miata, coming home from the retreat the morning before. After yet another zig when Hannah should have zagged—not to mention a surprising inability to read any signs while the car was in motion—Gus demanded that she pull over and let her drive.

"But I'm really good at it," Hannah'd protested, though Gus remained firm and got into the driver's seat, placating Hannah by showing her how to lower the convertible top.

"I switched the wipers on four times trying to figure that out on Friday," she'd said. But it hadn't been a smooth drive with Gus at the wheel, either: she hadn't driven a stick shift in over twenty years.

"Remind me not to ask you for driving lessons," smirked Hannah, as she let her hair blow in the wind, watching the Hudson Valley scenery stream by.

Now Gus rummaged around the cupboard for some acetaminophen. She went to the sink for a bit of water and glanced out the window, expected to admire her pansies. Instead, she saw Hannah, in a T-shirt and shorts, crisscrossing her fingers and stretching her arms back, back, back over her head.

Gus rapped on the window before opening it. "You're here early," she said. Hannah waved and continued her exercises for several more minutes before coming in through the patio door.

"Actually you're up late, Gus," she said. "It's past eight. I've already done a run up the road and back."

"What?"

"I went for a jog, outside, like any normal person," said Hannah. "And I did not wear a ball cap, sunglasses, or even a hoodie."

"Good for you. I can only imagine that you fell under the spell of Gary Rose and his can-do spirit over the weekend."

"Nope." Hannah reached for an orange out of the fruit bowl on Gus's counter. "I just got reacquainted with Hannah Joy Levine."

"Opting out of the candy diet?"

"This is just supplemental," she said, mounding up her orange peel on the counter. She ambled over to peek in the fridge. "Ooh, smoked salmon," said Hannah. "Wouldn't that taste good on eggs?"

"It might," said Gus. "Are you going to make me some breakfast?"

Hannah pretended to be confused. "If I watch you, then I can learn a thing or two."

Gus laid out a bowl and a whisk on the counter, a suspicious look on her face. "All right, Hannah Joy Levine, I'll bite," she said. "What's with the sudden interest in cooking?"

"I'm taking up Alan's offer," said Hannah. "I've decided that I'm coming onto the show."

"Are you sure? They're going to exploit you like nobody's business."

"I just felt so . . . alive this weekend," Hannah said, reaching into the cupboard for a cup and taking it to the coffeepot. "I thought, I'm thirty-six years old. Am I going to stay at home forever?"

"You were thirty-six a few weeks ago and afraid to come down the stairs for the show," said Gus. "But if you're breaking out of the pattern, then good for you."

She yawned. "I can't believe I slept in. Normally I set everything out for you, cups and such. It's a bit odd to have you do it for yourself."

"It's okay," said Hannah. "It's not like you have to do that for me. We don't want to get stuck in our roles now, do we?" She got a second mug, poured coffee and put in a dash of milk. Slowly she carried it over to her friend. "Sit down and spill it," she said. "And I don't mean the coffee. I barely saw you over the weekend, and it was impossible to talk over the noise of the thruway on the way back."

"What's there to tell?" Gus said, feeling a little weepy.

"Look, the money thing is all over the entertainment news. What with the kettle fire coverage just a few weeks ago and now this . . . you're everywhere."

"I wasn't the only one who got suckered, you know."

"Don't worry, you've got some pretty highbrow company. And I don't just mean Alan."

"Well, my Q ratings must be going through the roof," said Gus. "If you're serious about coming on the show, we'll be getting even more coverage." She took a sip of her coffee. "Remember when I was just a quiet old lady with a cooking show? Now I'm ringleader of a very out-of-control circus."

"Whatever you do, Gus, you must hold your head high," said Hannah. "You've done nothing to be ashamed of, and even if you did, there's no life in hiding out."

"So that's it, then?" She handed Hannah a plate of smoked salmon and eggs. "One weekend and you're free?"

"Ha! If that were the case, I'd run 'get over it' retreats for agoraphobics everywhere. I'd make a mint." She tucked into her plate and took several bites. "I'm freaked out of my wits," she confessed. "But I'm scared to wind up ninety years old and alone. And let's face it, Gus, you're most likely going to be dead by then. I wouldn't have anyone to feed me." She polished off her breakfast and wiped her lips with a napkin.

"There's nothing wrong with being alone," Gus said, piling up the dirty saucepan, cutting board, and plates in the sink. "It doesn't mean there's anything the matter with you just because you don't have a man in your life."

Hannah choked on her coffee and began coughing.

"Don't have a man in my life! Hell's bells, Gus, I haven't gone on a date in fifteen years," croaked Hannah. "Not everyone has relationships, you know? Besides, who said anything about romance? I was just hoping to make another friend. Carmen and I hung out a bit and it was kinda cool."

"You're barking up the wrong tree there," said Gus. "She's the kind of friend who'd climb over your dead body to get to the top of the heap."

"I just said she was nice to me," murmured Hannah. "I didn't make her a friendship bracelet and offer to lend her my *Toto* album. Sheesh!"

"Sorry, I'm on edge," said Gus.

"Why do you suddenly have men on the brain?" Hannah mused aloud. "That's unusual. That's interesting."

"No, it isn't. There's nothing to tell." Gus wasn't about to reveal her dream to Hannah, the way the water had glistened on Oliver's broad shoulders and the disarming way he'd gazed at her. That made her want to move closer, closer . . .

"Nothing?" Hannah asked, interrupting her thoughts. "Or did something else happen this weekend that you want to tell me about? You and Gary Rose? C'mon, you can confess . . ."

"No, Hannah, the only man on my brain is named David Fazio, and he's laughing all the way to the bank."

Gus went over to her laptop to see if she had received any email messages from Alan about the situation. Nothing.

"So what'd you think about the contest winner, Priya?" she asked Hannah.

"A bit under a cloud, I'd say. Or maybe just obsessive. She talked about you nonstop."

"I thought she was nice enough. Tired, maybe. But she's got three kids. She was kind of sweet, really."

"Speaking of kids . . . what's up with the girls?" asked Hannah.

"Ah, right, that. You saw my public humiliation with the rest of the crew. I'm officially a bad mom."

"Not true, Gus. I meant where did you leave things?"

"We're trying, I guess," Gus said. "Big talks, just getting some things out there. Aimee feels too much pressure, and Sabrina's overprotected. Or something like that." In fact, the conversations with her daughters—there had been another long one on Sunday night—had been tremendously fatiguing, and it was difficult to absorb everything they wanted to say. Mostly Gus felt blamed and worried. But her girls had seemed so hopeful when they were together, as if somehow, even as they were telling Gus to leave them be, she would be able to fix it all and make everything all right.

Sometimes old habits were hard to break. And sometimes there were no easy answers.

Clearly Gus required a publicist: she'd come home from the retreat to a phone ringing off the hook. All reporters, hoping to get a tasty quote about being bamboozled. She'd turned off the ringer, ignoring the constant flash on the call display, and pretended not to be home. And she hadn't bothered to turn on the phone that morning, either. Instead, she put on a pair of well-worn chinos and a faded denim shirt—her gardening clothes, she called them—and went out to spend some quality time with her roses, which, despite being surrounded by thorns, never complained, talked back, or called her out in public.

"But how will you feel when I can't afford your pricey rose feed?" she murmured. "Will you still love me then?" She carried a handful of blooms to the laundry room sink to be trimmed and washed her hands before crossing the foyer to the dining room to choose some containers from her china cabinet. Gus spent more time choosing vases than was necessary that afternoon, because she liked the distraction and because she enjoyed reflecting on the story behind each piece. She had just selected the cut crystal bud vase that had been her great-grandmother's—which she'd been planning to pick out all along—when the doorbell rang.

She looked at the clock on the wall: it was well past four. That was pretty much the middle of the workday for a New Yorker, which put the majority of her friends and family out of the running. Her daughters would never have rung the bell, and Hannah pretty much came through the gate between their yards and in from the patio. It wasn't the day for the paperboy to pick up payment, and the meter reader didn't need to come to the door. Another writer in search of a story, thought Gus. Strange how when she was engrossed in a news article she'd never spent much time thinking about the people who were quoted, about whether they'd wanted to chat off a reporter's ear or whether they had to be hounded and cajoled.

*Ding dong*! *Ding dong*! *Ding dong*! Goodness, thought Gus, she was trapped in her own dining room. She tried to peek out the window to see who was at the front door but she could only make out a tall figure, and when the figure turned in her direction, she hunkered down immediately. Omigod, she was turning into Hannah, just like that. No wonder Hannah had hidden out all these years: the sense of being hunted was overpowering.

"Gus? Are you in there?" She could hear a muffled voice coming through the door. "Gus, it's Oliver. Let me in."

Oliver. She felt a surge of relief, followed by a heavy dose of irritation. Just what was he doing here in the middle of the day?

"Hello, Oliver," she said, opening the door wide. "A patient man doesn't ring a doorbell four times."

"Sure he does," he said. "He keeps at it until it opens."

"So to what do I owe this surprise?"

"I've come to go swimming," he said.

Gus's face went red. "But I don't have a bathing suit," she said.

"Okay," Oliver said, pausing for a moment to consider what she'd said. He shrugged. "I think you do need a bit of a break to distract you from all the hubbub. Keep your wheels from spinning."

Oh, that's what he'd said. He had come to keep her wheels from spinning. Of course. No one was going to do any swimming. Of any kind.

"I'm really fine," she said.

"Aren't you even going to invite me into the house?"

Embarrassed, she stepped back to let Oliver inside. He was carrying a large box.

"What's that?"

"Dinner," he said. "I made some fresh pasta this morning, then picked up a good loaf of crusty bread and a couple pounds of fresh mussels. Two bottles of Fumé Blanc and we've got ourselves a feast."

"I've already eaten," Gus said, which wasn't the least bit true. She had barely eaten any of the breakfast she made for Hannah and had then traded in her coffee for endless cups of tea. Hannah had her all-candy diet; Gus's version was all-caffeine.

"Gus, it's four thirty in the afternoon," said Oliver. Of all the New Yorkers he knew—and he knew many—none of them ate dinner before eight. They simply worked long, late hours.

He put the box down on the counter he knew so well from their live shoots and began unpacking.

"You can't just barge in and start cooking," Gus said, feeling very nervous having just Oliver here, without anyone else around. She hadn't been alone with a man in, well, forever.

"I didn't force my way in here," he said. "You invited me."

"But that was just out of politeness. I didn't mean it. You should probably go." She picked up a tomato he'd just placed on a cutting board and put it back into the box.

"Nice," said Oliver. "That's pretty clear."

"It's not the right time, Oliver. I'm just not...ready for this kind of thing."

"There's not ready," said Oliver, "and there's running away. It's fine to wait, Augusta, for the right guy, but you still have to recognize him when he shows up."

"Do you know how old I am? I could be your...big sister."

"I don't have a sister," he replied. "Just two brothers."

"You know what I mean," she said, repacking a clove of garlic. "I'm older. You're younger."

"We're basically both in our forties," he said. "What's the difference?"

She felt flattered and considered—just for a moment—letting him think her age still began with a four.

"I'm fifty," she said flatly. "What do you think about that?"

"Fifty is fabulous," he ventured. "Fifty is nifty. Fifty is a number and guess what? Oliver Cooper doesn't care."

"But I do," said Gus. "It's unseemly."

"Gus, I'm a grown man. I'm not a high school freshman with a crush on my teacher. You are the classiest, most stimulating woman I have met in, well, ever."

He put his hand over hers inside the box and gently coaxed the garlic clove from her fingers. "And we love to cook together," he said. "I don't see how it has to be any more complicated than that."

Uncertain, Gus moved to the other side of the island, putting a barrier between them.

"I don't know," she began. "There are the girls, for one thing."

"Right, right," said Oliver. "The girl who's going to get married, maybe, and the girl who is saving the world's agriculture. I can see how you going on a date is really going to blow up their world."

"And I have to sort out my finances."

"I heard you when you said you didn't have time for a date," he said. "I thought I'd bring a date to you. I'll cook *and* clean. You can sit at the table with your abacus."

"It's been a real blow," she said. "Who knows what's going to happen if the show isn't renewed?"

"Worrying ahead of time won't change the outcome." Oliver strode over to the island and leaned across. He lowered his voice to a barely there whisper. "Look, I read the CookingChannel blogs. I know I'm good-lookin'. 'Smokin' hot,' if I may be so bold as to quote cyber fan crackedpot-one-twenty-two."

In spite of herself, Gus began to laugh.

"I kid you not," said Oliver. "I printed out that puppy and put it on the fridge. Makes me feel good when I'm reaching in to overindulge in a hunk of Brie. You have a little following yourself, by the way."

"So okay, you make dinner, and that's it."

"And a kiss," he said. "Just one kiss. That's all I ask. Then send me on my way and we won't even talk about it again."

It was all so silly, really, but it felt good. The attention. One dinner couldn't hurt.

"Okay," she said. "That's it."

"Let's do the kiss now," he urged. "Get it out of the way. Then we won't worry about mussel breath." He slid around the island so that he was next to her.

"Okay," Gus said, feeling a little breathless. Should her eyes remain open or closed? Should she lean her head back just so or wait for him to bring his hands up to her face?

Oliver moved closer, ever so slowly, and her eyelids lowered. She could barely keep still, the anticipation was delicious and he smelled so very good . . .

He pecked her on the cheek. Quick, dry lips on and off.

"Oh!" cried Gus, her eyes snapping open, disappointment and embarrassment flooding through her. "I thought—"

"Aha," Oliver said, quickly pulling Gus to him and placing his mouth firmly on her own, increasing his pressure ever so gently.

"And just one more," he said, breathing into her. "I probably should have told you I'm a tough negotiator."

# peas in a pod

# 24

He was good at twisting her arm, that Oliver. Not that she'd really minded, of course. Oliver had parlayed his kiss into the wonderful dinner of mussels, a trip to the movies on Thursday that was mostly about making out in the dark, an afternoon of gardening the following Monday, a "field trip" to the Culinary Institute of America on Wednesday, and another jaunt to the Union Square farmer's market on Saturday.

"It's June," he said. "Endless New Jersey blueberries and maybe even some strawberries. If we're lucky."

"Okay," she said. "Tonight is very important to me."

Oliver nodded, as though he was hearing this for the first time, when in fact Gus had been talking about Aimee and Sabrina arriving for days now. She'd spoken several times with her daughters since the retreat but had taken care to tread lightly, asking questions when warranted but trying not to push. Individually, she had asked them to come up to the house and stay the night before Sunday's show, which would be the first time since the retreat that *Eat Drink and Be* would air. It was their opportunity to prove that they truly could pull together as a team and produce an engrossing, chaos-free hour of food television. Priya Patel, as the winner of the contest, had been given a role in helping to choose the menu, and, in recognition of her personal beliefs, the show was going to be fully vegetarian. Not even any seafood, which Carmen hadn't taken lightly.

But tonight—Saturday—Gus didn't have the time or the inclination to think about her television program. Both of her daughters were arriving home and it was a chance for a new beginning.

Aimee and Sabrina arrived separately, each taking a cab from the train station, though within minutes of each other. Without knowing it, they'd been in separate cars on the same train and were somewhat peeved to discover the presence of the other.

"Does Mom know you're here?" Aimee asked as they met on the step in front of the manor house's front door. She had convinced herself—though Gus hadn't said so—that her mother wanted to spend some time alone with her, one on one.

"She and I are going to talk about the wedding," said Sabrina. "Why are you here?" Sabrina was under the impression that Gus wanted to talk about dresses and invitations, though in reality Gus had not mentioned anything about it.

Gus, who had heard the taxis come up the long driveway, opened the door while the two nattered, a collection of spoons in her hand.

"Don't you two look lovely!" she said, although both of her daughters were dressed all "casual Saturday," Aimee in a plain white top over a pair of jeans and Sabrina in a fitted turquoise shirt and chocolate-colored capris. Gus, on the other hand, was wearing a silver wrap shirt that tied to the side and a slim pencil skirt in a light green crepe, with a pair of gorgeous Jimmy Choos. Her hair, which she'd just had colored a bit lighter than its usual butterscotch color, had been blown out that afternoon.

"You look great, Mom," Aimee and Sabrina said in unison, as their mother stepped back into the foyer to let them inside. The chandelier in the formal dining room was turned on, though dimmed, and the rosewood dining table was spread with the good linens, and four places were set with the very best plates and glasses.

"Wow, Mom, you went all out," Sabrina said, putting down her hobo bag that was heavy with bridal magazines and looking forlornly into the room. Aimee placed her canvas tote carefully on the foyer table and stared.

"Of course," Gus said, putting one spoon at each place. "This is a very important dinner. I wanted to get it just right."

Aimee felt as though she might just cry. "Who's coming?" she asked.

"The two of you, of course," said Gus. "Now let's go into the kitchen. There's something I want to show you."

But there was no one in the room other than Salt and Pepper, lounging on the wing chairs in the bay window, one cat snoozing and the other cleaning its paws with commitment to the task. The smell of pot roast hung in the air, rich and fragrant, and a pot boiled on the stove. Potatoes, most likely.

"What do you think?" Gus said, looking expectantly into their faces.

"Of what?"

"This," she said. "It's Sunday dinner like we used to have it." She led Aimee and Sabrina over to the counter, which was covered with mixing bowls holding oats, cocoa, chocolate chips, flour, and eggs at room temperature.

"We're going to make a birthday cake," said Gus. "For your father."

"His birthday was months ago," said Aimee.

"So we're a little belated," replied her mother. "About eighteen years and a few months."

"Dead people don't eat cake," said Sabrina.

"No," replied her mother. "But the living do."

Gus handed each of the girls a wooden spoon. "Let's celebrate for once," she said.

"Like remembering the good times?" asked Sabrina.

"Sure," said Gus. "We're going to honor your dad, and we're going to honor ourselves."

"What about the bad times," said Aimee, "and all the stuff that happened at the resort?"

"We're going to honor that, too," said Gus. "Everything all together, everything that gets us to where we are tonight. Even all the mistakes I've made."

Together, as a family, they mixed the ingredients and greased the pans, put the batter in the oven, and then made a simple icing out of butter, confectioners' sugar, and vanilla beans. There were no cameras, no need for witty banter, no one else to distract their mother's attention. And all the while, the pot roast simmered, making their mouths water.

"This was your father's favorite meal," said Gus. "And it's almost ready. But there's one last thing." She took the girls into the dining room and popped open some champagne, quickly pouring into four crystal flutes, handing a glass to each of her daughters and putting one at the fourth place on the table.

"Christopher always had a place at our table and he always will," she said. "Even when other people can't see him here, we'll know, won't we?"

Aimee and Sabrina nodded.

"I'd like to make a toast," continued Gus. "To Aimee, whose good deeds and hard work I've always seen but always assumed you knew how much I appreciated them. I want you to know that I am so very proud." She took a sip of champagne. "And to Sabrina, who's not a baby anymore, but a wonderfully creative woman with endless potential. You're all grown up and getting married, and I've never said congratulations."

"Mom," said Aimee. "I'm sorry for embarrassing you at the retreat."

"I can't say I enjoyed that," Gus said. "But even the painful things can be part of the plan."

"Thanks, Mom," said Sabrina. "I brought some wedding books to show you tonight but I want you to know that I've talked it over with Billy and we're going to pay for our wedding ourselves."

Sabrina had been surprised, when she returned from the retreat, at just how thrilled she was to see Billy and have him immediately sit down and want to hear all about *her* adventures before he even told her about his own weekend. She'd felt newly excited as she and Billy had looked at wedding dates, and talked about the life they wanted to lead together. About staying in New York, maybe moving to Brooklyn, and setting up Sabrina in her own studio as Billy continued to jockey with other execs. She'd pledged to take up golf, and he agreed to dye his hair whenever it eventually turned gray. They'd truly begun to connect.

"That's not necessary," Gus said about paying for the wedding. "I'm not entirely penniless. And I look forward to having you bring Billy over so I can properly get to know him—or I could meet you in the city. Calling ahead, of course."

"Thank you for saying that," said Sabrina. "But I want to do something to help after all that's happened. And if all I can do so far is simply stop asking for things, I'll start there."

"I'll help you with a budget," said Aimee.

"And I will make the cake," said Gus. "Because we're still in this together, even if the two of you are growing up."

"G*rown* up," said Sabrina.

"Yes, yes, well, let me just get adjusted first." Gus looked down at her beautifully set table. "Oh, look, there's nothing for a centerpiece. Well, Aimee, I guess this is where you come in."

"That's Sabrina, Mom."

"No, I think it's time you had a go for a change," said Gus. "Surprise me." And she took her glass with her to see how things were coming along in the Aga.

"What do I do?" Aimee asked Sabrina. "You're the designer."

"Mom didn't ask me to make this centerpiece," said Sabrina. "She asked you."

They could hear Gus bustling around in the kitchen.

"What about flowers?" Aimee asked. "I could go to the garden. Or wait, I know, we'll scatter beads around."

"Beads? Where are you going to get beads?"

"I don't know. Don't you carry that kind of stuff in your bag?"

"For impromptu whatever-the-hell-you-use-beads-for? Uh, that would be a no."

Aimee ran up the stairs to hunt around in the bedrooms, bringing down a handful of paper clips, a stuffed bear, and a box of tissues.

"Now I get why you're the economist," Sabrina laughed.

Aimee dumped her stash of items on the foyer table and took a deep breath.

"Ready?" Gus called from the kitchen.

And then she knew. Reaching into her tote bag for her wallet, Aimee brought to the center of the table a weathered old photograph, in which two laughing girls in bathing suits—Sabrina missing her front teeth and Aimee all skinny legs—ran through a sprinkler with their father. There was no Gus in view. But that's only because she had been the person behind the camera, taking it all into her heart.

After dinner, and thick slices of chocolate cake, the trio pored over old photo albums. Pictures they'd all seen before but that suddenly acquired new meaning as Gus told them all sorts of stories she'd found too painful to recall because it made the missing of him that much worse. She shared photos of the two of them in Africa, faces sunburned but smiling. She told her girls about how purposeful and necessary she'd felt, and how their father could dig wells faster than anyone she'd seen. She pulled out the wedding album, which they'd seen before, but were giddy to look at again. They giggled hearing about the Christmas when the water pipes burst (Sabrina was barely three months old)—it wasn't that funny, Gus said, when I was the one cleaning it up!—and the time Christopher insisted on taking two little kids and a cat on a road trip during an August heat wave.

"We got as far as Philly before I put my foot down," said Gus. "The car had no air-conditioning!"

"Will we ever stop missing him?" Sabrina asked suddenly. It was one of the questions that kept her awake at night.

"No," Gus said, showing her daughters a new respect by being genuinely, deeply honest. "I don't think we ever will."

And the Simpson girls sat all together then, quiet for a bit, until one of them turned the page of the album and they laughed at the photos some more.

There were things she chose not to tell them, too. That she and Christopher hadn't always gotten along. That she'd been a bit lost when they were small, trying to raise two kids while trying to find herself and rather confused about where she wanted to be and what she wanted to be doing. That Christopher was bored at his job—good at it, but not really satisfied. That she hadn't been easy to live with. (Though that probably wouldn't have been a shocker, she realized.) That both she and Christopher had made mistakes. Maybe someday she'd tell them everything but, then again, maybe she wouldn't. Because while Gus and Aimee and Sabrina were learning how to get to know one another as adults, she *was* still their mother, after all.

# 25

"It's better than I imagined it," Priya said, stepping into Gus's manor house as Hannah opened the door. Priya had been picked up at her North Jersey home and brought all the way to Rye. "It's even grander than on television."

"Nice, right?" Hannah was dressed for the show in her very best tracksuit, an olive green zip-up jacket and pants combo. "I live in a carriage house across the back. About one-tenth the size of this place."

"Even the floors gleam," Priya said, nodding with approval. "Gus is the real deal."

"That she is," agreed Hannah. "Come with me to the kitchen and we'll steal some of whatever Oliver's been prepping. He told me he cut extra in case I got hungry."

"Oh, I better save up my calories for the finished meal," said Priya.

"Are you on a diet?"

"No, not really. Okay, maybe a little bit. I'm a snacker, I guess. But I just have to look at food and it goes to my hips."

Hannah, out of consideration, left her Milky Way bar in her pocket.

"Where someone else would gain one pound, I put on three," continued Priya. "I used to be slimmer. No skinny minny, but not quite so puffy." She blew air into her cheeks, copping a chipmunk look.

"Well, you don't have to worry about anything here," explained Hannah. "We never really eat after the show. It's pretty much been a disaster every episode, and then everyone goes away mad at everyone else. You know. The true CookingChannel Hollywood story."

"I see. I had hoped it would be social. Like the retreat."

"Okay, you two," Gus said, coming out of the library with Oliver and Porter. "You'd better get a touch of makeup on those faces if you're going to be on the air. No shiny noses!"

"I prefer to do my own makeup," said Priya. "I'm quite particular about my eyebrows. They're not quite as full as they used to be and I have filled them in with pencil."

Hannah moved in closer. "Oh yeah," she said. "I see what you mean."

"Hannah!" admonished Gus. "You look fine, Priya. But a little more lipstick won't hurt. Just don't take a big bite out of anything on camera or it'll end up on your chin. Rookie mistake, trust me."

Soon enough the team was assembled in the kitchen, ready to execute ratatouille, seitan stir fry in ginger sauce, and a vegan mocha cake made with gluten-free flour and vinegar instead of eggs.

"C'mon, guys," said Porter. "Let's do it for Gary Rose and Alan Holt. Work together, have fun, and make it look goddamn easy."

Gus noticed the glint in Carmen's eyes and tried nonchalantly to lift the lids off the pots on the stove.

"What are you doing over there?" said Oliver. "I've got sauce simmering."

"I'm looking for octopus," Gus said, in a low voice and barely moving her lips.

"I don't think she brought any." He mimicked her stone face. "We're clear."

"What about pepper spray in the oven mitts?" she asked. "I hear that's the kind of prank they pull at beauty pageants."

"Carmen hasn't been in the kitchen alone all day," said Oliver. "I've got my eye on her. I've got you, Gus."

"Places, everyone," yelled a member of the crew, as the last-minute get-ready swirl started.

Troy and Sabrina remained awkward with each other, so Troy was dispatched to cut carrots with Priya while Sabrina and Aimee sat on stools near the island and watched, though they remained in the camera shot.

"Thank God," said Aimee. "I was getting sick of chopping."

Hannah—in her inaugural official appearance as a member of the *Eat Drink and Be* team—stood at the central island between Gus and Carmen.

"Just for introductions, Carmen," Porter said, when she complained. "Then Hannah will assist Priya and Troy."

"Five . . . four . . . three," said an assistant producer, before switching to counting off "two . . . one" silently with wide hand gestures but no words. The red light was on.

"Welcome, everyone. I'm Gus Simpson. Tonight is one of the most special episodes of *Eat Drink and Be* we've ever had. We're joined by the lucky winner of our contest, Priya Patel—and thanks to so many of you who entered—who has inspired tonight's all-vegetarian menu. And we're also adding a new, permanent member of our cooking team here." She turned to Hannah and gave her a big hug in front of the world.

"This is my dearest friend, Hannah Joy Levine. She's a former tennis player who's learned from some big mistakes. She can't cook at all but you know what? Who cares? Because *Eat Drink and Be* isn't about being good. It's about being happy. And once you get to know her, you are going to love her as much as I do. So sit back and enjoy the show."

"And I'm still Carmen Vega," piped up Carmen, afraid Gus would "forget" to introduce her. "But I like Hannah, too," she added. "Let's cook!"

And they did.

"We're out!" Porter screamed nearly an hour later. "That was the best show we've ever done! If we keep going like this, no one's gonna be able to touch us. We'll be back for another season for sure."

For once, the entire cast of *Eat Drink and Be* sat down after a program and actually ate together, carrying dishes into the breakfast room and gathering around the painted white table.

"Perfectly seasoned," Oliver said, his mouth full of seitan stir fry.

"Priya, you're a wonderful cook," said Gus. "You have the heart of a chef."

"Oh, I am not so sure," said Priya. "These are just what I have always done, a little cardamom, a bit of turmeric. Sprinkle, sprinkle." She felt perfectly bright and shiny under Gus's compliments and watched with pride as Oliver reached over for seconds.

"Next time we grill!" said Oliver.

"That's right," said Porter. "Next time we go live for a July Fourth barbecue, here in Gus's backyard."

"What's the menu plan for the next episode?" asked Troy. "I was hoping we could do fruit kebabs . . ."

"We typically have a private meeting to plan the menu," interrupted Carmen. "Don't worry about it, Troy. Just show up and wear your damn FarmFresh T-shirt and leave the real cooking to us." She turned to Priya.

"Your appearance was just another stunt," she said. "Though it was very nice to meet you, and we all thank you for coming."

The hurt and disappointment was all over Priya's face. "Of course," she said. "I didn't think I was anything special."

"Well, that's not true," Gus said, fighting the urge to kick Carmen under the table. Her ability to be threatened by everyone was boundless. "You are special, Priya. A very nice lady and a good cook."

Gus locked eyes with Porter, who knew her well enough to see where she was going with this.

"It's very nice being here with all of you," Priya said, getting up to leave. "I thank you for inviting me to enter this contest."

"Would you do me the favor of coming to my July Fourth party, Priya?" asked Gus. "You could bring your family that you told me about at the retreat—I'm sure they'd have a very nice time. We'll be broadcasting some of the party, of course, and the cooking, but mostly it's going to be a wonderful, lazy day filled with delicious food and even sweeter people. I couldn't think of a better guest."

Priya was overwhelmed. She was being invited to one of Gus Simpson's world-famous parties. Just like that.

"The Patel family would be honored," she said. "We'll pick up some traditional sweets and drive in from New Jersey."

"Oh, that reminds me!" cried Hannah. "Can any of you drive a stick shift?"

"Yeah," Troy said. "I've been on a tractor or two."

"Awesome," said Hannah. "I accept."

"Huh?"

"You can be my driving teacher. I'm going to get my license."

The following Saturday found Hannah and Troy going around in circles—literally—as she tried to navigate her way around a nearby church parking lot.

"Trying to buy yourself a bit of extra insurance?" she asked, tilting her head toward the sign out front. "I'm not sure you picked the right place—I'm Jewish, you know."

"Quit stalling, pun intended, and release the clutch," said Troy, who had put on a helmet as soon as he sat down in the car. "I've heard about your driving from Gus. How do I lock?"

"Oh, now he's a funny man," said Hannah "Well, you should know I don't give in to taunting." She paused. "Anymore."

For more than two hours she maneuvered her little red Miata through the parking lot, trying to practice her parallel parking (turn the wheel, Troy shouted, no, the other way!) and her angle parking (watch the lines!) and keep her speed even (more gas, he encouraged, before screaming for her to brake! brake!).

"Oh my God," she said, turning off the car finally. She rested her head against the back of the seat and closed her eyes. "And no, I'm not trying to be funny." Hannah lolled her head to the side and looked at Troy, who had persisted in wearing his damn helmet as soon as he was certain it bugged her. He grinned.

"You suck," Troy said matter-of-factly.

"Damn straight," said Hannah. "I just got to get into training."

"I think you gave me whiplash. Ever done an article on that?"

Hannah rolled her eyes. "No, but I'm sure you would make a great source," she said. "So now what?"

"Time to trade this puppy in. Get yourself an automatic."

"I can't go car shopping," she said.

"I'll go with you."

"Do you drive an automatic?" asked Hannah. "That seems almost too easy. Like you haven't earned being on the road."

"Uh, I live in Manhattan," he said. "My existence is car-free until I go home to Oregon."

"Right." She nodded. "That must be nice, out there with your family. Lucky."

"Yeah," he agreed. "It is. Okay, you, let's switch seats so we can get out of here and get you home."

There was no lurching or mid-intersection stalls as Troy drove, his helmet resting on the backseat, all of which irritated Hannah tremendously. She hated when she wasn't very good at some sort of physical activity.

"Stop!" she shouted, as they made their way down the street.

"What the hell?" said Troy, who hit the brake, afraid he was about to run over a squirrel or something.

"Over there." Hannah pointed to a public park across the road. "It's a tennis court."

"You brake for tennis?" Troy shook his head. "That's not funny. We could have had an accident."

"No, let's go play," she said. "You wanna?"

"You have a racket in here?"

"I tucked a couple in just in case," she said. "You being the big tennis camp man and all that."

"You may be on the show now but playing on a public court near Rye?" asked Troy. "If someone recognizes you... are you ready for that?"

"Let's find out." Hannah wasn't entirely sure if she meant that, but she wanted to do something in which she was better than Troy.

He continued driving until the next light. "All right, you talked me into it," he said, though she hadn't said another word. Troy turned the car around and went back in the direction of the public courts.

"We won't play a full match," he said as he shut off the car. "Just a bit of volleying and that's it. I gotta get back into the city—we're close to landing a new investor."

"Sure," said Hannah. "But we'll keep score, just a few points. Otherwise, why bother?"

"You know what?" said Troy. "I've always wanted to beat Hannah Joy Levine."

"Not happening." She pulled out a bag of rackets and slung it over her shoulder.

"Can you imagine the crowd if I did?"

"No crowd here."

"What about them?" He pointed to a collection of what looked to be six or seven middle-school-aged kids loitering about on the court.

"You guys here to play?" Hannah shouted, practicing a few serves while Troy stood beside her.

The kids shrugged. They seemed to have only one wonky old wooden racket among the group of them.

"Come on over here," she called.

"You really have been locked at home for fifteen years," said Troy. "It's not okay anymore to just speak to kids you don't know."

*Thwack!* Hannah served another ball. Oh, the real thing was even better than she'd imagined.

"You're fast, lady," said one of the kids, coming nearer. "Just like Venus."

"Yup," said Hannah. "And I used to be even faster!"

"Whoa." The kids were clearly impressed.

"This guy here is about to be beaten by me" she said, gesturing to Troy.

"Ha!" Troy said, shaking his head at the kids. "It won't happen."

"You sure have a lot of rackets," said the shortest child in the group. "Why did you bring so many?"

Hannah looked at the kids, and then at Troy, and then back at the kids.

"For sharing," she said, unzipping the bag and handing out two rackets. "Just to borrow, and everyone gets a turn. Okay by you?" The last words she had addressed to Troy.

"I'm all good," he said. "Let's start volleying. Everybody put two feet on the line closest to the net!"

The kids scurried up, making more noise than he could have imagined possible. Like a little herd of elephants.

"Pull back and swing," Hannah said, marching up and down

behind them like a drill sergeant. She waved her arm over her head to gesture to Troy to go to the other side.

"Here," she said, putting her hand on one young girl's. "Grip the racket like this. And when the ball comes over the net, smack it like you mean it!"

The little girl giggled. "You're funny, you know that?"

"And I'm also good at tennis," said Hannah. "So who's next? Get in line and hit 'em as they come over. Troy, serve!"

They played for a long time, until even Hannah, who thought she would never be able to get enough when she'd first stepped onto the court that day, owned up to being exhausted. The kids handed the rackets back to her reluctantly.

"Thanks, lady," they said.

"Too tired for car shopping, then?" teased Troy.

"I'm not ready to trade in my Miata," she said as she put the rackets back into her case. "I'm going to master that sucker with just a few more lessons, I know it. Same time next week?"

"Wouldn't miss it," said Troy. "I'll bring my own racket this time."

On the edge of the court, the "crowd" went wild with cheers.

Gus heard the toot of a horn in front of the house and raced outside, dragging a suitcase behind her. She was in a breezy blue dress and carried a light cotton wrap over her arm, though it had actually been challenging to figure out what to wear for the day's events. She'd had to ask Sabrina for some input, and she advised avoiding green and opting for something comfortable.

"Though that's just off the top of my head, Mom," she said. "I've never heard of fashion for meeting the Feds."

Indeed. The call had come in only a few days before: the FBI, intensely pursuing David Fazio, wanted her to come in to make a statement and offer whatever information she might have.

"But I don't know anything," she explained for the umpteenth time to the agent over the phone. Still, he persisted, setting up an appointment and requesting that she bring documents. Oliver had encouraged her to go, and Aimee had offered to meet her at Federal Plaza in downtown New York, where the interview was set to take place.

"It just makes it all feel even worse," she told them. "Not only has my money gone missing but the government is going to walk me, step by step, through how I was so stupid."

"Or they'll catch him and maybe get some of it back," Aimee pointed out. "Either way, you have to stand up for yourself, even if it hurts."

She locked the door to the manor house behind her as Joe, the car service driver who'd taken her to the *Today* show, grabbed her rolling bag and placed it in the trunk of the car.

"That's heavy," he said. "What you got in there? Gold bricks?"

"Something like that," she said. "A lot of papers."

Joe held open the door as she climbed into the backseat and reached behind herself to put on her seat belt.

"Aha," he said. "Good for you."

Gus was nervous, no doubt about it. She hadn't even made anything for Hannah to eat that morning.

"No chow?" Hannah had said, looking forlornly at the counter when she came over at seven thirty. "People stop feeding stray cats when they don't want them to come by."

"It's not that, Hannah," Gus said, though she did feel a bit guilty because she'd been spending a lot of time with Oliver and not bringing dinner over to Hannah as often as she used to. "I'm just preoccupied."

"You look nice," said Hannah. "More relaxed than usual."

"Thank you. Your tracksuit looks stellar, as always."

"Yeah, about that," said Hannah. "I was thinking maybe it's time

I invested in a new wardrobe. Nothing earth-shattering, maybe just something that can't double as workout clothes."

"What about your gray jacket-dress?" Gus said absentmindedly as she rechecked her purse. "It's what you've always worn before."

"Do you have time to take me shopping?" asked Hannah. "I know you have all this stuff going on, but I was hoping." She waited but Gus didn't respond.

"I'll drive," offered Hannah.

Gus looked up. "Oh, definitely not that," she teased. And then a thought came to her: what about Sabrina? She could probably do a much better job outfitting Hannah than Gus could.

She put two slices of bread in the toaster.

"Finally, some food," cried Hannah.

"You could have done this yourself. You're not the least bit helpless."

Hannah pulled out a Reese's peanut butter cup. "I love peanut butter on toast," she said, biting into the candy bar while she waited. "Yum!"

"See there? You even had your own. Right there in your pocket."

"I've been giving some thought to Priya."

"Oh, goodness, I've been getting an earful from Carmen. The meetings at the CookingChannel have been very screechy."

"No, not about her coming to the cookout show," said Hannah. "Her health. I think I've figured it out."

"Hannah," Gus said, not hiding her irritation very well. "You're always diagnosing, even characters on TV shows. You're not actually a doctor."

"I'm right this time," Hannah said confidently. Indeed, something about Priya had lingered in her mind after the show, though she hadn't been able to put a finger on what it was. "It was the eyebrows," she explained now.

"Priya Patel is just a fortysomething mom with too much to do. It's like that when you've got a young family."

"Ouch." Hannah made a face. "But that's not her problem, I'm telling you."

"You can't go around barging in other people's lives," insisted Gus, who caught the expression on Hannah's face very well. "No comment from the peanut butter cup gallery, thank you very much."

"Okay there, Ms. I've-never-butted-in-anywhere," said Hannah. "Look, she's got a thyroid problem, Gus, and she doesn't even know it."

"I hope you're not planning on ambushing Priya at the Fourth party?"

"Of course not," Hannah said, as though Gus was being ridiculous. "I contacted Porter for her email address."

Joe had arrived with the car then, and Gus left Hannah to her toast, pulling the rolling bag of bank statements behind her. She had felt a rising dread as they drove down FDR Drive, watching the UN, the NYU medical center, and the Williamsburg Bridge as they nudged their way down the road, just one of endless cars heading into Manhattan. Off to work, off to play, off to go talk to the FBI.

Aimee was standing on the sidewalk as the car pulled up close to Federal Plaza, waiting to walk with her inside. She'd taken the day off, for which Gus was very grateful, and had told her so.

A line of people stretched around the block.

"Oh no," said Gus, "We'll never make our appointment now."

"That's the immigration line, Mom," Aimee said, grabbing the suitcase. "We go in over here."

After a short line at the security area—it was just like the airport with its security screeners—they took an elevator upstairs.

"Hello," said the brown-haired man who came into the waiting room. He was of medium build, a little bit shorter than six feet, wearing wireless glasses and a dark blue suit. His expression was solemn but he was younger than Gus had expected after hearing the deep voice on the phone.

"I'm Jeremy Brewer," he said, shaking her hand firmly. "I spoke with you earlier, Mrs. Simpson."

Gus nodded.

"No need to be nervous," Agent Brewer said, handing both of them his card. "I'm a forensic accountant. My weapon of choice is a calculator."

Aimee laughed. Gus did not.

They made their way to a small office, and Gus spent several hours drinking coffee and going over the faked statements she'd received, as the agent took detailed notes. Aimee, who was familiar with the papers from going through them in recent weeks, chimed in with an occasional comment or two.

"Let's take a break." Agent Brewer stood up. "Get some lunch and reconvene."

"I didn't think I'd have anything much to say," said Gus.

"But you knew this guy for a decade, professionally and socially," he said, moving to open the office door. "People often are aware of much more than they realize."

"Knock knock," said a voice belonging to a tall woman in a dark suit. "Saw that you were breaking and thought I'd take my chance to say hello to *the* Gus Simpson." She whipped out a cookbook from behind her back. "And I was hoping . . ."

"Of course," Gus said, accepting a pen and moving back into the office to sit down again. "Now who shall I make it out to?"

"She'll be busy with that for a few minutes," Aimee said, good-naturedly. "Probably made her feel a little better."

"Great," said Agent Brewer. "Though I have to confess I've never watched any of those food television shows."

"You've never even seen my mom?"

"No offense intended."

"And none taken." She beamed from ear to ear.

"So tell me about this UN stuff," said Agent Brewer. "Sounds like interesting work." He reached into his pocket to give her a card.

"You already gave me one," said Aimee.

"Did I?" he said, feigning surprise. "Well, here's another one. Just want to make sure you have my number."

"Yeah?" said Aimee.

"Yes, ma'am."

# 26

Every year since she started on the CookingChannel, Gus had hosted her entire cast and crew for a wonderful wrap party. But, with the future of the show still uncertain, she didn't want to wait until everything was wrapped. She could imagine all sorts of downcast faces if she put off the celebrations until the end of the season and it turned out the program was not to be renewed. No, far better to use the occasion of the Fourth of July to thank everyone for their hard work and commitment, when spirits—and hopes—remained high.

Her theme was obvious: eat, drink, and be merry. The menu? Crab cake ciabatta rolls, *bollos preñados*—chorizo "hot dogs"—for a Spanish homage, tomato-watermelon cubes on toothpicks, and a chilled green papaya salad. It was different working with Oliver in the kitchen now but the two of them, although giddy and often caressing a cheek or enjoying a deep kiss in private, made a point to be professional and discreet in public.

Everyone's families had been invited, including Priya Patel's, and Gus gleefully anticipated having loads of kids running around her backyard. In preparation, she purchased a handful of remote control boats that could be raced in the pond and a box of sidewalk chalk for patio doodling, and she set out a series of rented picnic tables on the lawn so there would be lots of room for every guest to relax. It wasn't as lavish as many occasions she'd thrown, but seemed appropriate given the uncertainty surrounding the show. Most of all, it was heartfelt. And that, Gus knew, was the most important ingredient of all.

The house was already half-full by the time the first guests arrived; Sabrina and Aimee had come up to stay for the weekend, and Hannah, as usual, helped Gus greet the day with a cup of steaming coffee and a chat. The difference, however, was that for once Hannah had moved beyond her well-worn tracksuit collection and was dressed, of all things, in an aubergine-colored skirt and a simple white top that Sabrina had helped her to choose. Her feet, out of sneakers for the first time in decades, were very pale inside a pair of metallic sandals, her toes painted a deep coral. And her red hair, free of its ponytail, shone (thanks to a conditioning treatment from Sabrina) in a sleek new cut.

There was something that made the manor house come alive when there were so many voices, Gus thought, and she loved having her rooms full. Porter and his wife, Ellie, rang the bell at 4 PM on the dot, their new grandchild in tow, and Gary Rose—yes, she'd even invited the facilitator from the retreat—followed soon after, then the grip, the gaffer, the sound guy, and the camera operator, all accompanied by spouses and significant others. Alan Holt made an unexpected appearance, too, carrying a bottle of champagne, which he handed to her at the door.

"I just heard from Porter the other day that Sabrina is getting married," he said, kissing Gus on the check. "Congratulations!"

He handed her the bottle, a vintage Henri Giraud, *Fût de Chêne*, and steered her into the dining room.

"Look, now that we've got a moment," he said, "I wanted to talk to you. 'Cause I've just had a stellar idea I'd like to run by you—"

The doorbell rang and more guests arrived, including members of the CookingChannel publicity department assigned to the show and the website editor. Then Priya was on the step, wearing a deep pink sari and bindi, introducing her brood with pride to Gus: Bina, Chitt, and Kiran.

"You look stunning, Priya," Gus said, forgetting her own anger for a moment. "Your clothes, yes, but it's something else about you that's quite different. You seem brighter somehow."

"I must thank Hannah," Priya replied, pushing Kiran forward to hand Gus a platter of *badam pista* rolls and *jalebi*. "She sent me an email that very much changed my life."

"And I am very happy about it," said her husband, Raj, stepping across the threshold to shake Gus's hand. "If it weren't for your show, Mrs. Simpson, Priya would never have met this Hannah. She doesn't even know it but she is quite a friend to the Patel family."

"I hope you tell her that." Gus ushered them inside. Later, she planned to surprise Priya by giving her the grand tour, just because she knew it would make her feel special. For now, she directed her to the pond, where Hannah was organizing competitive remote control boat races.

But the get-together had its challenges, as well.

Sabrina had very elaborately tried to keep Billy and Troy from meeting during the festivities. She recognized that Troy deserved to be there, and even wanted him to enjoy himself, but didn't relish any sort of showdown. What she hadn't counted on, however, was that Troy was just as desperate to steer clear of her fiancé.

And then it happened, the moment he had strenuously avoided

throughout the entire evening. Meeting William Angle. At the door to Gus's powder room.

"Hi," said the broad-shouldered man. "I'm Billy." He looked like a deer caught in headlights, but he didn't back away.

"Troy."

There was a drawn-out silence as both men considered their next move. And then Troy did something he never expected or imagined he was capable of. "Congratulations," he said. And he meant it.

"Thanks," said Billy, who looked as though a weight had lifted. "Sabrina's a great girl."

Troy nodded thoughtfully. "Yes," he said. "She is."

Then he strolled casually away, his back straight and stiff. That was enough for him; he lacked the ability and the inclination to play buddy-buddy with Sabrina's fiancé. He had wanted the girl and he'd lost. Though that wasn't quite the end of the story. He hoped she'd figured it out, finally, had sorted through her options and made a choice she could stick with. He could see Sabrina's future—her new future—better than he suspected she could. And he very much hoped it would be happy. Troy had realized, when they were at the retreat, that what he once saw as Sabrina's amazing spontaneity now struck him as indecision and a lack of impulse control. He loved her. But he didn't want to be with her.

The timing had been off. That was all. They'd moved in different directions, and by chasing her, he'd gotten himself a little lost in the process.

Out the kitchen window he could see Sabrina on the patio, animatedly acting out some anecdote to a laughing Priya and Ellie. He thought to himself that she seemed both lighter, somehow, than the day she walked into his office and swept him off his feet, and more serious. Quite by accident she glanced in his direction and he waved, as if by instinct. She saw him and returned the gesture, and then turned her head to greet Billy as he rejoined the group.

Troy wondered, as he watched his former girlfriend, her glossy black hair pinned loosely atop her head and wearing a cobalt blue sundress, when enough time and distance would have passed between them, in its natural way, that they would no longer be on a first-name-only basis. When he'd have to use his last name if ever he called her mother to discuss FarmFresh and Sabrina answered the line.

"Hello," he imagined himself saying. "It's Troy. Troy Park."

And there would be a pause and then a warmth in her voice as she said hello, hello, Troy, remembering—as he would—the special moments they'd shared.

"Gather round, friends," Alan was saying, as the sky grew dark and the guests were contentedly tired, full of watermelon and punch and Gus's fresh strawberry shortcake piled high with vanilla-flavored whipped cream. Amid all the hubbub, the *Eat Drink and Be* team had managed to sneak in a live show of Oliver showing Troy how to grill fruit and make a sweet yogurt and honey dipping sauce, Gus mixing cake in the kitchen, and Carmen explaining the wonderful spiciness of chorizo, interspersed with real-time action from the party. The crew had been delighted to have their loved ones finally see what it is they actually did on set, and the lightheartedness of the cast had made the episode a joy to film.

Even Alan had had a good time.

"It's been such a thrill to literally be a part of an episode," he was saying now. "You have all impressed me this season with how hard you've worked, and I know, with two episodes left to go on the schedule, you'll no doubt race it to the finish line."

No one picked up on the comment, too eager to hear what the president was about to say. Would the series be renewed?

"We have two episodes of *Eat Drink and Be* left, and Gus has already informed me that your final scheduled show is going to be a wonderful selection of family favorites," he said. "And I've just learned that Gus's daughter Sabrina is getting married, to this fine gentleman, Billy. I call him a fine gentleman though in fact I've only just met him."

Everyone laughed along with Alan. He was the boss, of course.

"But what most of the rest of you don't know is that . . ."

The cast and crew leaned in closer.

"I've added an extra episode," Alan shouted, raising his glass of punch in the air and spilling a few drops on his sleeve. He ignored the group's collective moan of frustration. "This is pure genius, if I do say so myself: our season ender is now going to be a live, on-air wedding. It'll be a ratings bonanza!"

And he tilted back his cup of punch and drank every last drop.

# 27

It was all coming together. Finally. A quick breath mint in her mouth to freshen up and she was good to go. Bad breath just wouldn't do.

She'd gotten the call three days ago. Somehow it had slipped her mind to tell Gus, even though she'd talked to her twice about the cookout episode. Besides, she'd had to share attention for quite a while now, and to be honest, she truly believed she deserved to have the spotlight all to herself.

"Carmen, hi!" said a short blond woman wearing a headset. "We've been waiting for you to arrive. Diane and Robin are so excited to meet you."

With a veritable skip in her fire-engine-red Christian Louboutin slingback heels (which added an impressive four inches), Carmen entered the set of *Good Morning America* in triumph. She made understanding murmurs when Robin told her it was too bad that Gus couldn't join her, and put on a neutral expression when Diane commented on how losing all that money seemed to have skyrocketed Gus Simpson to the front page of all the tabloids.

"And all the attention means her cookbooks have been selling like mad," Diane said. "They can't keep them in stock at my local bookstore. I know, I went to find one!"

"Yes," piped up the pert supervising producer. "You're really lucky to learn from one of the best in the business. Ready to go on?"

"Gus?" Oliver was watching her sleep, staring down at her. "Are you awake?" She hadn't been and so his voice startled her. It had been eighteen years since she'd woken next to a man, and all sorts of worries flashed through her mind: Had she been snoring? Did her face have those pillow wrinkles from sleeping too hard—or worse, actual wrinkles that flashed her maturity like a neon sign? Wisely, she kept her mouth shut as a barrier against morning breath. She wanted to clean up a bit but she wasn't quite ready to parade about in her nightie in front of Oliver just yet. Though he clearly had no such worries, wearing only a half-wet towel tied loosely at his waist, his chest bare and looking very touchable.

"You look fantastic," he said, moving his face closer for a kiss.

"Mmmm," she said, still keeping those lips zipped. If only she'd thought to wake up early and brush her teeth. Then again, she hadn't quite planned on this. They'd just been watching a movie the night before in her den—lying about on the sofa—with her pedicured feet on Oliver's lap. He was smooth, that man, the way he massaged her toes, and then her ankles, then leaned in for a kiss, then went back to massaging her. Gus had practically melted under the caress of his strong hands, hadn't thought to resist when he pulled her toward him to sit on his lap.

She hadn't wanted to resist.

Instead, she'd unbuttoned Oliver's shirt, insistent on getting her hands on his skin, until, in her clumsy eagerness, she popped one of those buttons right off. It went flying.

"Oh!" Gus said, blushing with embarrassment, her lack of practice obvious.

"Not a problem," Oliver said, lifting his shirt over his head and tossing it to the floor. "Screw the buttons."

He brought her face close to his own and kissed her hungrily. "No, on second thought," he said. "Screw *me*."

Gus had pushed him back against the cushions then. Not to hesitate. No, to really take in this man, the shape of his jaw and the crinkles near his eyes and the look of raw desire on his face. For her.

And then she did what he'd asked.

Later they'd gone upstairs, to the master suite, trying out her bed and, after that, her shower.

She'd forgotten what it was like to feel that sweet, achy soreness. The kind of ache that made her feel so desired, so feminine.

Sex with Oliver had been well worth the wait.

"I brought you up a coffee," he said now, "but there's something you've simply got to see."

Oliver clicked on the television on the far wall of her bedroom; the jingle for household cleansers was just ending.

"And we're back," said Diane Sawyer, "with one of the most popular new cooks on television. Carmen Vega, from CookingChannel's *Eat Drink and Be*, here to fix us a little something."

"Hey, that's my line," Gus said, forgetting about her breath and nightie and throwing back the covers. She jumped out of the bed to move closer to the TV, as though seeing Carmen's close-up would help.

"I can't believe she went and booked herself a solo spot," she said, pacing around on the carpeted floor. "Why does she always behave this way? It's infuriating."

"She's jealous of you." Oliver took off his towel and stretched front-down across the end of the bed. "You can be intimidating."

"That's not true," Gus said, trying not to stare but enjoying the view nonetheless.

"Sure it is. You're a survivor, and a gorgeous one. It's hard to compete."

He made a lazy grab for Gus, who bobbed out of his reach.

"I've got to call Porter," she said, grabbing the cordless phone from the night table.

"And do what?"

Gus took in a long breath and let it out, slowly.

"I don't know," she said. She tapped her teeth together for a few seconds. "Maybe all I have to do is nothing."

". . . and someday soon I plan to have my own restaurant," TV Carmen was telling Robin Roberts. "Something that celebrates my Spanish heritage and my mother's cooking."

Gus put a hand on her hip and listened, very closely, to Carmen babble on about how much she loved inventing new dishes.

"At home I like to play around with making lobster foam," she giggled to Diane, as though it was something everyone liked to do. It was more than she'd ever shared with Gus in the kitchen, and Gus, for her part, was transfixed. Carmen was actually quite perky and amusing when you didn't have to work next to her.

"I think she's telling the truth," Gus said to Oliver. "The girl just wants to cook."

"No, she also wants to be famous," said Oliver. "But, yeah, she wants to be famous for the food."

Gus put the phone back on its base and enticed Oliver to come back to bed. He didn't require much convincing.

Later, without putting on a robe, she went down to the kitchen in her nightie. "What's going on down here that smells so good?" she shouted up to Oliver, who had ducked into the bathroom for a quick second. "I think I can hear cinnamon rolls calling my name."

Salt and Pepper were meowing over an empty saucer in the middle of the floor.

"Did someone give you a little milk, hmm?" she asked, reaching over to rub their furry heads.

Just then Hannah rapped impatiently on the patio door, which Gus quickly unlocked.

"You're never going to believe this," said Hannah.

"But Carmen is on *Good Morning America*," finished Gus. "I just saw it. I had no idea."

"That's some *chutzpah*, if you ask me," Hannah said, a drop of admiration sneaking into her voice. "You gotta respect a tough competitor."

"Yeah. But you know what? I'm not going anywhere."

"Are those cinnamon rolls?" Hannah asked, sniffing the air. "My favorite!" She literally ran to the stool at the island and sat down, waiting to be served.

"You like those, do you?" Oliver said, coming into the kitchen. "I put them in a bit ago and they're almost done."

Hannah's eyes went from Oliver, in just his jeans, to Gus, in her nightie, and back again. "Oh," she said, her face turning red. "I didn't realize... I mean, I knew you were spending time together. But I didn't think it was serious and... wow." She turned around so she wasn't facing them anymore. "I should just go," she said. "I didn't mean to intrude."

"Hannah Levine, all you've walked in on is Oliver and I having breakfast," Gus said. "I am quite sure that would garner us a 'G' rating."

"I'm sorry . . ." stammered Hannah. "I'm just a bit blown away, that's all."

"Let's go onto the patio and have a talk," Gus said, meeting glances with Oliver. Then she put an arm around Hannah and led her outside.

"Oh my God, Oliver slept over!" said Hannah. "Did you know that?"

Gus could not keep the grin off her face. "Yes, I was an active participant," she said. "It may have been the first time but it definitely won't be the last, I can tell you that much."

Hannah tried to force a smile.

"What's all this?" Gus asked, as they strolled over to the roses, the patio cold under her bare feet, arm in arm with Hannah.

"I suppose I just thought we were the same," said Hannah. "Single. The kind of people who just don't do that sort of thing. Dating. Sex."

"I didn't, for a long time," admitted Gus. It wasn't as though she'd forgotten Christopher in one night, or that she ever would. But she was now ready to restart this part of her life. She was ready to let herself feel.

"But now I think differently," she said to Hannah. "I want something new. Besides, you're the one who asked me if I met anyone at the retreat!"

"Yeah, but that doesn't mean I thought you should go off and get all serious."

"Who says it's serious?"

"I know you, Gus," said Hannah. "Guest bedroom or not, you wouldn't have had a man stay the night if you weren't falling for him."

"Shhh. Don't want Oliver to hear."

"Ha," said Hannah, her lip trembling slightly. "From the way he was looking at you, I'm pretty sure the feeling is mutual."

Gus felt a thrill run up her spine but, with great difficulty, managed to keep a solemn face to listen to Hannah. In spite of her new situation, she was genuinely concerned for her friend.

"I'm going to be all alone," said Hannah. "At best the third wheel. And when you sit around making up pet names for each other, I'm going to have nothing to say. Because I've never even had a boyfriend. And all that might go along with that, if you know what I mean."

"Baby steps, Hannah," Gus said, rubbing her back. "You've only been out of the house a few weeks."

And together they returned to the kitchen, where Oliver was placing rolls on a platter. He presented one, still warm, to Hannah, with a wink at Gus over her head.

"Do you like me again, Hannah?" he asked as she bit into the sugary glaze.

"Yeah," she said, her mouth full. "You're not half-bad, Oliver."

But if Hannah reacted poorly to the news of her relationship with Oliver, Gus worried even more what Aimee and Sabrina might think. There'd been no point in talking about it with them before she knew how she felt about things, but now that she was certain she wanted to continue seeing Oliver, it was better to get it all out in the open. A family, as she had so often said to her daughters, should not have secrets.

"I am dating someone—and it's Oliver," she told her daughters, over the phone because she was—quite frankly—more than a little nervous.

"As in a *date* kind of date?" asked Aimee.

"Like a boyfriend?" asked Sabrina.

Gus had prepared a big speech, about no one taking Christopher's place and being single for so long and the excitement she was feeling now. How she felt rejuvenated. Like she had felt when she was just out of Wellesley, in love, and eager to change the world. When anything seemed possible. But she decided that it wasn't necessary to explain why she was doing what she was doing, or to rationalize her feelings. She could just let it be.

"I'm happy," she said simply. "And I wanted you to know."

"Well," said Sabrina. "Then I guess that's what matters. It's still weird, though."

"I like Oliver," said Aimee. "Good choice, Mom."

The four of them met later at a new Spanish restaurant on the Upper East Side, which was awkward for a few moments, until they all relaxed and realized they were the same people, just mixed around in a new configuration. They made a toast to Carmen, naturally, who had passed along Oliver's name to Alan Holt, and to *Eat Drink and Be*. Ratings remained high, though the other Sunday night programs in Alan's "smorgasbord of destination television" were also doing well, and they'd aired another successful episode since the July Fourth party, centering on using only local organic products from tristate farms within a hundred miles of Gus's home. Eating locally was one food trend that Gus supported, thank you very much.

All in all they had just two more shows—including Sabrina's early autumn wedding to Billy—and then they would finally know whether or not Alan was going to renew.

"To making it work," Gus said. "To the future."

# 28

Priya had been cooking for two days, and planning her menu for the four before that, visiting the Indian market to see what was fresh and to spark ideas. She had sent out a formal invitation to Hannah Joy Levine, asking her to be a very special guest at the Patel family table.

"I have not seen you so intent in a long time," Raj said, clearly pleased, as she crushed cumin seeds.

"You just want to eat everything up," she said, popping a piece of cucumber in his mouth.

"True," he said, chewing eagerly. "But I am not just pleased to see you cooking. I am happy to see you so cheerful."

And she was. Everything was different now, once she had taken Hannah's articles in to her doctor and told him how she was feeling.

A few blood tests and it was confirmed: Hannah Joy Levine could have been a doctor. Well, maybe not quite, seeing as she didn't go to college. But she had read Priya correctly in guessing at a slow thyroid gland, and in doing so had brought joy back into her life. Even to the parts of her life with Raj where'd she have definitely told someone to MYOB. No more did Priya find herself awash in fatigue, or wanting to cry for no reason. In time, her doctor had said, her hair might not be so thin and her eyebrows might fill in on their own. It was all so simple when you saw it from the other side.

She would never have guessed at how quickly the medicine made a difference in just a few weeks. One afternoon, watching another repeat of Gus's old show *Cooking with Gusto!*, as Kiran played Chutes and Ladders with Bina nearby, she noticed—as though for the very first time—the light that came in through the window and shone on the wood floor. It looked so inviting that she went over and stood in the warmth, closing her eyes and imagining all the negative energies melting away. And when she looked up again and saw her house, she could see that it was a very happy home indeed.

The meal she was preparing for Hannah was a traditional *thali*, a multi-item platter consisting of *bhaat*, *farsan*, dal, curry, veggies, sweet and sour pickles, *raita*, chutney, with plenty of *roti* wheat bread. And, because she knew how much her new friend enjoyed sweets, she made plenty of those Indian delicacies as well, plus a large tub of good old-fashioned American-style vanilla ice cream over which she planned to drizzle chocolate sauce after mixing in an assortment of chocolate chips, peanuts, coconut flakes, and every candy she could think to include.

The children had been enlisted to clean their rooms—it didn't matter that Hannah might not see them—and Raj had pitched in by getting a new flat-screen television so they could all watch the U.S. Open after dinner. If Hannah wanted to. If she was up for it.

Her buddy Troy was coming for dinner as well, since Hannah insisted on driving to New Jersey in her red car and had only a learner's permit. Not even Gus would ride in the car with her, Hannah had explained when she RSVP'd and asked if she could bring a plus-one. ("A plus what?" Priya had asked.) But of course it was more than fine. One person made it a party, but two guests made it an occasion.

Gus met with Porter, Oliver, and Carmen two days after Labor Day to plan the last episodes of *Eat Drink and Be*. The wedding episode was the simplest to organize, even though it had been extended to ninety minutes, because the majority of the food was being made ahead of time and catered by a chef friend of Gus's.

"I'm the mother of the bride," she said. "I'll have enough stresses walking her down the aisle." Everyone had agreed that only a handful of easy hors d'oeuvres would be prepared by the team on air in the first fifty minutes, followed by a brief ceremony and then several minutes of the reception.

"Everybody loves a wedding," said Porter. "The SaTroy fans are up in arms over this development—been writing in to the message boards without ceasing—and we're generating quite a lot of buzz. Yet again."

"This has been quite a show, Porter," said Gus.

"It's been the best thing you've ever done. And a damn fine first turn at bat, Carmen."

"Which leaves us with the second-to-last episode," said Oliver. "We've done octopus, brunch, veggie, grilling, local foods, and we'll finish with the wedding. But how do we sum it all up?"

"How about our favorite dishes from childhood?" Carmen said. "Wasn't that what we were supposed to learn at our retreat—finding our outer child?"

"*Inner* child, yeah," said Porter. "That seems good."

"How about we call them family favorites," Gus said. "We can come up with one item for everyone who's appeared on the show."

"That's pretty ambitious," said Oliver. "I don't know if we can squeeze it in."

"Let's try—we'll just show a few quick tips from each," she said. "For example, when I was young, my grandmother always made the most delicious homemade buns. I don't think we could show everyone how to make bread and do all the other stuff we have to do, but I could talk about it and show the finished product."

"And since it's fall, we can work in a bit of a harvest theme," suggested Oliver. "Like a fruit crisp using pears and apples in recognition of Troy's family."

"And I love meat loaf," said Porter. "We never make any good old-fashioned meat loaf on this channel."

"What'll be our Spanish touch?" sniffed Carmen. "I want to recognize what matters to me, as well."

"If octopus is your family favorite, then just tell us and by all means bring it in," said Gus. "This show is going to be for everyone."

Gus went directly from her meeting to Bar 44 at the Royalton. There, she found Sabrina and Billy eagerly awaiting her arrival. She'd been surprised, as she had spent more time with her daughter and her fiancé, at how simpatico they were, and how Billy seemed able to read Sabrina's moods quite well. He still looked like a Ken doll, with his conventionally handsome features, but there was clearly much more to him than that. Billy was, in fact, a very sensitive, caring man.

"We've just had a big talk about the food for the wedding," she told them now. "Lobster, and filet, and shrimp, and even a bit of truffle."

"Thank you, Gus," said Billy. "I'm completely overwhelmed. I know we had a rocky start but I am thrilled to become a part of your family."

"Well, that's good because if the season doesn't get picked up, I could be looking for a new home," she said, laughing.

"You're always welcome with us," he said.

They shared a good bottle of cabernet as Sabrina proudly showed them the dress she had picked out for Aimee, her maid of honor, and the bow ties she planned to force upon Salt and Pepper.

"I've an idea," Gus said. "Aimee knows we're doing wedding stuff but why don't I ask her to join us for dinner?"

"Perfect," said Billy. "I completely want to talk to her about an article I read about cassava production in Central Africa. She's great to talk to."

"Blah blah blah," said Sabrina. "The two of you can be so boring sometimes."

Gus held up her hand. "Wait, she's answering," she said, before asking Aimee to meet them. There was a long pause on the other end of the line.

"I'd love to, Mom, but I have plans."

"Tell her to turn off her game shows and come on down," piped up Sabrina, directing her comments toward the phone.

"Oh?" asked Gus. "What sort of plans?"

"I've met someone," said Aimee. "And that's all I'm going to say about that."

A slew of questions popped into Gus's brain: she had to know more, more, more. But she stopped herself. She was learning.

"Okay," she said. "I can't wait to hear all about it when you're ready."

It was getting rather late when Carmen returned to the test kitchen at the studio. Oliver was there, putting together some of the dishes for the next episode. He was just straightening up after placing a pan in the oven when Carmen came up and put her arms around him.

"Hey, you," she said, leaning in to give him a big smoochy kiss on each cheek. "Want to have some fun?"

"Hey, Carmen," he said, picking her arms off him though gazing at her fondly. "That's enough of that, okay."

"I've got a new idea," she said. "Let's get back together."

"We barely dated, and that was years ago, Carmen. You've got Alan now. And besides, I'm in love."

"*Vale, vale,*" Carmen said, making a face. "Who is it?"

"Someone whose last name is Simpson," he said.

"Aimee?"

"Gus," corrected Oliver.

"But she's older than you!"

"I know. That's part of her charm. She knows who she is."

Carmen crossed her arms. Now what? In her mind, she'd always considered Oliver her back-pocket guy, the one she could pull out for comfort when life wasn't working out.

"She can't have babies," she said. "I can do that for you."

"Ah, I'm not one for kids," said Oliver. "They're a bit chewy."

"Everyone wants children, Oliver."

"I don't. I'm good with the nieces and nephews. Uncle Oliver, you know. It's enough for me."

"What if you stop being happy?" she said. "Then what?"

He shrugged.

"I'm not happy," she admitted.

"Ah," said Oliver. "We're really talking about you, not me. Now I get it."

"Why am I not happy?"

"Well, if I had to hazard a guess, I'd say you take yourself far too seriously," he said. "And I strongly suspect your relationship with Alan is pretty much a means to an end. Is that what you really need in your personal life?"

"Everything is a means to an end, Oliver. I don't think it's fair that I've had to be on a show with Gus."

"It's not," said Oliver. "To her."

"I just feel thwarted," said Carmen. "Don't I work hard?"

"Do you feel good? That's what matters."

"Have you ever thought about bankrolling a restaurant?" Carmen leaned back on her arms and tilted her head, affecting a pose. "A Carmen Vega restaurant."

"I would have loved to. But I just made a huge investment in something else."

"You gave it to Gus?" Carmen toyed with an oven mitt that Oliver had taken off his hand.

"Hell, no, she'd never have taken it anyway," said Oliver. "I've just become the major shareholder in FarmFresh."

"Troy's dinky little company?"

"Ah, that's the beauty," said Oliver. "I don't think it's going to be small for too much longer."

"Everybody gets what they want except for me." Carmen threw the oven mitt onto the floor. "I don't understand, when I've sacrificed so much."

"Give it time."

"Sometimes I do things I'm not proud of, Oliver," she admitted, tilting her head back to stare at the ceiling. "But I tell myself it's okay. I just want to get ahead so much."

"Life isn't a straightforward climb up the ladder," he said, dishing up a bowl of the chicken soup he'd just prepared and handing it to her. "It can take a few slips to really gain perspective."

# comfort food

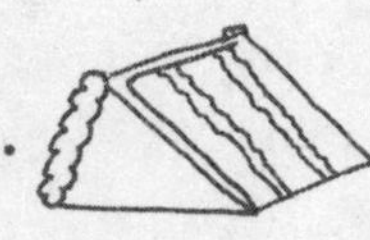

# 29

The mood in Gus's kitchen as the crew prepped was ebullient; Alan still hadn't announced the fate of *Eat Drink and Be* but he'd let Porter know that he was coming to personally be in the "audience" of the second-to-last show.

"He does remember there isn't actually a group of fans here, right?" asked Gus. "He's going to end up on an equipment box wedged in between Salt and Pepper."

"I'll make sure he has a chair," Porter said drily. "I try to go all out when the boss comes over."

Alan Holt arrived with an elegantly attired blonde on his arm, who towered over him in her heels.

"This is Melanie," he said. "She's a model."

"So nice to meet you," said Gus. "You'll find the 'set' is right down that hall. But do you mind if I have a quick word with Alan?"

She and Alan stepped into the dining room.

"What about Carmen?" she asked.

"What about her?"

"She's your girlfriend," hissed Gus. "Or was. And now you've brought another date to our show."

Alan stared at her as though she'd lost her mind.

"*Melanie*," he said, "is my girlfriend. For quite a while now. Months."

"What?"

"Melanie, my girlfriend, you just shook her hand." Alan patted her on the shoulder. "Maybe I do work you too hard."

"Are you saying Carmen is not your girlfriend?"

"It's an intriguing idea," Alan said. "But she's a little volatile, even for me."

"Well, everyone's been tiptoeing around her all season because they think you're her sugar daddy." Gus's voice was growing.

"Where'd they get that idea?"

"From everything," said Gus. "You brought her to my show from your house, and then she told Porter you okayed the octopus, and every time someone so much as stresses in her direction, she drops your name."

Alan chuckled.

"I've been played, haven't I?" Gus was not amused.

"I gotta say, there's more to that Carmen than I thought," said Alan. He patted a fuming Gus on the shoulder and walked away.

"You've still got a show to do, my dear. I look forward to it." And he strolled off to take a seat near Porter.

"Ten minutes, people," Porter called out. "If you need to use the facilities, do it now."

Gus was so angry she practically jet-propelled herself into the kitchen.

"Carmen," she said. "In the library. Alone. Now."

"I'm busy," Carmen replied, wiping the counter with a dry towel. "Tidying."

Gus brought her hand down quickly on the towel to stop Carmen's movements. "Since when," she asked, "do you do any tidying around here? Let's go. It's time to have a talk."

The rest of the team stared, then pretended not to be watching, then began making eye contact and mouthing, "What's going on?" to one another as Carmen was marched out of the room by Gus.

"Old habits die hard," mused Aimee, thinking of the times she and Sabrina had been reprimanded for various infractions when they were young.

"Just stay in the zone, people," Porter called out, sneaking glances at Alan and his blond guest and wondering just what, exactly, he'd said to Gus to set her off. And the series had been going so well.

"Sit," Gus said, as she and Carmen entered the library. Gus remained standing.

"Alan's not your boyfriend?"

"No." Carmen stared out the window, refusing to look Gus in the eye.

Gus took a deep breath, held it, and let it out.

"Carmen," Gus said slowly, in a calm, clear voice. "I want you to know that I was struck, particularly at the weekend retreat, by your absolute talent in the kitchen. You love food in a way few people do. That's something we have in common."

Carmen sat motionless in the chair, shocked still by what Gus was saying.

"I think you have a great future ahead, and I genuinely look forward to the day when you have what you want—the solo show, the fame, the restaurant, the cheese slicers bearing your name."

"Don't lie," said Carmen. "You've never wanted me to succeed. You should have seen the look on your face the day I walked into your kitchen. You wanted to scream but you were too proper to do it."

"You're right," admitted Gus. "But for right now, all we have is this program. We've got a few chances left to learn to work together. It's not for one of us to be successful at the *expense* of the other."

Carmen got up and began to pace, looking at Gus every few seconds. She'd always been an individual, competing by herself, for herself, from the beauty pageants to the Internet cooking program. She'd never considered there could be any other approach. Until now.

"I'm sorry, Gus." She looked her cohost full in the face. "Can you forgive me?"

"Oh, you mustn't be all bad, Carmen," Gus said, gently touching her arm. "Otherwise you wouldn't look quite so guilty."

Gus walked her back into the kitchen, where the rest of the team waited, salivating for an update.

"I have an announcement to make," Carmen said when she entered the room. "I want all of you to know that I am not dating Alan, nor have I ever been. I made it up to force all of you to respect me."

Troy dropped the pear he was cutting onto the floor. "But you've been so . . . difficult," he said. "Downright mean."

"My mother has been stressed out for six months," shouted Aimee.

"You lied," Sabrina said, somewhat shocked.

"You really do have *chutzpah*," said Hannah.

"Oh, Carmen," sighed Oliver.

"And I just want to say that Gus and I talked about it and she's not a bitch," Carmen said.

"What?"

"No, wait, that came out wrong. Gus, I expected you to be harsh, and I thought I'd beat you to the punch line. But you've never treated me anything other than decently, and I am sorry."

"Oh, this is huge," said Hannah. "I need a Milky Way."

Oliver came over and gave Carmen a long hug, then turned and kissed Gus full on the mouth.

The camera crew burst into applause.

"Lipstick! Lipstick!" shouted Porter.

"Okay, everyone, okay," Gus said, pushing Oliver back gently. "We're going live in . . . how long, Porter?"

"Three minutes!"

"Three minutes," she repeated. Gus motioned everyone closer to her: Troy, Aimee, Sabrina, Hannah, Oliver, and—when she stayed several steps back—Carmen.

"Tonight we are going to cook with love," she said quietly. "Everything's out in the open now so let's just forge ahead. This program is about food, and it's about family, and we just may be a rather dysfunctional lot, but it's what we have. Let's make this show hot!"

And when the red light came on, Gus was as warm and welcoming as she'd ever been.

"Thanks for tuning in tonight," she said. "I'm Gus Simpson, and this is *Eat Drink and Be*." She picked up an already-baked bun, warm from the oven. "See this? It's a roll, just like my own grandmother used to make. And when I bite into one of these, it takes me back to being a girl. So on this episode we've collected all sorts of comfort foods that are inspired by all the folks on our show."

"And I'm Carmen Vega. What are we making tonight, Gus?" For once, Carmen was deferential.

"Well, you're going to show us your mother's delicious gazpacho, aren't you?"

"I'd be happy to," said Carmen. Even though the tomatoes and peppers and cucumbers had all been prepped, she had half-expected that Gus would nix her project. It's what she would have done if the situation were reversed. I guess, she thought to herself, there's a reason why Gus is Gus.

"Two minutes until end of commercial," called out Porter. "Get ready to do that meat loaf with peach-apricot chutney."

"Chutney? Isn't that kinda weird on meat loaf?" asked Aimee.

"Oh, I had something like it at Priya's house and it was delish," said Hannah. "I told Gus all about it."

"I thought you were making chicken soup?" Sabrina said.

"Oh, I'm doing that, too," said Hannah.

"Don't forget we've got veggie chili and easy roasted fall vegetables to round out the menu," said Oliver.

"And my dad's chocolate cake," said Aimee. "We've that, too."

After sixty frantic minutes, the group had managed to showcase each of their dishes briefly—there were a lot of "look, here it is already done" moments—and taken a bite out of absolutely everything.

"Don't forget to check the website for the recipes," said Carmen. "All of this stuff is easy to make and fun to share."

"Remember," said Gus. "Food is family and family is food."

She paused to smile into the camera.

"My hope is that all of you make a point to savor what's on your plate. From all of us, have a good night, and, please, eat drink and be." She took a mouthful of Troy's pear and apple crisp as Carmen spooned gazpacho from a small cup. Both were delicious.

"And we're out," yelled Porter. "Great job! Next up is Sabrina's wedding, and then we'll break. Hopefully we'll be coming back after that."

Alan cleared his throat.

"About that," he said. "I'd like to see Porter, Gus, and Carmen in the study, please. If you don't mind me commandeering the room, of course, Gus."

"Not at all," she said, putting down the bowl in her hand and reaching for Oliver's to give it a squeeze before making her way to the library.

"Okay, gang," said Alan. "I just want to thank the three of you for a great run. Good job."

"That's it?" asked Porter.

"Pretty much. And, oh yeah, I'm renewing *Eat Drink and Be* with Gus Simpson!"

"And Carmen Vega," said Carmen.

"No," Alan said. "Just Gus is going to be on *Eat Drink and Be* from now on. It's always been her show anyway."

"*¡No lo creo!*" cried Carmen, sinking into a chair.

"Oh, it's not all over for you, Carmen," Alan said, putting his arm around her. "I'm giving you your own program."

"Really?"

"Yeah, I'm going to run the same episodes on both the Cooking-Channel and the new Spanish-language channel I've just bought into," he said. "*Eat Drink and Be* has been a great setup."

"I'm not understanding you," said Carmen.

"Me neither," said Gus.

"It's obvious," said Alan. "I had to build up Carmen's brand by piggybacking onto Gus. Get her a head start on a new fan base."

"Why didn't you let me in on it?" Gus asked.

"Tension makes for great television. Remember: it's business, Gus, business. Besides, I had faith you could handle it. I've always been able to depend on you."

"Wait a second here," said Carmen. "You didn't think I could hold my own?"

"You had a ten-minute Internet show about yourself, Carmen. I wanted you to learn how to host a show about the viewers."

"A Spanish-language channel?"

"And the CookingChannel," Alan said. "You'll be on both. The show will be bilingual, too—it's one of my best concepts. It'll be accessible and yet have that European sophistication, like Giada De Laurentiis."

"*Vale, vale,*" said Carmen. "I don't know whether to be happy or to cry. But finally I have my own show."

Gus still had questions.

"So I've never been in danger of losing my job?" she asked.

"I wouldn't go that far," said Alan. "Your ratings were dropping faster than a thermostat in a snowstorm. But with Porter's guidance, you made it through."

"Were you in on it, Porter?"

"Hell, no," said Porter. "I've barely slept in six months for worrying."

"Water under the bridge," said Alan. "Especially when I tell you, Porter, that you've just been promoted to head of programming for both channels."

"And a raise, I presume?"

"A big, fat raise."

"Gus?" asked Porter.

"Okay," she said. "Another season."

"Fantastic," Alan said. "I knew I hadn't lost the touch."

"Oh?" said Gus. She was more than a little exasperated with Alan, and quite ready to send him out the door and curl up on the couch with Oliver, maybe with some of the fruit crisp, and sort through the day's events. It had all been a bit much.

"I've always been able to put together such winning combinations," he said. "Carmen was the spice and Oliver was the beefcake."

"And what was I?"

"You, Gus?" Alan said. "Well, you've always been the heart and soul."

# 30

And then, after weeks of preparations that seemed to be mere moments, the day of Sabrina's wedding finally arrived. A white tent had been erected in the backyard of Gus's manor house, complete with a parquet tile dance floor and lights running up the tent poles. Gus arose even earlier than usual to awaken Sabrina and Aimee, whom she found sleeping together in the guest bedroom that overlooked the driveway. In just a few hours, thought Gus, watching her girls sleep for a few more moments, everything would change. The wedding dress, carefully chosen after endless try-ons, hung pressed inside a garment bag on the back of the bedroom door—the only spot high enough to hang it so that the skirt didn't crumple—while Aimee's strapless mauve gown waited inside the closet. Aimee had resisted her sister's styling for as long as possible (she'd wanted to wear a simple business suit, had even suggested as much to Sabrina, who had been quite fussed over it all) but in the end she relented, agreeing even to the too-high heels she'd had to practice walking in for days.

"Don't galumph around like that when you're coming down the aisle," Sabrina had moaned at her sister the night before. "Be light on your feet and smile."

"I can't smile and walk in these things at the same time," Aimee insisted.

"Just wear them for the ceremony and then change later," Gus said, ready to broker a truce although her daughters, it appeared, were quite fine sorting things out between themselves.

Now, hovering in the darkened bedroom listening to her no-longer-little girls breathe in their sleep, Gus was overwhelmed by the overlapping emotions of excitement, nostalgia, and melancholy. Was this how every mother of the bride felt? she wondered. Somehow, Gus realized, she'd assumed that her girls would always be the same, and that she would stay that way, too. Without ever meaning to, Alan Holt had given her a wonderful gift when he forced *Cooking with Gusto!* to transform into *Eat Drink and Be*. His actions had ultimately reminded her that change is nothing to be afraid of, that taking risks sometimes leads to unexpected dividends, and that even her mistakes could result in welcome discoveries.

Today was an auspicious day. Christopher would have been proud.

Gus ran through a mental checklist in her mind: the hairstylist was coming at 9 AM, the florist at ten, and the catered food at eleven. By 2 PM the guests would start arriving, and by three o'clock the cameras would be on.

What had she been thinking? No mother of the bride who wanted to keep her sanity would dream of hosting a live television program the same day her daughter was getting married. It was going to be a crazy day, thank you very much. At least there was Oliver to handle much of the meal preparation. He was quite useful, that fellow, in all sorts of ways.

Gus and Aimee and Sabrina were upstairs getting ready when Oliver let himself in. He'd come up from the city on an early Metro-North train; Carmen and Troy were coming an hour later. Hannah was already in the kitchen, for once not waiting on Gus to make her breakfast, but nibbling on some peeled and sectioned oranges she'd found in the fridge. She was busy, too, having printed out several Heimlich maneuver posters that she thought could be taped up inside the tent and had brought along several extra fire extinguishers. Just in case.

"Hey," said Oliver. "You better not be eating what I think you are." He didn't look worried in the least.

"It's just some oranges," said Hannah.

"Don't let Gus catch you," he joked. "She'll chop your fingers off. She and I prepared all of that last night to use in the fruit salad."

He went into the pantry and carried out a box of tomatoes, several cloves of fresh garlic, and green onions. He took Gus's special scissors into the back garden and, a large tray in hand, began cutting fresh herbs to use in the day's dishes.

By the time Carmen, Troy, and Porter entered the kitchen, the area was prepped and ready for the few hors d'oeuvres they planned to make live on the air. The rest of the food for the 120 guests was on its way in a catering truck from the city. It was, for an episode of *Eat Drink and Be*, going to be a fairly easy day.

Or so they thought.

"Where's the food?" Carmen asked Hannah a few hours before the show, as she was chopping tomatoes. The caterers had not arrived, and Oliver was talking animatedly into his cell phone. He waved at Carmen, Troy, and Hannah to get their attention.

"The catering truck blew a tire about two miles down the road," he said. "The back door blew open and most of the meals that were going to be served are now covering I-95."

"We have no food for the reception?"

"Pretty much," said Oliver. "We don't need to tell Gus yet—there's nothing she can do. We're going to have to solve this one for ourselves."

"I'll take Hannah's car and see if there's anything still good at the truck," said Troy, who immediately ran with Hannah to her carriage house to get the keys.

"From inside the truck, Troy," Oliver shouted after him. "No five-second rule!"

Carmen turned around and left the room.

"Get back here," muttered Oliver, being careful to keep his voice down so he wouldn't be heard inside the house. He didn't want to disturb Gus and her daughters.

Carmen returned to the kitchen with a bag of potatoes in each hand. She very calmly opened drawers to find a peeler, not responding to Oliver's queries about what she was doing, and then positioned herself near the sink.

"Oliver," she said, without looking up from her work. "Write out a list for Porter and send him to the store. Tell him to buy every shrimp he can find—any size at all—and if they have lobster or lamb, get that, too. We're going to make the best selection of *tapas* anyone has ever put together in two hours, and Gus's guests are never going to know the difference. I'm starting with potato galettes that we'll cover with whatever different cheeses Porter brings back. This wedding reception will be spectacular."

"You'd really do that, Carmen?"

"I owe her, Oliver," she explained. "And I want to pay my debts."

Forty-five minutes later, Troy and Hannah returned with a speeding ticket, a pan of fresh salmon, one black truffle, three tins of caviar, a covered box of mushrooms, and twelve filet mignons that had originally been intended to be served with a spicy Gorgonzola sauce of shiitake mushrooms and chipotle chilies. That sauce now coated a good portion of the highway.

"Start slicing the beef," ordered Carmen, "and make it paper thin. We're going to wrap it around the green onions we already have here, and God help me, we're going to make it stretch."

The salmon was quickly thrown into the Aga to bake, then drizzled with a vanilla-infused vegetable oil and sprinkled with roe.

"We're going to run out of plates," said Oliver.

"Good thing I saw more potatoes in the pantry," said Carmen. "We'll make smaller galettes, and use them as though they were plates."

"What do you want me to do with these mushrooms?" Troy was rubbing each mushroom with a clean soft cloth, as Oliver had instructed him.

"Get them started in a pan with a little olive oil, and we'll brown them with some of our fresh garlic and the thyme from Gus's garden," said Carmen. "We'll finish them with a few drops of sherry. Hannah!"

Hannah waited for her marching orders.

"Find those oranges I saw you pigging out on earlier, and bring them to the stovetop."

"And then what?" said Hannah.

"Then it's time for you to learn how to cook," said Carmen. "You're going to create a syrup from red wine, a little zest, cinnamon, and sugar, and let it simmer for a half hour. We'll cool it in an ice bath and drench the oranges. You've never had anything like it."

Breathless, Porter ran into the kitchen, bags of groceries spilling out of his arms, as various members of his camera crew leaped in to help.

"How's it going, guys?" he asked.

"*Muy bien*," said Carmen, who was not in the least bit nervous. "We're going to show our viewers how to make some of the best *tapas* in the world."

• • •

It was forty-five minutes before the show, and the Simpsons were almost ready. Gus's hair was sleekly blown out, Aimee's was straight and shiny, and Sabrina had an updo, with loose tendrils framing her face.

"Aren't we the gorgeous ones," Gus said, as she unzipped the garment bag around Sabrina's dress for a peek. The gown was elegantly simple, an off-the-shoulder silk sheath dress in the palest of pinks—it was like white that was a tad more excited. With great care, she helped Sabrina put it on.

"And let's not forget the purple people eater," she teased, dancing around with Aimee's dress.

"It's mauve, Mom," said Sabrina. "Aimee is going to look lovely."

"Or something," said Aimee, calculating just how many minutes she'd have to suffer in the damn shoes her sister had picked. Ah, well, it wasn't every day her little sister got married. She smiled as her mother pinned flowers in Sabrina's hair.

"And now you're a bride." Gus smoothed out Sabrina's veil and kissed her lightly on the cheek.

"Ready to get hitched, Sabrina?" teased Aimee, going through Gus's jewelry box to pick out a pair of good earrings.

"Yes," Sabrina said, before turning around to face herself in the mirror. She saw the layers of lace and tulle and the glittering crystals beaded into the waistline. She'd never gotten this far before with any of her previous fiancés. This is real, she thought. This is definitely happening. I am going to marry Billy today. And in an instant her stomach constricted, her heart raced, and the air was squeezed out of her lungs even as she gasped for more.

"I can barely breathe," Sabrina said, and she began to hyperventilate, her eyes stinging. "I'm not. I'm not ready. I can't do it."

# 31

Get Billy. Those were the words her mother had said, and Aimee fairly flew down the stairs to look for him. In just over five minutes, Sabrina had morphed from a perky bride-to-be into a hysterical raving lunatic, alternately crying that maybe she really loved Troy after all to declaring that she would just never be ready. Billy, outfitted in a black tuxedo even though it was a daytime wedding—because that's what Sabrina wanted and Gus recognized it was her right to choose no matter what etiquette dictated—beamed as Aimee drew nearer.

"How are things upstairs?" he asked, before reading Aimee's face and rapidly taking the stairs, two at a time, until he came upon Sabrina, crying on her mother's shoulder.

"Let's give you two a few minutes," Gus said, though she could hear Porter calling for everyone to remember their marks and get ready to go live in a half hour. She and Aimee waited anxiously in the hallway until Sabrina and Billy emerged, holding hands, about twenty minutes later.

"So we're back on," shouted Gus, ecstatic.

"No," said Sabrina. "We've decided to call off the wedding."

"For now," corrected Billy.

"I've got cold feet, that's true," admitted Sabrina. "But mostly I just feel as though I've rushed things."

"We're going to take some more time to get to know one another," added Billy. "This is unorthodox, I know, but we feel it's the right thing to do. Our guests will be disappointed, but our marriage isn't simply about today."

"Oh, Sabrina," said Gus. "As your mother, I support you one hundred percent. But as the host of a TV show going live in a few minutes, I could shake you."

Sabrina was sheepish, especially as Porter came up the stairs to find Gus, his energy electric. He could barely stand still.

"This show is going to be phenomenal," he said. "Carmen has saved the day, Gus. You wouldn't believe it but we had a catering disaster. All fixed now—don't worry. It's delicious."

Gus hugged Porter.

"So sorry to tell you this, old friend, but we're not having a wedding today," she said.

Porter stopped moving and gaped at her.

"Now what are we going to do?" he asked when he'd recovered his voice.

Gus threw up her hands. "Who knows," she said. "Let's just take it as it comes. We'll be having a party today, that much I know."

"So this is where you make fun of me, big sister," said Sabrina. "Always a fiancée, never a bride."

"Oh, shut up," Aimee said, though her tone was gentle. "You're finally sticking with something, in your own weird way. If Billy's okay with it, then so am I."

"And now someone's got to go down and say something to our guests," said Gus. "Not to mention our viewers."

"I'm a big girl," said Sabrina. "I can make my own announcement."

Billy put his arm around her. "I'll stand with you, too."

The day had been a roller coaster and Troy was exhausted, physically and emotionally. He would have expected to feel relieved about how things had unfolded, but he didn't. Troy was hardly surprised, and more than a little concerned for Sabrina, but he wasn't about to make another bid for her. He had really and truly moved forward.

The show had been frenzied but fun, and the guests seemed to bounce back rapidly from their initial shock. Cushioned, no doubt, by the sense that Sabrina and Billy were merely postponing their big day, and by all the sumptuous delights that Carmen had produced for them to enjoy. Personally, he'd eaten much more than his fair share, and he didn't regret it one bit.

He was ready to call it a night, though he needed to be polite and thank his host before leaving. He might also, if he could find her, say goodbye to Hannah.

Out on the dance floor, Hannah was doing the Twist with Priya's youngest, Kiran.

". . . and it goes like this," she was singing to the little boy, her red hair flying with each shake of her hips, as Kiran copied her moves. She looked absolutely ridiculous, thought Troy, and completely oblivious.

He strode onto the dance floor as the music was dying down and tapped Kiran on the shoulder.

"May I cut in?" he asked.

"I dunno," said Kiran. "What's that mean?"

"I want to dance with Hannah," said Troy.

"Yeah, okay," she said, her stomach jumping.

The band started up a quick beat.

"No wait," Troy said, apparently changing his mind. "I want our first dance to be a slow one."

The cameras had long been turned off and several guests had left when Alan strolled up to the microphone to make a special announcement about Carmen's new show and the renewal of *Eat Drink and Be.* Such news wouldn't have been appropriate at a wedding reception, of course, but seeing as how the marriage didn't take place . . . Gus thought it was fine. She rather enjoyed Alan's effusive praise of her years on the CookingChannel and his excitement about the program.

"Gus, would you like to say a few words?" asked Alan.

She jumped up the few steps to the dais.

"Thank you for coming," she said. "It's been such a pleasure. But I'm afraid Alan's wrong about one thing tonight, and that is the fact that I'm not going to be returning for another season of *Eat Drink and Be.* As much as I have loved working with all of you."

She caught Carmen's eye. "With *all* of you," she repeated. "But it's time for me to go."

In the weeks following Alan's offer of renewal, Gus initially felt as though she'd received exactly what she had wanted and she was relieved. But another idea nibbled at her, as well—the feeling that, with Sabrina and Aimee successfully living their own lives, she was suddenly unburdened by the responsibilities she'd so long carried. And that's when she knew: now was her opportunity to recapture and reinvent herself.

"And I'm not only leaving the CookingChannel, which has been my home for twelve years," Gus said, "but I am also leaving Rye and New York and this house, which has been such a special place. I'm hitting the road and touring the world."

Aimee and Sabrina looked at each other in shock; Hannah was dumbfounded, freezing in position with a shrimp halfway to her mouth.

It was as though Gus had become a different person.

"I didn't say I'm disappearing," Gus said, speaking directly to them even as she addressed everyone in the tent. "You'll all be seeing more than enough of me, and getting a lot of calls and emails. But it's time for some new adventures in my life. It's time to explore."

She stepped off the dais and was immediately surrounded by a mix of well-wishers and stunned CookingChannel colleagues. Within seconds, she felt Oliver's hand on her arm, pulling her out of the crowd.

"Gus," he said. "What the hell? What am I? A little summer fun?"

"Don't demean yourself, Oliver," Gus said emphatically. "You've made a huge difference in my life."

"That's all well and good," he said. "But I thought our relationship meant . . . something."

Oliver held his hand to his forehead as he tried to collect his thoughts.

"I've been circling around for a long time," she said. "And I feel as though I've finally figured out where I want to land."

"Look," he said, his voice cracking just a little. "I know well enough that we've all got to follow our dreams. If this is what you want, I support you."

"Thank you, Oliver," said Gus, feeling very relieved. "That means everything to me."

"But don't think I'm just going to wait around." He picked up his tuxedo jacket off a nearby chair as if to go.

"Yes, about that," Gus said, lightly placing her hand on his arm to stop him. "You see, I was very much hoping that you'd be coming with me."

# the icing on the cake

# 32

APRIL 2008

It came in the mail: a formal invitation to one of Gus Simpson's world-famous parties. What was surprising was the location—a private loft overlooking the Union Square farmer's market—and the occasion. Gus Simpson was coming back to television in a new show produced by her very own production company, 50/50 Ventures, and she was throwing a huge party to launch the first episode.

She and Oliver had been away from New York for almost a year, traveling to twenty countries to research and film *Local Food Far Away*, a program dedicated to showcasing great places, great foods, and great crafts, and making those items (all fair trade, naturally) available for purchase by American viewers. Gus had finally found a way to unify the altruism of her youth with her professional success and her belief in the importance of fresh local ingredients. She'd had to sell the house for capital, of course, though she felt it was worth it. The house and its nineteen rooms had been precisely what she'd needed at a previous point in her life but she had been ready to move on.

Hannah was through the door of the loft before anyone else had appeared, eager to reconnect with her old friend since the last time they'd emailed, and to tell her all about the latest developments in the Hannah Joy Levine Love Yourself tennis program, designed to help at-risk youth boost their physical fitness and self-esteem. And although she had rather enjoyed her time on television with Gus, she ultimately turned down the Hollywood producers who approached the once-scandalized sports star to host *Take That Back*, a catty exploration of celebrities' most embarrassing moments caught on tape. Instead, she'd kept up with her health writing, taken on a few clients for private tennis lessons (Priya, wanting to shed a few pounds, was her first customer), and finally passed her driving test, with Troy proudly waiting at the DMV to celebrate.

Troy had been busy, as well, having gone national with the FarmFresh healthy vending machines in all fifty states, then sending his equipment into Canadian schools and ultimately hooking up with *Naked Chef* Jamie Oliver to take them across the Atlantic to the United Kingdom. FarmFresh apples were available in airports, train stations, shopping malls, and, most important, in schools. Apples from his parents' orchard were even available in the local elementary school in Hood River, and his father made a special trip some days simply to watch with pride as the students punched a button to select the Park family produce.

Fresh food was on Carmen's mind, too. Her bilingual show was popular on both the Spanish-language network and the Cooking Channel, and she worked closely with Porter, who was run ragged with his new position and loving it. But most important to Carmen was that she had managed to secure funding—thanks to Oliver calling a few friends—to open her very own restaurant, *Pulpo*. And she chose a stylish up-and-coming designer to keep the look of her *cocina* fresh, fun, and, above all, bright.

Because Carmen's designer, Sabrina, had gotten past her aversion to making over kitchens—finding a way to integrate her mother's history with her ability to decorate. Sabrina's business was growing. She and Billy were still happily dating, thinking every so often about making things more permanent, but in no rush to do so. He was the one to finally figure out how to get the girl: he waited.

FBI Agent Jeremy Brewer had gotten his Aimee, too, as well as solving the case of the year. He'd discovered money manager David Fazio moving funds to Europe when Fazio sought treatment for a social disease he'd acquired while partying with other people's money.

All in all, it was a festive atmosphere, with many friends and an abundance of delicious nibbles. Everyone milled about, chatting with Oliver, but not so secretly keeping a lookout for Gus. Problem was, she was nowhere to be found.

Not until the strains of music started and Gus appeared in the doorway in a cream linen pantsuit, holding a single rose in her hand, did the assembled guests have any clue that the launch party was about starting much more than just a new show.

Aimee and Sabrina, in on the secret, stood on either side of their mother and walked her toward Oliver, who was standing patiently by the window through which the lights of the city sparkled.

It was a perfect moment.

Gus Simpson adored wedding cake.

# homemade buns

*Gus's favorite comfort food, and mine as well.*
*From my grandmother's secret recipe and known in*
*my family as Nannybuns.*

INGREDIENTS:

*For the buns:*

½ teaspoon sugar
¼ cup warm water (100–115°F—if the water is too hot it will kill the yeast)
1 packet dry yeast
¼ cup sugar
¼ cup shortening or unsalted butter
2 eggs
8 to 10 cups all purpose white flour (or a mixture of 1:3 wheat to white flour)
½ tsp salt (mixed into the flour)
5 cups warm water
⅓ cup canola oil

*For the glaze:*

¼ cup heavy cream
¼ cup sugar

DIRECTIONS:

Proof the yeast: whisk sugar and water together in a bowl, then sprinkle yeast over the mixture. Stir to combine. Allow mixture to sit for approximately 7 minutes until frothy.

In a large bowl, cream together sugar and shortening (or butter) using an electric mixer with beaters on medium speed. Add eggs and mix until incorporated. Remove beaters and place dough hook on the mixer. Sift together flour and salt. Add 2 cups of the warm water and 2 cups of the flour. Mix until thoroughly combined. Add proofed yeast and mix thoroughly.

Add another cup of flour and another cup of water, and mix at medium speed. Add yet another cup of flour and cup of water, mixing again at medium. Add one more cup of flour and the final cup of water and mix. You will use up all the water but should have flour left over. Your dough is ready if it moves in a circle around the dough hook—it should be fairly stiff and thick but not dry. If it does not circle around the dough hook, then add more flour.

Place approximately 1 cup of flour in the bottom of a large bowl. (You'll need a big bowl because the dough will double in size). Place the dough in the bowl and add ½ cup of flour on top of the dough. Knead the dough, adding more flour if necessary so that you can knead without all the dough sticking to your hands. Keep kneading until all flour is incorporated. Form the dough into a ball (it will be slightly sticky). Wash your hands, coat them with a little oil, and oil the ball of dough so that it doesn't stick to the sides of the bowl as it rises.

Place the bowl with the oiled ball in an unheated oven (but leave the light on to provide a slight amount of heat). Make sure there are no drafts in the room because drafts will make the ball collapse. Let dough sit until it doubles in size, approximately one hour.

Grease several cookie sheets or 9×13 pans. Remove the dough from the bowl, place on a floured surface, and punch down for a few minutes until all the air is popped out and the dough returns to its original size. (Knead in a little more flour if the ball is too sticky.) Place canola oil in a soup bowl. Shape the dough into tennis ball–sized buns and dip the top into the oil. Arrange the dough balls on cookie sheets approximately three across and four lengthwise: about a dozen on a full-size cookie sheet. (If you want to make soft-sided buns, let the balls touch in a 9×13 pan.) Place sheets or pans in an unheated oven (again, with the light on) and allow to rise for an hour to an hour and twenty minutes. Remove dough from oven, again making sure there are no drafts in the kitchen.

Preheat oven to 375°F. Bake for 20 minutes, or until buns are golden brown and sound hollow when tapped.

For the glaze mix heavy cream with sugar. Lightly brush mixture on top of the warm buns to give them a nice shine and a little sweetness!

*Yield: 2 dozen buns*

# gus's golden cupcakes

*Nice moist crumb texture—almost muffinlike—with light sweetness and dotted with bursts of chocolate chips.*

INGREDIENTS:

2½ cups flour
2½ tsp baking powder
¾ tsp baking soda
½ tsp salt
⅔ cup butter, softened
2 cups white sugar
2 tsp vanilla
2 eggs, room temperature
1¼ cups buttermilk
1 cup miniature chocolate chips, semi-sweet

DIRECTIONS:

Preheat oven to 375 degrees.

Line muffin tin with paper cups.

Mix flour, baking powder, baking soda, and salt in a bowl and set aside. (You need the baking soda to offset the tang of the buttermilk.)

In a separate bowl, using a mixer, cream the butter until light and fluffy. Then add the sugar, and cream until smooth. Add vanilla, mix.

Add room temperature eggs one at a time, mixing well after each addition. After both eggs are incorporated, mix again on medium-high for 30 seconds.

Alternate adding the flour mixture and the buttermilk, a little at a time, mixing on low until just combined. When all milk and flour is added, mix together on medium-high for 30 seconds.

Chocolate chips offer a pleasant counterbalance to the cupcake. Fold in now.

Fill muffin cups ¾ full. Do not overfill or muffins will overflow when they rise!

If intending to serve the chocolate chip cupcakes without frosting, put a few chocolate chips on top before baking for appearance's sake.

Bake for 22–26 minutes. Check through the oven window before opening the oven door. (With homemade cakes and cupcakes made from scratch, opening the oven before baking is complete can result in fallen cakes.)

Icing flavors from chocolate to vanilla to peppermint will work; go to www.comfortfoodnovel.com for ideas.

*Yield: 18–24 cupcakes*

# ACKNOWLEDGMENTS

Recently, a reader told me that the acknowledgments are her favorite part of any book. (What does that say about the rest of the pages? I wondered.) Well, believe me when I tell you I had a lot of support—a great deal of comfort, if you will—as I wrote this novel. It was deeply appreciated during what has been a hectic and tumultuous year.

Many thanks to everyone at Putnam, especially Ivan Held, the ever cheery and always helpful Eve Adler and Rachel Holtzman, and above all to Rachel Kahan, the smartest and most understanding editor in New York. Equally patient were Sue Fletcher and Swati Gamble in London. And I'm very grateful for the attention that this book has received from everyone in sales, marketing, publicity, editorial, production, and design.

Deserving of her very own paragraph is my insightful and caring agent, Dorian Karchmar, of the William Morris Agency. I leave every conversation with Dorian having laughed and learned, and few things reassure a writer more than having an agent in her corner who is also such a steadfast friend. Thank you.

I'm indebted to my parents and siblings for their constant encouragement and willingness to listen, and to my dear friends who read early chapters that often arrived late at night: Rhonda Hilario-Cagiuat, Kim Jacobs, Shawneen Jacobs, Tina Kaiser, Alissa MacMillan, Robin Moore, Sara-Lynne Levine, and Christine Tyson. A special mention goes to my mother and sister, with whom I enjoyed many hours reminiscing about favorite family foods, such as the smell of my grandmother's homemade buns and her fragrant chicken soup with fresh noodles.

In particular, I'd like to recognize Althea Saldanha and Tamara MacMillan, who opened windows into Indian and Spanish food and culture, and Sandra Lee, who shared tales from culinary school and restaurant kitchens. I appreciate your insights tremendously. And thanks to Kevin MacMillan and David Berger for their steady and wise counsel; to Dorian's great assistant, Adam Schear, who is always on top of things; and to all of the wonderful readers who have emailed me over the past few months to say they were eager for my next book! It's always a delight to hear from you.

Finally, I want to recognize the home team. To my dog, Baxter, who loves a good tennis ball and was always eager to play fetch when I wanted to step away from the computer (and even when I didn't). And to my husband, Jonathan Bieley, who alarmed me with a bit of a health scare and then bounced back good as new, ready to stay awake late, get up early, make (order!) dinner, reorganize our home office, and proofread every chapter. Thanks for being such a comfort.

READERS GUIDE

# comfort food

## by Kate Jacobs

You can also visit www.comfortfoodnovel.com for more recipes! Go to www.katejacobs.com to sign up for Kate's newsletter and to learn more about her upcoming events.

And you can even ask Kate to call in to your very own book club!

1. When we first meet Gus, she's on the cusp of her fiftieth birthday. Suddenly, the woman known for her lavish celebrations "woke up one morning and realized she hadn't done a thing to plan. She, who never missed a chance to have a party. And that's when she realized she didn't want to do anything about celebrating, either." Is Gus in an emotional rut simply because she's hit a milestone birthday? What else in her life might not be worth celebrating? Which of the other characters appear to be in the same rut as the novel begins?

2. Gus's two daughters, Sabrina and Aimee, seem to be complete opposites, and yet both seem to be at odds with Gus. Is one daughter more like Gus than the other, or do they represent different facets of their mother's personality? Does this change over the course of the novel? By the end of the story, do you think Gus has incorporated lessons from her daughters into her own life?

3. We meet several characters who are grappling with their sense of purpose and identity: Priya, the underappreciated housewife; Hannah, with her candy habit and a secret past; and Carmen, the beauty queen who just wants to be respected. In what way do the women around Gus prompt her to examine or change her own life? Who do you think is most helpful in this way?

4. Carmen Vega's defining feature is her beauty—her viewers "loved to talk about how she looked as much as what she cooked." Does Carmen seem conflicted about using her beauty to get what she wants? How is she typical—or not typical—of women who get ahead by using their looks as well as their brains? Did your opinion of her change by the end of the book?

5. When we first meet Oliver, we learn that over the course of his lucrative Wall Street career: "ambitious Oliver morphed into an older, far less interesting man. Only he was the only who didn't know it." Does this also describe the very successful Gus Simpson? And if so, what do you make of Oliver's attraction to her?

6. As the characters begin to pair off, were there any couples you found surprising? Who is your favorite new couple? Would you have had things turn out differently for any of them?

7. One of the big mysteries of this story is why Hannah lives such a secluded life. Once you discovered the root of her angst, did you sympathize with her, or think she was overreacting? Why do you think Hannah latched onto her friendship with Gus when she shunned everyone else's company? And how does Hannah's journey out of the house and toward a fuller life mirror Gus's own journey in the course of this novel?

8. We only hear about Christopher, Gus's late husband, a few times, but it's clear that his death was the pivotal event in the lives of Gus and her daughters. Would Gus have achieved the same level of success had Christopher lived? What kind of life would she and her daughters have had if Gus had stayed at home and never become a CookingChannel celebrity?

9. At the end of the novel, Gus "decided that it wasn't necessary to explain why she was doing what she was doing, or to rationalize her feelings. She could just let it be." Is this a total change from the Gus we first met? Why do you think she feels so serene? Is it because of the romance with Oliver, or having cleared the air with her daughters, or perhaps something else?

10. Not all of the characters cook, but they're each affected by food or cooking in some way. In what way does food serve to connect or reassure them? Are there times when food seems like a divisive or negative element in relationships? Have you had these food-related experiences with your own friends and loved ones?

11. In your opinion, is there a "lesson" to *Comfort Food*? What, if anything, do you think Kate Jacobs most wants you to take away from this story? And what is your own favorite "comfort food"?

# beginner

Seeing a pattern doesn't mean you know how to put it all together. Take baby steps: don't focus on the folks whose skills are far beyond your own. When you're new to something—or you haven't tried it in a while—it can feel impossibly hard to get it right. Every misstep feels like a reason to quit. You envy everyone else who seems to know what they're doing. What keeps you going? The belief that one day you'll also be like that: Elegant. Capable. Confident. Experienced. And you can be. All you need now is enthusiasm. A little bravery. And—always—a sense of humor.

It was after hours at Walker and Daughter: Knitters, and Dakota stood in the center of the Manhattan yarn shop and wrestled with the cellophane tape. She had spent more than twenty minutes trying to surround a canvas Peg Perego double stroller in shimmery yellow wrapping paper, the cardboard roll repeatedly flopping out of the paper onto the floor of the shop and the seeming miles of gift wrap crinkling and tearing with each move. What a disaster! The simpler move would be to just tie a balloon on the thing, she thought, but Peri had been quite insistent that all the items be wrapped and ribboned.

Gifts, smothered in bunny paper or decorated with cartoonish jungle animals, were piled in a mound atop the sturdy wooden table that was the focal point of the knitting store. The wall of yarn had been tidied so not one shelf—from the raspberry reds to the celery greens—was out of hue. Peri had also planned out a series of cringe-inducing guessing games (Guess how much the baby will weigh! Eat different baby foods and try to determine the flavor! Estimate the size of the mother's stomach!) that would have caused Dakota's mother to shake her head. Georgia Walker had never been a fan of silly games.

"It'll be fun," said Peri when Dakota protested. "We haven't had a Friday Night baby since Lucie had Ginger five years ago. Besides, who doesn't like baby showers? All those tiny little footie pajamas and those cute towels with animal ears. I mean, it just gives you goose bumps. Don't you love it?"

"Uh, no," said Dakota. "And double no. My friends and I are a little busy with college." Her hands rested on the waist of her deep indigo jeans as she watched Peri pretend not to fuss over the job she'd done. The stroller looked like a giant yellow banana. A wrinkled, torn banana. She sighed. Dakota was a striking young woman, with her creamy mocha skin and her mother's height and long, curly dark hair. But she retained an element of gangliness, gave the impression that she was not quite comfortable with the transformation of her figure. At eighteen, she was still growing into herself.

"Thank God for that," replied Peri, discreetly trying to peel the tape off the yellow paper so she could redo the edges. Whether it was operating the store or designing the handbags in her side business, she approached everything with precision now. Working with Georgia had been the best training she could ever have received for running a business—two businesses, really. Her own handbag company, Peri Pocketbook, as well as Georgia's store. Still, Peri felt she had done a lot to keep things going since Georgia passed away, and now that she was pushing thirty, she was beginning to feel a desire to move. In what direction, she wasn't sure. But there would be no more Walker and Daughter without her. Of that she was certain.

Sometimes it wasn't very satisfying to work so hard for something that essentially belonged to someone else. It was hers but not really hers at all.

For one thing, Dakota had seemed less and less interested in the store during the last year or so, grumbling on the Saturdays when she came in to work, typically late and sometimes appearing to simply roll out of bed and throw on whatever clothes she could find. It was quite a change from her early teens when she seemed to relish her time at the shop. And yet there were brief moments when her world-weary attitude would disappear and Peri could see the whispers of the bright-eyed, wisecracking little kid who loved to bake and could spend hours knitting with her mother in the store's back office or the apartment they had shared one floor above the yarn shop.

The shop was located on Seventy-seventh and Broadway, just above Marty's deli, amid boutiques and restaurants in Manhattan's Upper West Side. Only a few blocks from the green of Central Park and the cool of the Hudson River in the opposite direction, it was a lovely part of the city. Oh, certainly there was lots of noise—honking taxis, the rumble of the subway underneath the streets, the sound of heels on the sidewalk and cell phone conversations swirling all around—but that was the type of commotion that had appealed to Georgia Walker when she moved in. She didn't mind the beeping of the Coke truck at five a.m. bringing supplies to the deli on the street level. Not if it meant she got to live right inside the action, showing her daughter the world she had barely imagined herself when growing up on a farm in Pennsylvania.

Of course, now Peri lived in the upstairs apartment that had been Georgia's and the back office was no more. The wall had recently been blown out to make a separate showcase for the handbags she designed and sold; each purse was individually displayed on a clear acrylic shelf mounted onto a wall painted a deep gray.

The change to the store had come together after much discussion with Anita and with Dakota, and they'd consulted Dakota's father, James, too, of course, though mostly for his architectural expertise. But it made financial sense: Peri had turned Dakota's childhood bedroom in the apartment into an office so there was no need to tally up receipts in the shop anymore. Why waste the store's valuable real estate? And there *had* always been the understanding—with Georgia and with James and Anita after Georgia died—that her handbag business would have the chance to flourish. She had reminded them of that while purposefully avoiding the one ultimatum she knew everyone most feared: she would leave the store if she wasn't able to remodel. The concern hung in the air, and she saved voicing it unless it was absolutely necessary.

After all, what would happen to the store if Peri left? Anita, who had turned seventy-eight on her last birthday, though she still looked just barely old enough to collect Social Security, certainly wouldn't be about to take over. Though she continued to arrive two days a week to help out and keep busy, as she said, Anita and Marty spent a lot of their time going on quick trips, by train or car, to wonderful country inns in New England and in Canada. Those two were on a perpetual vacation, and Peri was happy for them. Envious, a little bit. Definitely. Hopeful that she'd have the same thing someday. And if that legal department coworker her pal KC kept mentioning was half as cute as he'd been described, who knew what could happen?

And then there was Dakota, who had nearly finished up her first year at NYU. It wasn't as though she could step in to run the store—or that she even seemed to want to do so anymore.

Not everyone wants to go into the family business.

Peri's decision to work at the yarn shop, and create her own designs, had not been popular within her own family. Her parents had wanted her to become a lawyer, and she'd dutifully taken her LSAT and earned a place at law school, only to turn it down and leave everyone guessing. Georgia hadn't been cowed by Peri's mother, who flew in from Chicago to pressure Georgia into firing her, and Peri had never forgotten that fact. Even when difficulties arose over the shop, Peri reflected on how Georgia had helped her and she stuck it out. Still, the work of two businesses took up all of her days and many of her evenings, and the past five years seemed to have moved quickly. It was as though one day Peri woke up and realized she was almost thirty, still single, and not happy with the situation. It was hard to meet guys in New York, she thought. No, not guys. Men. Men like James Foster. Peri had had a mild crush on the man ever since he'd come back for Georgia, and he remained, for her, the very epitome of the successful, confident partner she longed for.

Of course, James had only ever been interested in the store from the standpoint of keeping an eye on Georgia's legacy to Dakota. And Georgia's old friend Catherine was surrounded by crap up in the Hudson Valley, thought Peri, where she managed her antiques-and-wonderful-things-blah-blah-blah store. Besides, Catherine couldn't even knit. And she and Peri had never really connected; it was more as though they shared several mutual friends but hadn't quite managed, even after all this time, to get to know each other. Peri often felt judged whenever Catherine glided into the shop, soaking in everything with her perfectly made-up smoky eyes, every blond hair in place.

No, over the years the feeling had become more definite that either Peri would keep things going at Walker and Daughter or it would be time to close up the doors to the yarn shop. The desire to keep everything just as it once had been—to freeze time—remained very strong among the group of friends. So even as she advocated change, Peri felt guilty. It was almost overwhelming. Stemming from some natural fantasy they all shared but never discussed: that everything needed to be kept just so for Georgia. For what? To want to come back? To feel at home? Because making changes to Georgia's store, without her presence or consultation, would mean things were really final. Wouldn't it? That all the moments the members of the Friday Night Knitting Club and the family of Georgia Walker had experienced, the good and the bad, *had* truly happened.

That Georgia's yarn shop was the place where an unlikely group of women became friends around the table in the center of the room. Where Anita, the elegant older woman who was Georgia's biggest supporter, learned to accept Catherine, Georgia's old high school friend, and cheered as Catherine rediscovered her own capacity for self-respect and left an empty and unfulfilling marriage. It was at Georgia's that dour and lonely graduate student Darwin found a true friend in director Lucie, who had embarked on first-time motherhood in her forties, and that Darwin realized just how much she wanted to sustain her marriage to her husband, Dan, after a brief night of infidelity. It was at Georgia's store that her employee Peri admitted she didn't want to go to law school, and at Georgia's store that her longtime friend KC confessed that she did. It was here that Georgia's former flame James had walked back into her life and the two discovered their love had never lost its spark. And it was at the store that Georgia and James's only child, Dakota, had once done her homework and shared her homemade muffins with her mother's friends and flaked out on the couch in her mother's office, waiting for the workday to be finished so the two of them could eat a simple supper and go on up to bed in the apartment upstairs.

And if that all had happened, then it also meant that Georgia Walker had fallen ill with late-stage ovarian cancer and died unexpectedly from complications, leaving her group to manage without her.

For just over five years they'd all kept on just as they'd done—still meeting up for regular get-togethers even though KC never picked up a stick and Darwin's mistake-ridden sweater for her husband remained the most complex item she'd ever put together—and Peri had left everything mostly the same in the store. Year after year, she resisted her impulse to change the decor, to redesign the lavender bags with the Walker and Daughter logo, to muck out the back office with its faded couch or to update the old wooden table that anchored the room. She kept everything intact and ran the store with the energy and attention to detail Georgia had demonstrated, had turned a profit every quarter—always doing best in winter, of course—and furiously created her line of knitted and felted handbags with every spare moment. She even found the energy to branch out in new lines, new designs.

Until, finally, she'd had enough working on her handbags late at night and never feeling rested. She put down her needles and jammed out an e-mail in the middle of the night. She required a meeting, she'd written, had broached the remodel. It had been an impossible concept, of course, the idea of changing things. And it took a long while for Anita and Dakota to agree. Still, Peri stood firm, and ultimately the wall came down, some new paint went up, and even the always serviceable chairs around the center table were replaced with cushier, newly upholstered versions. The shop was revitalized: still cozy, but fresher and sleeker. As a surprise—and in an attempt to woo Dakota's emotional approval—Peri had asked Lucie to print an outtake from her documentary about the shop, the first film she had shown in the festival circuit, and had framed a photograph of Dakota and Georgia ringing up sales together, back when Dakota was only twelve and Georgia was robustly healthy. Appropriately, the picture hung behind the register, the Walker and Daughter logo next to it.

"She would have liked that," Dakota said, nodding. "But I don't know about the changes to the store. Maybe we should put the wall back up."

"Georgia believed in forging ahead," said Peri. "She tried new things with the shop. Think of the club, for example."

"I dunno," said Dakota. "What if I forget what it used to be like? What if it all just fades away? Then what?"

Tonight, for the first time, the entire group would see the updated store in its completed form. It was a pleasantly warm April night, and the Friday Night Knitting Club was getting together for its regular monthly meeting. Whereas once the women had gathered in Georgia's store every week, the combination of their busy careers and changing family situations made it more difficult to meet as often as they once did. And yet every meeting began with hugs and kisses and a launch, without preamble, into the serious dramas of their days. There was no pretense with these women anymore, no concern about how they looked or how they acted, just a sense of community that didn't change whether they saw each other once a week or once a year. It had been Georgia's final and most beautiful gift to each of them: the gift of true and unconditional sisterhood.

But if time had not changed their feelings for one another, it had not spared the natural toll on their bodies and their careers and their love lives and their hair. Much had happened in the preceding five years.

KC Silverman had made law review at Columbia, passed the bar with flying colors, and ended up back at Churchill Publishing—the very company that had laid her off from her editorial job five years ago—as part of in-house counsel.

"Finally, I'm invaluable," she had told the group upon starting the job. "I know every side of the business."

Her new salary was transformed, with some guidance from Peri, into a fabulous collection of suits. And her hair was longer than the pixie cut she'd had in the old days, shaped into a more lawyerly layered style. She'd experimented—for a millisecond—with letting her hair go its natural gray, but she decided she was too young for that much seriousness at fifty-two and opted for a light brown.

"If I had your gorgeous silver," she told Anita, "it would be a different story."

Lucie Brennan's documentary circulating on the festival circuit had led to a gig directing a video for a musician who liked to knit at Walker and Daughter. When the song went to the Top Ten in *Billboard*, Lucie quickly transitioned from part-time producer for local cable to directing a steady stream of music videos, her little girl Ginger lip-synching by her side in footie pajamas.

At forty-eight, she was busier and more successful than she ever imagined—and her apartment reflected the change. She no longer rented, but had purchased a high and sunny two-bedroom on the

Upper West Side with a gorgeous camelback sofa that Lucie, still an occasional insomniac, would curl up on in the middle of the night. Only now, instead of knitting herself to sleep, she typically mapped out shots for the next day's shoot.

And the tortoiseshell glasses she'd once worn every day had been joined by an array of frames and contacts for her blue eyes. Her hair, if left to its natural sandy brown, was quite... salty. So she colored it just a few shades darker than little Ginger's strawberry blond, aiming for a russet shade.

Darwin Chiu finished her dissertation, published her very first book (on the convergence of craft, the Internet, and the women's movement) based on her research at Walker and Daughter, and secured a teaching job at Hunter College while her husband, Dan Leung, found a spot at a local ER. They also found a small apartment on the East Side, close to the hospital and college, the living room walls lined with inexpensive bookshelves overflowing with papers and notes. Unlike other women, Darwin had hair free of gray though she'd hit her thirties, and she still wore it long, without bangs, making her look almost as young as her women's studies students.

Peri Gayle, striking with her deep brown eyes, mahogany skin, and meticulous cornrows that fell just past her shoulders, ran the store, of course.

Anita Lowenstein had settled into a happy arrangement with her friend Marty, although their decision not to marry came up now and again.

"I'm living my life in reverse," she told the group. "Now that my mother can't do a damn thing about it, I'm rebelling against society's expectations." She'd been joking, of course. Moving in together was a simpler solution, quite frankly, in terms of estate planning and inheritance, and. as the movie stars say, neither she nor Marty needed a piece of paper to demonstrate their commitment.

"We'll just call him my partner," corrected Anita when yet

another of her friends tripped over how to describe her relationship. "It seems overreaching to call him my boyfriend at this age."

They had, however, purchased a new apartment together and moved out of the garden apartment in Marty's Upper West Side brownstone, allowing Marty's niece to incorporate that level into her family home. Anita was seventy-eight, though she'd lie about it if anyone ever asked, and certainly appeared younger, with her layered, silvery hair and her well-cared-for hands. Thanks to Anita, Catherine truly appreciated the value of high SPF.

Catherine Anderson's little business flourished north of the city in Cold Spring, though many days she continued to take the train in, spending some days in the tidy, expensively furnished cottage she'd recently purchased and others in the San Remo apartment that Anita had shared with her late husband, Stan.

It seemed that five years was about right for all that had happened to settle in, and for the urge to try something different to begin to swell.

"Not much of a surprise if the presents are all out there," exclaimed KC at the entrance to Walker and Daughter as she wheeled in a red wagon filled with stuffed animals perched inside: a monkey, a giraffe, and two fluffy white teddy bears. Peri stopped trying to rewrap Dakota's gift for a moment to wave hello.

"We should try to hide in the back office and then jump out and surprise her!" said KC, waving back even though she was mere steps away. "What do you say?"

She and Peri were from different generations—KC was twenty-three years older than Peri—but they were, as the volume-impaired and talkative KC explained to anyone who cared and often to those who didn't, the very epitome of BFFs.

"We help each other get ahead," KC explained when Dakota asked at one meeting why the two of them spent so much time together when, on the surface, they looked and acted so different from each other. "We gossip, we go to movies, she picks out my clothes, and

I give her legal advice for her pocketbook business." Their shared devotion to career—and KC's years of experience—also kept up the connection. As proud as she was about her professional reinvention, KC had ultimately traded one workaholic lifestyle for another. Just as she'd put in long days at the office when she was an editor and followed it up with nights reading manuscripts, now she spent her evenings reading contracts on the sofa in the prewar rent-stabilized apartment on the West Side that had been her parents' home.

But while Peri kept up with a steady crowd of pals from the design courses she'd taken, KC's relationship with Peri filled a bit of the gap that had been left by Georgia, who had been a young assistant when KC met her. For a woman who would never describe herself as a nurturer, KC made it a practice to look out for others and to mentor them. And she had a deep fondness for Dakota, who seemed exasperated with her latest concept.

"For one thing, no back office anymore," muttered Dakota, inclining her head toward KC and motioning for her to take a look behind her. "So it wouldn't work."

"And for two, we have a no-scaring-pregnant-women policy," added Anita, who was two steps behind KC and coming through the doorway. As she did every day, Anita wore an elegant pantsuit and a selection of tasteful jewelry. The oldest and wealthiest member of the club, Anita was also—everyone would agree—the kindest and most thoughtful. In her arms Anita carried a giant hydrangea plant in blue; Marty carried a second one in pink. She nodded solemnly.

"The renovations are excellent, my dear," she said, though Peri suspected her words were meant mainly to bolster Dakota's uncertainty since Anita had checked on the shop's progress repeatedly.

"I'm here, I'm here," came a voice from the stairwell. It was Catherine, sweeping into the room with a bit of self-created fanfare and an armful of professionally wrapped presents in brightly colored paper and a large canvas bag filled with several bottles.

"Hello, darlings," she said, blowing enough air kisses that everyone in the room got three each.

"Hello, grumpy," Catherine said to Dakota, lightly wrapping an arm around her shoulders as they surveyed the room.

"I was afraid I was late," said Catherine. "Is she here yet?" The store phone rang as Lucie called to say she wasn't able to get away from work and not to wait. Peri looked at her watch and let out a cry of concern. Quickly, KC pulled out a box of cupcakes from the bottom of the red wagon, and Catherine opened a magnum of chilled champagne without a pop.

"When I think of the Friday Night Knitting Club, I always think of plastic glasses," said Catherine to Dakota. "It adds a certain je ne sais quoi." She winked at Dakota, managing to charm a shrug out of her young pal. The two had forged a big sister–little sister bond since Georgia had taken Catherine in years ago and let her bunk on Dakota's floor during her divorce; many times in the ensuing years since Georgia died, Catherine's cynicism and over-the-top drama had been the perfect antidote to Dakota's teenage moodiness. Anita remained Dakota's source for unconditional love; Catherine was good at keeping secrets and seemed willing to become her partner in crime, if only they could think up a scheme.

"To Walker and Daughter," said Catherine, taking one sip and then another. "To the reno, to my favorite kid, and to the club." The rest of the women raised their glasses.

Even though the vague unease about the remodel persisted, Peri could tell it was going to be a happy night. Anybody could see that. The gang was all here, together again; the volume was already deafening as everyone spoke at once, trying to cram a month's worth of news into a few minutes. She began to relax as she saw Dakota flop into one of the new chairs, throw her jeans-clad leg over the arm, and bum a sip of champagne off Catherine, the two of them glancing to see if Anita had noticed.

Tonight, the Friday Night Knitting Club would have made Georgia proud. They were holding a special meeting to throw a surprise baby shower for one Darwin Chiu, who was finally, after many long years of trying and hoping, expecting her first children.

Darwin and Dan were having twins.